Great Afterschool Programs and Spaces That Wow!

Also from Redleaf Press by Linda J. Armstrong
Family Child Care Homes: Creative Spaces for Children to Learn

Great Afterschool Programs and Spaces That Wow!

Linda J. Armstrong
Christine A. Schmidt

Redleaf Press®
www.redleafpress.org
800-423-8309

Published by Redleaf Press
10 Yorkton Court
St. Paul, MN 55117
www.redleafpress.org

Interest Survey 2 on pages 265–267 is adapted from the Virginia Department of
Social Services, Division of Child Care and Early Childhood Development, Course
Title: "Using the Environment to Connect with School-Age Children" Copyright ©
2005, 2011. All rights reserved.

Portions of this text are adapted from *Family Child Care Homes* by Linda J.
Armstrong. © 2012 by Redleaf Press.

First edition 2013
Cover design by Jim Handrigan
Photograph of Linda J. Armstrong by Erin Heim
Photograph of Christine A. Schmidt by Emily Crosby
Interior design by Brian Donahue / bedesign, inc. and typeset in Adelle Light
Interior photos by Linda J. Armstrong and Christine A. Schmidt
Illustrations on pages 166–69 by Roberta Fultz.
Printed in the United States of America
Printed on acid-free paper

20 19 18 17 16 15 14 13   1 2 3 4 5 6 7 8

Library of Congress Cataloging-in-Publication Data
Armstrong, Linda J., 1946–
    Great afterschool programs and spaces that wow! / Linda J. Armstrong,
      Christine A. Schmidt.
          pages cm
    Includes bibliographical references and index.
    ISBN 978-1-60554-122-8 (pbk. : alk. paper)
    1 School-age child care. 2. After school programs.   I. Schmidt, Christine A. II. Title.
  HQ778.6.A76 2013
  371.8—dc23
                    2013006795

We salute everyone working with
school-age children for all you do for them
and their families each day.

An environment is a living, changing system.
More than the physical space, it includes the way time
is structured and the roles we are expected to play.
It conditions how we feel, think, and behave;
and it dramatically affects the quality of our lives.

—Jim Greenman

Contents

Acknowledgments

WRITING A BOOK IS MORE THAN having writers put words on a page. It is much like cooking—start with two women who have a passion and years of experience working with children, add staff at a great publishing company, stir in two understanding husbands, mix together for many months, and send off to be printed; recipe serves all individuals working with children in school-age programs.

Linda Armstrong

First, last, and always I want to thank my best friend and husband, John, whose never-ending support, great meals, and 24-7 reminder that I really could write this book kept me going. My daughters, Sarah and Beth, continue to remind me that what we do (or did) for our children every day makes a big difference in their lives. And lastly, my grandchildren's excitement and joy in learning remind me that children need and deserve amazing places to give them a good start as lifelong learners.

Christine Schmidt

To my husband, Rick, thank you for always believing in me, encouraging me when times were hard, and bringing laughter and love into my life. Your constant support and encouragement have allowed me to create this book. To my children, Rick, Mandy, Katie, and Beth, thank you for understanding and supporting my passion for children and afterschool programs. To my grand-children, who are constant reminders of the vast potential and unique inner spirit of children.

Linda and Christine

Many thanks to Peggy, Theresa, Donna, Jen, Tracey, Becky, April, Nikki, Cheryl, Sharon, Gail, and Lee for opening their doors to share the many faces of the afterschool world, and for their appreciation, encouragement, support, and belief in this project. And to Kyra Ostendorf at Redleaf Press, thanks for always being there for us. Your kind words and gentle guidance helped so much as we struggled to keep our focus and channel our energies. Last but not least, we want to thank each other. We have been a good team and developed a lasting friendship during the many months of working and writing together. We are both proud of what we have been able to do together and realize it is far more than either of us could have done working alone.

Preface

THIS BOOK IS FOR INDIVIDUALS who work in programs that provide care to children from kindergarten through early adolescence when they are not in school. The name for these programs varies. Titles include "afterschool," "school-age," and "before-and-after" care. You will find these three titles used interchangeably in this book. Just as the names of programs differ, so each program has unique characteristics. School-age programs come in all sizes, from six children in a family child care home, to before-school programs that offer care to twenty children only during the hours before school, to programs that offer care to a hundred or more children before and after school and during times when school is not in session. Some programs offer care only during the summer. The program purpose can also vary. Some programs are based in academics, others are recreational, and still others are a combination of academic, recreational, and social development programs. Regardless of their variations, one critical element of quality programs for school-age children should be a constant: providing a safe place for children to play, develop social skills, increase learning, and make friends.

School-age programs are important in the lives of children and their families. According to a 2009 Afterschool Alliance fact sheet, "8.4 million K–12 children (15 percent) participate in afterschool programs. An additional 18.5 million would participate if a quality program were available in their community." The daunting number of children who need quality programs offers a great opportunity and a large responsibility to those designing environments and caring for children when they are not in school. Afterschool programs can provide a safe haven where children can flourish and be accepted for who they are while learning about others and the community around them. Creating a community within the school-age program allows children to develop socially and cognitively and helps them master self-help skills in a safe, nurturing environment.

But creating environments that meet the needs of all the children—regardless of size, age, gender, ethnicity, or ability—requires time, planning, and information gathering. Often before-and-after care programs become spaces that warehouse children for a period of time when they are not in school. Programs can be devoid of inviting and appropriate physical spaces, engaging learning experiences, and opportunities for social skill building.

Some programs do the same things day after day, month after month, year after year, providing the same games and activities, and then staff wonder why children are bored or no longer want to come to the program.

The goal of this book is to help you think about how your program environment affects children and to provide you with strategies to create a program that will keep children coming back. Whether you have little or no experience working with children or you have been in the field for a considerable time, you can create an environment that engages children. The ideas may challenge your current thinking. Start out with baby steps if that is easier for you. Trying just a few new things can be the beginning of a new environment, creating excitement in and renewed engagement with your afterschool program. While the book does not cover every detail you might need, it does compile information from a variety of sources and from our years of experience. The ideas and information are based on hundreds of visits to school-age programs around the world; input from afterschool program staff, field experts, and parents; brain research; and our experiences as school-age professionals, mothers, and grandmothers. Our goal is to help you think about your space in a new way while sparking your imagination and creativity.

Before-and-after care personnel are busy people, frequently working split shifts and having to tear down and re-create a school-age environment each day. Afterschool programs often do not have large budgets, an abundance of staff, or planning time. The absence of time limits the staff's ability to research and become aware of new ideas and cutting-edge information. Limited budgets may restrict what changes can be made to the environment. This book addresses these limitations by providing many low-cost or no-cost solutions to common struggles in the school-age environment. We hope the information in this book will motivate you to look critically at your program and become inspired to make necessary changes to create an exciting and supportive environment for the children you serve.

CHAPTER 1

The Many Faces of School-Age Care

CREATING A SCHOOL-AGE PROGRAM that "wows" children and supports their needs can seem overwhelming. You might be asking, *Where do I start? How do I know what is supposed to be included or excluded? How much is too much? How do I know when the environment is working or not working? How can I do this alone?*

Never fear, help is here. This book takes you through all the considerations that affect your school-age program environment and then lays out a process for creating your environment. This chapter looks at the wide variety of afterschool programs, both in terms of the type of program and the type of space that houses the program. Based on the children and on where your program falls within the spectrum of school-age programs, you can begin to formulate some goals for your environment.

Types of Programs

The need for accessible and affordable care for school-age children is well documented, but providing afterschool care to meet the needs of families and communities can be challenging. There is no cookie-cutter way to provide school-age care. The National AfterSchool Association's (NAA) "Code of Ethics" defines afterschool programming as "any organized program provided for children and youth ages 5–18 during a time when they are not in school" (2009). While the NAA does not specifically mention before-school care in its definition, many programs provide care before the school bell rings. Each program is unique, offering a variety of educational, recreational, and enrichment activities that are based on the needs of the children, families, and community and on the organization's mission and goals. Some programs have limited hours. Some operate only on days children are in school. Others operate seven days a week; still others, just on weekends. Some operate only during the summer. Some offer overnight care.

Also, the size and age range of children can vary greatly among school-age programs. Some programs separate children by ages. Most, however, have children spanning several grades within the same space. While these multi-age groupings provide great opportunities for peer interaction and mentoring, they also present some challenges. How can you create an environment that will meet the physical, social-emotional, and cognitive needs of all children in your program? The diversity in types of programs helps meet the needs of children and of changing family dynamics in today's society; however, not all options are available in all areas.

Types of Facilities

Just as afterschool programs come in many shapes and sizes, so too do the facilities in which they are housed. School-age programs can be located in a classroom, cafeteria, gym, or library in a school building or in a community or faith-based organization. Some school-age programs are part of a child care facility and may be held in a room within the larger facility. Others may have their own facility that has been designed solely for the afterschool program. Regardless of their location, school-age facilities fall into two basic categories: shared space and dedicated space.

Photo 1.1

The initial impression of a building housing a school-age program should send a message that this is a good place for children.

SHARED SPACE

The majority of programs share part or all of their space. Shared space is defined as space that is used by others either during the school day, when you are not using it, or simultaneously, during your program time. Setting up and taking down the environment daily is a key indicator that your space is shared space.

These shared spaces come with opportunities and challenges. The inability to use or move desks or other items in the room can limit group activities and active play. A library offers an area for quiet activities but leaves little room for active play. Sporting events, science fairs, school fundraisers, or other events can temporarily force you out of your space, causing the frustration and disruption of dislocation.

Shared-space programs are often located in school cafeterias, libraries, or other large rooms such as this one. These large spaces offer ample room for many activities to take place at one time, but reducing noise and softening the institutional appearance can be challenging.

On the plus side, however, shared space can offer access to additional areas where children can experience different types of activities. Explore the options that exist in your building. Consider using an indoor gym or large-motor space for needed physical activities on a cold or rainy day. A cafeteria provides a clean and safe space for food preparation and serving snacks. A library can provide a quiet place for studying and doing homework. Children can access reference materials, computers, and reading materials for information and enjoyment. While shared spaces can be trying at times, with flexibility and planning they can provide a variety of areas to expand your program spaces.

Perhaps one of the most daunting challenges in shared spaces is the need to set up the environment and take it down daily. How do you turn a blank space into an eye-catching, welcoming environment where children want to be? The good news is that school-age children are very energetic and willing to help, so let them. With a little creativity and help from the children, the transformation can be quick and painless. To create a setup plan, answer these questions:

Photo 1.3

With the use of portable furniture dividers, the space in this room has been distributed so many activities can occur at one time. By using lightweight furniture or furniture with locking wheels, the room can be arranged and rearranged easily and quickly.

- What items in the space can be moved?
- What items need to be added for the afterschool program?
- What are your storage options for the items you would like to add?
- Where is the water source for drinking, hand washing, and preparation and cleanup of snacks and projects?

Once you have answered these basic questions, you can begin to plan the logistical details of how to set up your space each day. Each type of shared space—cafeteria, gym, classroom, library—comes with its own setup difficulties. The following questions and answers may help solve some of these challenges. The answers are meant to help you think about your own shared space environment. Throughout this book you will find additional information that will give you a more complete understanding of how to set up an ideal after-school environment in your shared space.

Photo 1.4

Photo 1.5

This portable storage container on wheels can carry a variety of equipment, go wherever needed to support the children's play, and then be stored when not in use.

Are you unable to leave permanent displays in your space? Use three-paneled display boards to showcase artwork, create a parent area, or define activity areas. This allows you to make the space inviting while minimizing storage needs. The displays can be folded up and placed flat on top of a storage cabinet.

Does your space lack storage facilities? Do you ever have to move to a temporary location to accommodate the need for others to use your space? Use rolling carts and handled bins to store and transport materials and supplies. These "grab-and-go" caddies enable you to move quickly even without advance notice, and you will still be able to provide the consistency of familiar games and materials. (See the "Arranging and Displaying Materials" section in chapter 8 for more on grab-and-go caddies.)

Does your space lack furniture? Bring in a folding table and chairs to serve snack or to set up the art or homework area. Look for other areas in the building that might provide storage space for items when not in use or provide space large enough to store unused furniture such as couches, area rugs, bookshelves, tables, and chairs. Smaller storage areas should be used to store

Photo 1.6

This gallery displaying children's artwork is located in a highly visible place where everyone can enjoy it. When children's projects are displayed with respect, the message is sent that their efforts are appreciated and valued, and it is easy to put up and tear down as needed.

materials not in use or supplies that need to be accessed quickly, such as extra crayons or paper. Folding chairs and tables can be stored easily alongside or on top of a cabinet. To protect the floor in a gym, place a drop cloth or quilt under the furniture.

If bringing in furniture is not possible, use floor coverings to designate different activity areas. Small rugs or gym mats can define an area for construction and dramatic play, or along with a few pillows can create a cozy place for children to relax and read. A colorful quilt can provide an area for art or for picnic-style snacks. Floor coverings help minimize noise, and they roll or fold up for easy storage.

Are your activities restricted? Look to other spaces to fill the gap. For example, if you are in the library, you may not be able to eat snack, be physically active, or use any books or computers. See if you can use the cafeteria, hallways, and other areas in the building or outside for the children to eat snack and participate in large-motor activities.

Photo 1.7

Children need both permission and places to slow down for a while after a busy day in school. This child has found a musical instrument and comfy place to unwind.

Are you unable to move the furniture in your space? If you are in a

Photo 1.8

Photo 1.9

school classroom or cafeteria, you may be limited to individual desks or cafeteria tables. Use bright tablecloths on the desks or tables to define space and help children know where an activity will take place. Use pillows and gym mats to create a comfortable area on the floor where children can read, listen to music, talk with friends, or just chill out, relax, and de-stress after a long day at school.

Is your water source in another room? Use a bucket to hold clean water (changed regularly) so children can wipe off table tops after a messy activity. Placing a rubber bath mat on the floor below the bucket will minimize accidents and damage if water gets on the floor.

DEDICATED SPACE

School-age programs that operate in facilities or space in a building that is solely for their use are often referred to as *dedicated space programs*. Dedicated space for afterschool programming can be found in family child care homes, schools, churches and synagogues, and military facilities; however, most often it is located in a building called a "center." A significant aspect of selecting a facility—whether shared or dedicated—for school-age programming is ensuring that the health, safety, and well-being of children and staff are consistently maintained. Equally important is being housed in a

Photo 1.10

A Hundred Years From Now
...it will not matter what my bank account was,
the sort of house I lived in, or the kind of car I drove...
...but the world may be different because I was
important in the life of a child.

WELCOME

Photo 1.11

This program's entry area includes comfortable chairs and a cheery appearance, encouraging everyone who arrives to come in and stay for a while.

Photo 1.12

By using ceiling drops in only a few places, this program has defined activity areas and added a splash of bright color to the environment.

Photo 1.13

This whimsical snake hangs from the ceiling to invite children to the science and discovery area. An old broomstick, hand puppet, and artificial vines hung together from fishing wire were used for this low-cost signage.

building that is suitable for the intended purpose of the program. A facility such as a former library or an office building is more easily redesigned specifically for child care than a bowling alley or a skating rink. The amount of space available for children's use is another significant factor in the quality of care. The size of the facility dictates the maximum number of children in care.

Dedicated space environments are much more permanent than shared space and do not require the daily setup of program space. In addition, dedicated space can support many functions and activities, each of which can take place in a separate room or location in a center or building. Staff and children can create and control their environment according to program goals and needs. Those that operate in dedicated space often incur all the expenses of the building and grounds, including maintenance fees and security systems. Ask yourself the following questions to evaluate the physical limitations of your dedicated space:

- Can the space be divided to accommodate a variety of activities at one time?
- Are staff able to maintain line-of-sight supervision in all areas?
- Are there enough toileting and hand-washing facilities for the number of children enrolled?
- Can children be kept safe from harm in the building?
- Is the building healthy and safe?

Communication Is a Key to Success

No matter what kind of program space—shared or dedicated—you have, an essential key to success is communication. Communication directed to individuals or organizations takes many forms—verbal, written, electronic, paper.

Communication to families is the foundation of your program and can be a key marketing strategy. School-age program staff have a unique opportunity to talk to family members daily as they drop their children off in the morning and pick them up in the evening. This personal, face-to-face communication helps families feel valued and connected to your program. How and what you communicate can be a wonderful marketing tool. A positive comment about your program from one parent to another or from a community leader can create a favorable public image. Written materials such as newsletters and brochures can communicate your program's goals, mission, and vision. They can highlight program events, community resources, and parenting information, showing your commitment to the children and families enrolled.

You should communicate regularly with those in charge of scheduling your space, maintenance personnel, supervisors, staff, organizational leaders, and, if applicable, the owner of the building. The topics discussed with each of these stakeholders will vary, but a constant topic should be information about your program events, successes, and challenges. These stakeholders have a direct effect on your program, from budgeting to programming, so it is important to keep the lines of communication open.

Two-way communication with those who use the program space either during program time or when your program is not in session keeps after-school staff informed of upcoming uses and potential schedule conflicts. By scheduling regular meetings, you can avoid last-minute surprises that leave you scrambling to move your program to an alternate space. Regular communication allows you to be proactive and plan ahead so that you can minimize the disruption for children.

In addition, a communication network in your local community can be very beneficial. Tapping into community resources can provide you with a variety of opportunities, such as local field trips and access to indoor and outdoor program space when your space is being used by others. Community members can also furnish supplies such as computers, desks, bookshelves, and labor for painting the program space or creating a wonderful playground.

Defining the Environment

When we think of the word *environment*, many of us think of physical space—four walls, windows, furniture, rugs, the color of walls. Others think of outdoor space—the look of the sky, terrain, flora, and fauna. This book will help you look beyond the physical aspects of your school-age program and see other, equally important dimensions of this setting.

In the book *Beginnings and Beyond: Foundations in Early Childhood Education,* Ann Miles Gordon and Kathryn Williams Browne describe children's learning environments as having three dimensions: temporal, interpersonal, and physical (2011). While the authors focus on early childhood settings, their discussion of these three dimensions of the environment is equally applicable to school-age settings. Gordon and Browne maintain that all three dimensions must be met to ensure the overall environment will both appeal to children and support their needs. Gordon and Browne define these three dimensions as follows:

- **temporal environment:** schedules, routines, rules, regulations, and learning opportunities that meet children's needs
- **interpersonal environment:** the relationships and interactions of all individuals involved in the program, including the children, staff, parents, and the greater community
- **physical environment:** the indoor and outdoor setting, including furnishings, materials, and architectural elements of lighting, color, plumbing, and physical layout of the space

Child development researchers define a child's environment as the total of all things a child comes in contact with on a regular basis (Isbell and Exelby 2001; Curtis and Carter 2003; Greenman 2005). In school-age program settings, this includes physical places and spaces, learning experiences gained from the temporal environment, and social interactions with people. A quality school-age environment is a welcoming, dynamic place full of action and excited learners. How you design and equip the environment helps children be successful learners, grow in self-confidence and esteem, and establish a sense of community with peers and adults. The program environment generally affects the overall well-being of everyone who spends time in the school-age program.

The following questionnaire, A Day in the Life of Your School-Age Program, will help you to begin thinking about all three dimensions of your program environment—temporal, interpersonal, and physical. Pretend you are a first-time visitor to your program and answer the questions honestly, based on what you observe in the environment. (The questionnaire is also available at www.redleafpress.org for downloading and printing.)

A Day in the Life of Your School-Age Program

ARRIVAL TIME

1. What is the first thing children and their families see or hear when they enter your program?

2. Is there at least one place where each child can leave, find, and return personal belongings without adult assistance?

3. Is there a space designated only for older children?

4. What behavior do the children display when they arrive?

5. What areas do children go to when they arrive?

6. How much time is scheduled for children to transition into the program after they arrive?

7. Are children and families greeted by staff when they arrive?

CHILD-INITIATED PLAY

1. Can children move freely and independently in the environment?

2. Are there traffic jams when children go from one place to another, or are children running from place to place?

3. Do the pathways disrupt play areas?

4. Are the play areas too big or too small for the number of children in them?

5. Is it easy for children to find and return materials without adult assistance or asking questions?

6. What areas are used most? Least? Not at all?

7. Do children have uninterrupted playtime when they can choose what and whom to play with?

8. Are there places where children can be creative? Inventive?

9. Do children appear to be excited and challenged by materials in the environment?

10. Do staff provide help when asked or talk with children as they play?

MEALTIME AND SNACKTIME

1. Is there a peaceful mealtime environment free from distractions, overstimulation, and conflict?

2. Are children allowed and encouraged to relax and enjoy peers' company as they eat?

3. Is there enough space for children to sit comfortably and promote conversation during meals?

4. Is the room or eating space bright and attractive?

5. Is there a staff member who interacts with children while they are eating?

6. Is snacktime long enough so children can decide when they would like to eat?

QUIET TIME

1. Are there places for children to be alone and relax in comfortable furniture?

2. Are there places where children can be with only one or two other children?

3. Can the mood of an area be changed with the amount of light or by rearranging furniture?

4. Are children given permission and encouraged to relax and slow down for a while?

5. Are staff available to talk with children if need be?

INDOOR PLAY

1. Is there an indoor open area large enough for all children to sit, dance, put on a play, exercise, or play together?

2. Does the indoor space support activities for a team or large group as well as for one child or a small group?

3. Are there adequate lighting, ventilation, and sound-absorbing elements to support children's active play?

4. Are children encouraged to participate in exercise and fitness activities?

OUTDOOR ACTIVITIES

1. Does the outdoor environment connect children with nature?

2. Are there places outdoors where children are encouraged to be involved in a variety of sensory experiences, such as climbing trees, touching textural things, or listening to animal sounds?

3. Does the outdoor environment and staff support both children's quiet or passive play as well as active play?

4. Are all children able to use at least one piece of each type of playground equipment regardless of their size or disability?

5. Do staff guide and encourage children to participate in outdoor activities? Do they enter into these activities as a participant or role model of sportsmanship?

ADULT-LED ACTIVITIES

1. Are adult-led activities conducted to teach a skill or extend learning? If so, what skill or extended learning does the activity encourage?

2. Are adult-led activities conducted with the needs of the children in mind?

3. Do staff use adult-led or monitored activities to ensure the safety of children?

4. How often do adult-led activities occur?

5. Are the adult-led activities designed to engage the children?

6. Are children allowed to ask questions and modify the adult-led activities to meet their needs?

This wall mural is a visual reminder of the program's goal of character development for children. Programs that change goals periodically can use less permanent displays, such as quilts, posters, or bulletin boards, to be equally effective and reflective of their program goals.

Setting Goals for Your Environment

No matter where your program is located, how big or small your space is, or how many children attend, the ultimate goal for all school-age care programs is to support children's learning. Remember that *learning* is a broad term that includes how we react either consciously or unconsciously to what is going on around us. It is a process, not a product. Learning happens over a period of time by building on what we already know with new information to develop additional behaviors, skills, attitudes, and preferences. In other words, learning is more than memorizing facts or spelling words; it is making sense of these facts and words to understand the world around us and our role in it.

Setting the stage for learning success begins with the children. What you place in the environment depends on the children. For instance, if you have children in primary grades (grades K–3), having on hand early reader books, larger balls, and a variety of art supplies and providing additional staff supervision create an environment that supports children's learning. Children in intermediate grades (grades 4–6) and above benefit from activities with higher-level problem solving, challenging games, and staff who encourage children to think for themselves. There is no one design that fits all. Each environment should be as unique as the children and adults in the program while also being designed to develop children's love of learning, which ideally will last their lifetime.

Children learn best when they are in an environment where they are physically safe and comfortable, know what to expect, and feel emotionally secure. A strong link exists between children's experiences and surroundings and their overall brain development. For that reason and many more, children's environments should be rich in resources and learning opportunities (Strong-Wilson and Ellis 2007). Achieving this goal goes beyond tangible physical components to include how people, policies, and practices make children feel in the environment. When people walk through the door of a school-age environment, they form an impression of the program within a few minutes, if not seconds. What is in the environment signals the program's level of commitment to providing the best place for children.

In her book *Child Care Design Guide,* Anita Rui Olds, a well-known expert on children's environments, recommends designing the environment for miracles, not minimums (2001). If we see each child as a miracle full of learning potential and needing our help, we are well on our way to creating an ideal school-age environment. For better or worse, your program transforms the characteristics that the children bring to it. Make your program the best it can be, and you will help transform children into the best they can be.

All quality school-age programs have certain common threads regardless of the type of facility, size of space, number of children enrolled, shared or dedicated space, and location—inner-city, suburban, or rural. All these programs

- offer a safe environment that fosters total child development, and employ an adequate number of qualified, well-trained staff;
- are administered efficiently;
- encourage staff-parent interaction;
- balance activities to include structured and unstructured time, teacher-directed and child-initiated experiences, and a range of activities;
- capitalize on the interests of the children and opportunities for informal, social learning;
- use community resources as much as possible;
- communicate clear, consistent expectations and limits to children;
- provide indoor and outdoor space for active play and places for socialization and private time;
- meet the individual needs of the children;
- pursue the goals and mission of the program; and
- keep within budget and staffing limitations.

So how do you weave all these threads into your school-age program environment? How do you develop a program that wows everyone who walks through the door? Designing a quality school-age program is like putting together a puzzle. It requires many pieces that all fit together perfectly. While architects and engineers design buildings, people who know about children create learning environments. To create a quality school-age environment for your program, include the following in your goal setting:

- program goals
- curriculum
- group size
- staff-child ratios
- equipment and furniture
- staff's needs
- families' needs
- children's needs

In addition, the Day in the Life of Your School-Age Program questionnaire (see previous section) can help you begin to set some goals for your program environment. After answering the questionnaire, reread your answers and think about what messages your environment sends out. Circle or highlight the areas that concern you. You may find it helpful to number these in order of priority to decide where to focus first. Choose one or two that are the highest priorities. Ask yourself how you will know when you have succeeded in making positive changes. Answer the following questions:

- How will you measure success?
- How long, realistically, will it take to make the needed changes?
- What, if any, materials and supplies will you need to complete the changes?

Then outline your goals and strategies for the changes you plan to make. Remember, you cannot do everything at once, but with a lot of planning you can create an environment that is exciting and that supports children's needs every day.

It has been said that goals are dreams with a plan and a timeline. Goals provide a basis for a continual process of planning, implementing, and evaluating your program. This process helps you see what your program goals need to be. The environmental goals you set will help children to

- develop a sense of both independence and connectedness with others;
- strengthen their self-help life skills, such as study habits, personal hygiene, healthy lifestyle, and appropriate social interactions;
- appreciate themselves;
- learn to empathize and respect others;
- increase their feelings of self-worth and eagerness to learn; and
- experience more successes than failures.

Observational information helps you evaluate all you do in your school-age programs: your activities, schedules, routines, transitions, rules, and consequences. When you incorporate both spontaneous and scheduled observations into your program, they will open your eyes to the effectiveness of your environment. The next several chapters address the three environmental dimensions in greater detail. As you delve into each of these realms, you will continue to use observations as your guiding light:

- Observations are based on what you see and hear within the program environment.
- Program environment includes the physical, temporal, and interpersonal and is based on planning.
- Planning is based on reflection and careful thought.
- Reflection is based on observations.

As you explore the ideas and strategies presented in this book, you will learn practical information about how to incorporate the key components for an ideal environment into your program. You will also learn how to use information gained through observations to create an environment that supports each child's overall development. Throughout your exploration and planning, keep asking yourself, *If I could design an ideal environment for children, what would I include? How can I create a place where children love to be, love to learn, and do not want to leave? How can I create a place where staff like to work, want to stay, and want to come back to every day?* This book will help you answer these questions.

Activities and Questions

At the end of each chapter, you will be challenged to apply the information presented to your program. The following activities and questions are meant to help you think about your program in a holistic way and begin to intentionally design your program space to include the physical, temporal, and interpersonal dimensions of the environment.

1. Is your program located in shared or dedicated space? What are the limitations of your space? What are some strategies to minimize your limitations?

2. How do you communicate with the host of your site and those that use your program space? How often do these communications take place?

3. What do you see as the limitations of your environment (physical, temporal, and interpersonal)? How do these limitations hinder children's learning?

4. Describe your program goals. How and when were these developed? Are they relevant and useful? Do they serve as a guide for your environment? Do parents, staff, and children know about these goals?

5. What dreams do you have for your environment? List these and use them as you read this book to guide you in creating a quality school-age environment.

6. Review the list of common threads for all school-age programs presented in this chapter. Which of these does your program currently fulfill? Which items should you consider including as you design your environment?

CHAPTER 2

Considerations for Management

WHETHER YOUR PROGRAM IS IN SHARED or dedicated space, some aspects of school-age environmental design are administrative. As such, they go beyond the scope of most of the staff and fall squarely on the shoulders of management. Management can be as diverse as the program types and the components offered in each program. Job titles vary from one program to the next, but in general management roles fall into two categories: site administrator and organizational administrator. The site administrator takes care of the day-to-day operations within a defined program, such as payment of parent fees, environment setup, lesson plan development, compliance with all licensing and building regulations, and communication with the stakeholders. The organizational administrator oversees the overall and site budgets, hires program staff, maintains training records, conducts evaluations of the staff and program, markets the program, conducts enrollment, and purchases needed materials and supplies.

Because of the uniqueness of program types and organizational structures in the field of school-age care, the descriptions of these roles are only partial examples of the many tasks that administrators perform. If you are an administrator, your job title and responsibilities may differ from these two descriptions, but overall the administrative functions that need to be accomplished by someone in a program remain the same. Many of these functions have a direct impact on the environment of your afterschool program.

This chapter outlines steps for administrators to obtain information about various regulations and standards that can affect how you design school-age spaces. Checking with state and local community regulatory agencies can provide information to ensure your program is on the right path. The small business association in your area can assist in developing a business plan to provide a strong financial foundation as you begin to design your program. The chapter also includes information on communication, on supporting your staff, and on working with limited resources as you redesign your program environment. Whether you have shared or dedicated space, you must set goals, gather information, and engage in planning. Being a flexible, creative thinker as you begin designing your environment will make the process more successful and much easier too.

Regulations, Licensure, and Accreditation

A strong and successful school-age program design should begin with planning and information gathering. If you are considering a remodel, a move to a new location, or an expansion of your program facility, then you may need to look into community and state requirements. Requirements vary from state to state as well as from community to community. A good place to start your investigation is your local resource and referral agency or licensing agency. These agencies can often provide specific local and state information to help you expand your program, pursue local training opportunities, and discover grant opportunities.

Starting a New Program

If this is your first time operating a school-age program, obtain licensing requirements for afterschool programs from the appropriate agency in your community and from the local building inspection bureau. These requirements may affect group size, staff-child ratio, environment options, amount of square footage per child enrolled, required learning areas, age and level of education of staff, and types of activities offered. Regulations may also determine where programs can be housed and located.

In addition, conducting a community needs assessment will provide valuable information. This will help you determine how many families would be interested in your program; what days of the week, times of day, and times of the year they would use the program; and how much they would be willing to spend to send their child to the program. (For more information, see the sample Community Needs Assessment that follows.)

If you are making major changes to your environment, such as expanding or remodeling your space, you will need to understand building code regulations. They will guide your thinking as you begin planning. If you violate any regulations, you may be forced either to make costly renovations to your program space or to forfeit your license and close your program. Regulations undergo periodic revisions, so be aware of any changes in local and state regulations so you are not caught off guard. A simple change in regulations, such as the amount of fall zone required in outdoor play space or the amount or type of acceptable ground covering, may require changes to your environment before the space can be used.

Your local building and fire departments can provide current building codes and additional information that will provide a safe space for children in your care. Some local communities have a separate set of requirements for school-age and youth development programs serving children five through eighteen that can be more restrictive than state licensing requirements. You will be required to follow the most stringent rules for your area. Being proactive in obtaining the licensing requirements, building codes, and community regulations will help you plan a safe environment that is well within state and local regulations. (See chapter 3 for more information on how to create safe and healthy environments.)

Many states have a definition for the type of program considered a school-age program and requiring licensure. Not all states require afterschool programs to be licensed, or they may have an upper age limit for required licensing, such as fourteen or sixteen years of age. Some states include school-age licensure within early childhood guidelines. Other states have a specific set of regulations for school-age programs. Even if you are not required to go through a licensure process, your program must have clear evidence of the following:

- facility and grounds that protect children from harm
- staff who are responsible and well trained
- program goals that reflect an understanding of how children grow and learn

Community Needs Assessment

A community needs assessment is done to evaluate feasibility when you are considering changes in the services your program offers. Some specific reasons for doing one include

- evaluating a change of location;
- deciding whether to offer care to additional ages; and
- considering the need for additional hours, such as summer, evenings, or weekends.

In preparing a needs assessment, ask questions that determine if a family would be interested in a school-age program for their child, what hours and days they would need care, if they would need summer care, and how much they would be willing to pay. A needs assessment is typically done via a survey, but sometimes information shared in a follow-up phone call can identify additional needs, such as tutoring, extended hours, medical support, or accommodations for disabilities.

Give the needs assessment to local community organizations and businesses as well as families from the schools located in the proposed area for the afterschool program. Also include questions in the assessment about resources in your community. The community can play a key role in providing resources to set up the environment, program activities, supplies, and guest speakers. Tapping into resources in the community will maximize your program's resources and can provide children and families with information about services available in the community. The following is a sample needs assessment. It is available at www.redleafpress.org for downloading and distribution.

Dear Families and Community Leaders,

The _____ is conducting an assessment to determine if there is a need
(name of your organization)
for a school-age program in our community. If it is determined there is a need for this program, it will be

located at _____. Please answer the questions below to see if you
(name the specific location)
would be interested in enrolling your children in a school-age program. If you do not have school-age

children and you or your organization could provide services to support this effort, please skip to #11.

Thank you for taking the time to fill out this survey. Please return your completed survey to

_____
(fill in how to return survey)
_____ no later than _____ .
(fill in date here)

1. Do you have children between the ages of _____
   (fill in ages here)
   who are in need of a safe, nurturing place to be when they are not in school?

   Yes No
   (circle one)

2. What is the earliest time you would need care before school?

   6:00 a.m.   6:30 a.m.   7:00 a.m.   7:30 a.m.   8:00 a.m.
   (circle one)

   Other time not listed _____. I do not need care before school _____.

3. What is the latest time you would need care after school?

   3:00 p.m.   3:30 p.m.   4:00 p.m.   4:30 p.m.   5:00 p.m.   5:30 p.m.   6:00 p.m.   6:30 p.m.
   (circle one)

   Other time not listed _____. I do not need care after school _____.

4. I need care **part-time (three days or less)** or **full-time (four or five days)** days a week before and
   (circle one)
   after school or other time _____.

5. I need care only in the morning **part-time** or **full-time**
   _____ days a week.   (circle one)
   (number)

6. I need care only after school **part-time** or **full-time** _____ days a week.
   (circle one)   (number)

7. Would you be interested in full-day care when the children are out of school (M–F)?

   Yes No
   (circle one)

From *Great Afterschool Programs and Spaces That Wow!* by Linda J. Armstrong and Christine A. Schmidt, © 2013.
Published by Redleaf Press, www.redleafpress.org. This page may be reproduced for classroom use only.

8. Would you be interested in full-day care during the summer (M–F)?

Yes   No
(circle one)

9. Our tentative fee schedule is as follows:

- Before and after school, full-time is _____ ;
  (fill in amount here)
  part-time is _____
  (fill in amount here)

- After school only, full-time is _____ ;
  (fill in amount here)
  part-time is _____
  (fill in amount here)

- Before school, full-time is _____ ;
  (fill in amount here)
  part-time is _____
  (fill in amount here)

- Full-day care when school is not in session; per day rate is _____
  (fill in amount here)

- Weekly rate for summer program is _____
  (fill in amount here)

Do you qualify for child care subsidy? **Yes   No**
(circle one)

10. Please list the names and ages of the children that you would consider enrolling in the school-age program.

_____

_____

_____

_____

_____

11. As a community leader, I would like to support your program. Please call me to discuss.

Name: _____

Contact phone number: _____

E-mail: _____

X _____
(Signature)

In addition to state and local regulations, many states have a Quality Rating and Improvement System (QRIS) for school-age programs. A QRIS is usually a voluntary program designed to recognize child care programs, family child care, and afterschool programs that exceed the quality benchmarks outlined in licensing regulations. These standards can be vastly different from state to state. Find out if your state has a QRIS by searching on the Internet. The search words "quality rating system" and the name of your state should show you if this system exists in your state. Once you have identified the system for your state, make sure that afterschool programs are included in the system. Not all states that have QRIS offer it for afterschool programs. If yours does, find out what the requirements are and how to apply for the process. QRIS systems are usually linked to state licensing agencies. Each system has several levels of achievement that exceed state requirements. The top level usually meets or exceeds nationally recognized accreditation standards. In some states, additional funding, training, technical assistance, and resources are provided for each level achieved. Once you have all of the pertinent information, you can decide if applying for the process will benefit the children, families, and staff in your organization while staying within your program goals, mission, and vision.

Finally, another step to consider for your program is accreditation. An accrediting body is an organization that verifies that a program has met a set of prescribed standards. Accreditation can provide a blueprint for creating a quality, well-balanced, safe environment for school-age children. Going through the process of accreditation can be rewarding for children, families, and staff. Remember that accreditation is a walk on a path and not a destination. As staff change and as new children and families enter your program, the process of observations and self-study or formal assessment should be updated. This helps ensure the needs of the children, families, and staff are met in accordance with accreditation standards. (For more on observations and assessments, see The Administrator's Role in Evaluating the Environment later in this chapter and The Power of Observation section in chapter 4.)

Accreditation processes vary greatly from organization to organization. Many accreditation processes available to school-age programs include a self-study. Not all nationally accrediting bodies are recognized by all states. Some states have used the National AfterSchool Association's (NAA) *Standards for Quality School-Age Care* to develop their own statewide accreditation standards. Check with your state afterschool association to determine if a state accreditation process is available in your state, how to apply for it, and what it costs. A state process can provide your program with another accreditation option. In many states, programs that are accredited receive additional subsidy dollars per child and qualify for additional training dollars or grant opportunities. Once you have researched the options available, you can decide whether accreditation is right for your program. Appendix C lists a variety of assessment tools that can be used for evaluating a school-age program. While the list is not exhaustive, it does include many of the nationally recognized assessment tools, accrediting organizations, and information about each tool.

Americans with Disabilities Act

With the passage of the Americans with Disabilities Act (ADA), federal laws govern accessibility issues for anyone with a temporary or permanent disability. Titles II and III of the ADA and Section 504 of the Rehabilitation Act set mandatory guidelines for group care settings that enroll children with physical, psychological, or cognitive disabilities. This includes afterschool programs.

By law, school-age programs must be inclusive, and children with disabilities must be allowed to enroll. As required by the ADA, a team that includes the child's parents or guardians, school and medical personnel, and other individuals working directly with the child (such as school-age program staff) makes the final determination about placement for a child with special needs. But enrolling is not always the same as attending a program. If the needs of a child cannot be met *in the program in which he is enrolled,* the child poses a risk of harm to the health or safety of others, or the child's care would *fundamentally* alter the nature of the program, alternate programming should be considered to ensure the child's safety, well-being, and overall development.

While staff are responsible for ensuring that all children's needs are met in the program space, site administrators must determine how to create a safe and successful environment for children with disabilities. By law, these children must have equal opportunity to be enrolled and then freely participate in your program. You may not have a child with disabilities now, but school-age programs have a legal obligation to make reasonable environmental modifications or accommodations if a child with disabilities should enroll or if a child currently in your program has a temporary disability such as a broken leg. Reasonable modifications or accommodations means making needed changes to help a child with special needs reach her potential. Many of these modifications can be carried out without much difficulty or expense. For example, simple and inexpensive changes include the following:

- installing grab bars in the bathroom
- rearranging furniture to create broader pathways
- adding ramps or handrails to help a child with limited mobility

- purchasing or borrowing large-print books for a child with limited eyesight
- acquiring large-piece puzzles for a child with limited fine-motor skills

You should not simply assume your facility cannot accommodate a child with a disability without major and costly changes. As you research ADA compliance for your program, know that tax deductions are available for small businesses to offset the cost of making the changes needed to comply with the ADA; consult with your tax adviser or the Internal Revenue Service. Also, assistance in interpreting ADA guidelines is available free of charge from the U.S. Department of Justice at www .ada.gov or by phone at 800-514-0301.

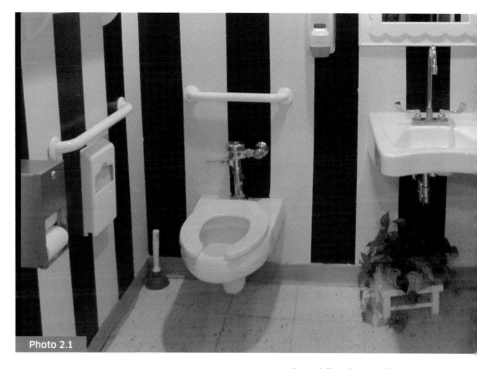

Photo 2.1

By adding handrails and a hand-washing sink that are usable by individuals with disabilities, this program has met the ADA requirements in an attractive and functional manner.

You can further support children with disabilities in your program by helping your staff understand their limitations and their abilities. When reviewing health forms completed by families and their children's doctors, decide what information the staff need to know to ensure children's needs are being met. Ensure that all staff members are aware of children's identified needs and learning potential by:

- Providing appropriate training on a particular diagnosed condition and on how best to support children's needs.
- Encouraging routine, systematic observations of children to plan appropriate learning experiences.
- Collaborating with families, school and medical personnel, and service agencies to develop common goals and expectations for children.

When designing your environment, work with staff to include children with disabilities by considering the accommodations that follow. In addition to helping those children who need a modified environment, these strategies help all children be successful.

Accommodations for hearing impairments

- Let the child initiate communication. Wait and observe; pointing, eye-gazing gestures, grunts, and crying all have meaning.
- Talk distinctly and be sure the child can see your face.
- Be at the same physical level; this makes you more aware of nonverbal and verbal initiations.
- Use gestures.
- Use sign language.
- Make sure there is adequate lighting.
- Use color codes and pictures along with words.
- Encourage communication by selecting activities that facilitate language.
- Seat the child close to a staff person when doing group activities.
- Avoid extra background noises when you are doing activities.

Accommodations for visual impairments

- Use large print and Braille in signs.
- Provide Braille materials.
- Use large-print books and pop-up books.
- When the child enters your program for the first time, walk her around the room. Some children will pace off the room so they know the number of steps from one space to another.
- Keep pathways clear of obstructions.
- Leave furniture and equipment in the same place at all times. If you need to move furniture, show and tell the child about the move.
- Describe activities.
- Use string around the room to make a path for the child to hold on to.
- Provide toys with texture.
- Provide toys with sounds.
- Use art materials and sensory materials, such as playdough, sand, and fingerpaints, to stimulate touch.

Accommodations for physical impairments

- Become knowledgeable about the child's physical limitations.
- Check with the family to see if there are any handling needs or adaptive equipment needed.
- Make sure the room is well lit.
- Provide adequate open spaces between furniture and at tables for wheelchairs, walkers, and other equipment.

- Provide rails and ramps where you have steps.
- Show and tell the child when you move furniture.
- Provide activities that use all parts of the body.
- Provide extra time during activities that require balance and coordination.
- Provide ways for the child to sit with the group.
- Make sure all activities and toys are accessible.
- Provide adaptive materials, such as large pencils, button puzzles, and easy-grip scissors.

Accommodations for ADD and ADHD

- Create and post a consistent, clearly defined schedule.
- Give the child positive attention—then she will demand less negative attention.
- Repeat, repeat, repeat.
- Designate a place for the children to regain control.
- Use positive consequences and do not use bribes.
- Model and teach socially appropriate behaviors.
- Offer choices whenever possible, but have limits and be prepared to meet the child's needs within the limits.
- Give the child responsibilities you know she can handle. Make sure it is meaningful and not busy work.
- Be there; it makes a difference.
- Make eye contact.

Accommodations for language learning or memory difficulties

- Provide a consistent, structured environment.
- Display posters and pictures at children's eye level.
- Use color codes, pictures, and words to help the child learn where an activity takes place or where materials belong.
- Break activities into small pieces.
- Use short, simple directions.
- Ask the child to repeat your directions.
- Show the child what to do instead of just telling her what to do.
- Believe in the child's ability to succeed.
- Do not interrupt the child or rush her.
- Do not pressure the child to talk.
- Name and label objects.

Accommodations for behavioral problems

- Maintain consistent rules and structure. Be fair, firm, and consistent.
- Maintain a full schedule of activities. Keep activities structured and well planned.
- Review rules before and during games and activities; ask the child to write down the rules for games and post them for everyone to see.
- Be aware of your body language, tone of voice, and eye contact.
- Intervene early before conflict occurs.
- Model and teach appropriate social interaction and friend-making skills.
- Help the child control her behavior by staying near. Gently put your hand on the child's arm or shoulder and give her an opportunity to make a different choice.
- Use stories, dramatic play, and puppets to teach appropriate ways to express positive and negative feelings.
- Give four positive statements for every negative or corrective statement.
- Inform the child and the family regularly of positive behaviors.

The Administrator's Role in Evaluating the Environment

Evaluating all aspects of your program should be an ongoing process of gathering and evaluating data and information. This process allows you to identify program successes, weaknesses, and underused areas so that you can plan specific changes to make in your environment. Gathering information can be done through formal assessments, which produce quantifiable results, and through observation. As an administrator, you may do some of the assessing and observing yourself, but you should also involve the staff in these processes. Staff members are key players in how well your program environment functions. When they conduct assessments and observations, they see things that can help them create a quality environment by making improvements. Your role as an administrator, then, is to take these actions:

1. Develop systems and schedules for gathering information about the environment.
2. Provide training for staff to assess and observe.
3. Ensure that you are getting all the information you need to effectively evaluate how well your environment is working.
4. Analyze the information and evaluate what needs to be changed in the environment.

Review Your Program Environment

To decide what needs changing in your program environment, you need to gather information about what is and is not working. Two ways are key:

• **Formal assessment:** a formal, research-based tool that asks the same questions each time you conduct a review so that the results can be calculated accurately. This tool is designed to measure your program against standardized criteria.

• **Observation:** the process of watching what is happening in a program and making notes about what you see and hear.

FORMAL ASSESSMENT

Formal assessments guide you through the evaluation of your program space in a systematic way and measure the program on a rating scale. These tools are based in research, have been tested in the field, and include an explanation of how each criterion is scored. Many assessment tools include training that helps observers understand the assessment criteria and scoring to ensure consistency of scoring. There are a variety of formal assessment tools for school-age environments. Some assessments look at the entire program while others look at specific areas. Some focus on regularly assessing staff to document their performance and to identify needed training. For example, the National AfterSchool Association "Code of Ethics" (2009) outlines the staff's role in afterschool programs and helps staff understand their ethical responsibilities to children and families related to the confidentiality of information gained through assessment. (See appendix C for more information about this and other assessment tools.)

Formal assessments are scheduled for a specific time and use a standardized tool that is designed to look at specific aspects of the program or the program as a whole. Some administrators choose to conduct assessments to gain a global understanding of how effectively the staff work together, design program environments, and meet the needs of the children. Formal assessments typically last for up to two to three hours so the observer can see most aspects of the program.

During formal assessment, the observer can use an existing tool, a checklist, or detailed notes on one or more behaviors, interactions, events, or aspects of the environment. Assessments can be conducted by program staff, administrators, an outside consultant, or a parent who is trained in the assessment tool. When program staff administer the assessment, they become aware of all of the areas observed and the expectations of each standard or criterion within the tool. Sometimes outside consultants are brought in to provide objective assessments since they do not have a vested interest in the program. When parents conduct the assessment, they become aware of the many aspects of afterschool programming and the expectations outlined in the tool.

The assessment process provides administrators with information about how well the environment supports the needs of the children, what areas and materials are working, and what needs to be changed. The first time you use a particular assessment tool, you acquire a baseline of information about your program. Subsequent assessments using the same tool will help you to track your progress, tell you whether the changes made were effective, and what other changes need to be made.

OBSERVATION

Observations can provide information on a variety of aspects of a program, from issues that arise among children to problematic areas in your program's environment. For example, observations can describe children's behaviors and interactions, accomplishments or challenges; play areas that are of interest and those that are not; and activities that children enjoy or avoid. Observations can be formal or informal.

Informal observations occur during the course of the day as the staff move to and from areas of the room or work with individuals and groups of children. School-age programs can have so much happening all at once that often observations are spontaneous and quick. The point is to record what you see and hear. An observation is a snapshot in time—what was happening on the specific day and at the time the observation was made. Thus, observations should not be a onetime thing; periodic scheduled observations are ideal. Some program staff feel, however, that frequent short observations allow program changes to occur in a timely fashion. When spontaneous daily observations are made for several weeks and then reviewed as a whole, they can give a clear picture of areas that are and are not being used, areas and materials that cause conflict, children's interactions, and staff struggles with a specific child.

Providing dedicated time, all the documents, and a quiet space to review them helps staff to determine children's areas of strength and areas that need improvement.

Photo 2.2

Regardless of the type of observation (formal or informal), an observer watches, listens, and records what children and staff do and say over a period of time without adding judgment or opinion. An observer does not interact with others in the program but rather takes a position that allows a view of the whole program without disrupting the activities. For more information of observations, see the section Recognizing the Observation Skills of Staff later in this chapter.

Working with Limited Resources

As always, change is limited by your creativity and money. School-age programs often operate on tight budgets with strict allocations for training, materials, and environmental changes. When deciding how best to use your money, remember all three dimensions of the environment: temporal, interpersonal, and physical. All of these dimensions need funding in various ways. The key to success is creating a balance so that all dimensions of the environment are supported. This balance, coupled with maximizing your program space and making use of community resources, will go a long way in helping you stretch your budget. For example, your observations may have indicated a need to train staff in making effective transitions, creating an effective daily schedule, scaffolding children's learning through problem-solving techniques, and partnering with families. Additionally, the observations may have pointed out the need for more exciting learning materials and for replacement of worn-out or broken furniture. No set formula governs how you use your funds, so you must allocate spending according to what the children and environment need to create an exciting and welcoming program space. So how do you stretch your budget to meet all these needs?

If you operate on a limited budget, you will need to unleash your creativity and maximize your community resources. When considering how you will afford changes in the environment, you have a number of options. For starters, ask families to volunteer in various ways, such as painting, building shelves, and creating inviting outdoor spaces. Provide families with a donations wish list of materials, furniture, equipment, and consumable supplies that will enhance the program (offer a letter of donation for their taxes).

Shop at resale shops and garage sales for major purchases, such as large wooden cabinets and overstuffed furniture, usually available at a significantly reduced price. If you hear of a program closing, see what you can purchase within your budget. Make sure that anything you purchase has not been recalled before you place it in your program, and examine used furniture carefully to ensure it is intact and sturdy enough for children to use safely. In addition, clean all used items to remove any potential health hazards. For smaller items, such as storage baskets or bins, take advantage of sales where you may be able to purchase these for considerably less money. And do not forget to contact local foundations and community organizations, which often offer grants to pay for or subsidize the cost of environmental changes.

Developing relationships with community organizations can help your program in other ways as well. For example, professional development organizations and resource and referral agencies may provide training for staff for free or at a low cost. Search for professional conferences that provide a variety of training topics for one price. Partner with other school-age programs to provide training for staff at half the price. Attend community meetings so you can build a network with organizations that support afterschool programming. These opportunities differ from location to location. Some examples are community roundtables such as directors' networks, health and human services meetings, chamber of commerce meetings, and local initiative meetings. Knowing what other community organizations are doing enables you to identify ways in which you might help them and they in turn might reciprocate.

The relationships you cultivate might even save your program some expenses. For example, an organization may be looking for a community service project that can meet a need you have, such as painting your classroom or creating a new outdoor play space. Or you may learn of an opportunity for the children in your program to provide a service to an organization, which then donates money, materials, or expertise to your program. One school-age program worked with an organization to separate donated clothing into sizes and gender so it could be shipped to a low-income area for needy families. In return, the organization donated money to the school-age program's field trip fund, which the children used to bring the mobile zoo to their program, something that was previously beyond their budget. Note that not all organizations will pay your program for completing a community service project. Nevertheless, exposing children to a project that supports others helps teach them understanding and empathy, a benefit to which you cannot attach a monetary value. When people in the broader community know you and what you are doing in your program, they will tell others about your program, helping you market it and meet your financial needs.

Your close working relationships with other community organizations will also keep you informed about resources that may be of interest to the families in your program. These opportunities can span a broad spectrum: movies, community activities, library events, parenting events, subsidy information, weather-related assistance such as flood relief or help with gas and electric bills, opportunities for English language learning, or assistance with medical or financial issues.

Communicating with Families

One of your jobs as an administrator is to ensure that the families in your program are getting the information they need. In so doing, you help them understand program activities and feel a sense of ownership in your program. One great way to inform parents about program events is to film or take snapshots of plays and activities. Connecting the recording equipment to a television or computer monitor allows you to show videos and digital photos during open houses and recruitment events. Media clips can also be used to advertise your program or show families the activities their children have been doing.

E-mailing and texting are often the communication of choice for day-to-day messages between the afterschool program, the parents, and the school. For example, you can send e-mail or text messages to parents to tell them about upcoming events, to request needed materials, and to remind them to provide up-to-date information. You can also send or post electronic monthly newsletters, which will reduce your printing costs. Remember, not all parents have e-mailing or texting capabilities, so make hard copies available to those parents who need or request them.

A program website can provide families and the community with valuable information about your program, fees, openings, services, and upcoming events. Updating the website can be a great project for older children, allowing them to write, design, and publish information to keep families and the community informed about the program. Again, before posting photos of children on the web, obtain a photo release from parents or legal guardians.

Refer to the table Communicating with Families in chapter 7 for a list of a marketing and informational options for your program.

PHOTO RELEASE REQUIREMENTS

Make sure you have a photo release on file for every child who appears in images you intend to use in program materials. Verify that the release states the ways in which you will use the images.

Supporting Your Staff

Your staff needs your guidance and support to help them be effective. They need you to communicate clear expectations about the program environment and their role in it. In their daily interactions with children and families, the staff can be the bridge to creative solutions that improve your program environment. Those staff members who work directly with children are in the best position to know what is most appropriate and interesting for them. As an administrator, the more you do to recognize and appreciate the value your staff brings to your program, the more support your staff will feel.

CONNECTING JOB EXPECTATIONS TO YOUR PROGRAM ENVIRONMENT

Hiring the right staff can be the hallmark of a quality program. Part of finding and keeping the right staff is developing job descriptions that clearly define duties. By clearly listing and reviewing job expectations with staff and job candidates, you can limit misunderstandings. To relate job duties to your program environment, you will need to identify specific tasks in each area of the environment. These may be defined by program area or by the dimension of environment (temporal, interpersonal, and physical). Be sure to include responsibilities that relate not only to the physical space but also to the temporal and interpersonal environment. Address not only daily tasks but also those that occur weekly, monthly, or yearly, and note the frequency next to the task in the job description. For example, duties might include the following:

Photo 2.3

When staff take time to engage in games that interest children, there are many opportunities to build relationships and teach social skills while extending their learning.

- designing physical space to meet the needs of all children
- planning activities, events, and field trips that promote learning and social skills
- creating lesson plans that reflect the interests and abilities of the children
- developing program goals
- designing policies and procedures to create a supportive environment
- maintaining a safe environment
- making anyone who enters your program feel welcome
- observing children to assess how well the program is meeting their needs
- establishing rules and enforcing consequences
- maintaining ethical behavior at all times

After you list the duties, write next to each one the skills you think are needed to accomplish these duties effectively. Develop a clear vision of the skills you want employees to possess. For example, skills might include the following:

- has good written and oral communication skills
- is flexible
- appears organized

- has creative ideas
- has experience working with target age group
- enjoys working with school-age children
- likes science, math, and analytical challenges
- loves being outdoors

Use the job duties and skills listed above and those listed in the *Core Knowledge and Competencies for Afterschool and Youth Development Professionals,* which was adopted by the National AfterSchool Association in 2011 to help develop job descriptions. This lists the competencies that school-age staff need to provide quality programming in the physical, temporal, and interpersonal environments. It rates each competency on a scale from one to five, with five being the highest level of proficiency. The competencies are formatted into ten content areas:

- child and youth growth and development
- learning environments and curriculum
- child/youth observation and assessment
- interactions with children and youth
- youth engagement
- cultural competency and responsiveness
- family, school, and community relationships
- safety and wellness
- program planning and development
- professional development and leadership

In addition to helping you create, revise, and refine job descriptions for your staff, this tool can help you assess staff members' level of competency in the ten areas. This assessment can then help you determine what training may be needed in each area.

Observe staff members at work, and conduct regular performance reviews to help staff remain focused and improve their skills. Sometimes you will find you need to add duties to a job description or reassign duties among staff. If this occurs, be sure to review the revised job duties with the staff affected. As a general rule, you should review job descriptions at least once a year and communicate any changes to the staff. Posting job descriptions allows everyone to be aware of their job responsibilities and those of others. Keeping all staff members aware of who is responsible for what ensures that no aspects of the program environment are neglected. When the program environment runs smoothly, everyone who enters senses the commitment to quality and to the well-being of children. Staff, children, and families all want to be there.

RECOGNIZING THE OBSERVATION SKILLS OF STAFF

The staff who work directly with and observe children every day have a wealth of information about your program and the children. Help staff understand the importance of what they see in the program from day to day. Their observations are essential to understanding how the program is functioning. Your recognition of this role allows the staff to feel that they are valued.

Often staff members try to recall information from weeks ago. As much as we would like our memories to be 100 percent correct, we are usually far from accurate. Encourage staff to write down what they are seeing, either throughout the day or during time scheduled at the end of the day. Assure staff that these observation notes usually take little time—just a few minutes to write down something they observed happening. Stress the importance of writing the note the same day they made the observation, while their memory is still fresh.

Observation sounds easy to some staff, while others find it daunting. With a little planning and preparation, you can make it easy for staff to record observations during their busy day. The following strategies will help your staff prepare and conduct effective observations:

Provide a clipboard with paper, and house it inside a cabinet. This ensures that all observations are kept confidential and accessible only to staff. Instead of plain notepaper, you might place adhesive mailing labels or a sticky notepad on a clipboard—the observation is recorded on the label. Periodically, sort the notes by program area, type of environment, or individual child, and stick them onto master sheets placed in folders for respective categories. This system also makes it easy for the observer to collect and evaluate observation notes at a later date. Additionally, these notes can serve as a great record when conducting conferences to document a child's progress and the skill areas that need support.

Rotate note taking. Sharing this responsibility relieves staff members from feeling burdened by conducting observations. Rotation can be done among staff or by placing children into groups and rotating groups among staff. This method provides an objective summation of each child based on the observations of several staff members over time and does not burden one staff member with the sole responsibility of conducting daily observations.

Encourage staff to note what worked well and what did not. They should record what areas children are not using and areas in which conflict always seems to be happening. Tell staff that recording this information for several weeks will make clear what the real issues are and what were just onetime occurrences. You may want staff to focus their observations on a specific area, segment, or child. If so, still emphasize the importance of recording everything they see, even if it was not something they originally set out to observe.

For more information on the administrator's role in observations, review The Administrator's Role in Evaluating the Environment earlier in this chapter. Observation is also addressed in The Power of Observation in chapter 4, which focuses on how to use observation to better understand children and support their learning.

ENCOURAGING STAFF TO BE AGENTS OF CHANGE

The only thing that is certain in life is change. As children grow and develop, new children enter the program. Some staff members leave, and you replace them with new employees. The evolution of the program environment is an ongoing process. With each change, the environment will need adjustments. The staff members who interact each day with the children are the natural agents of change. On any given day, the staff observe the interactions between children, between children and staff, and between children and the environment. These observations can help inform the staff about what works and what does not in the program space and with individual children. Not only do the staff members who work with the children understand the dynamic of the program space, but also they are often the ones responsible for making changes in the environment.

Maximize the benefits your staff bring to the program environment. Provide opportunities for their input on how the environment is set up and what changes need to be made. This topic could be a regular agenda item at staff meetings, or you may choose to cover it more informally during conversation with the staff members. Sometimes you know that something is not working but are unsure of how to fix it. Work together as a team. Discuss the situation, brainstorm possible solutions, and ask the children for their input. After all, it is their program. Make sure your staff understands any budget constraints that might affect possible solutions, especially if you are exploring a major redesigning of the space. Do not discourage staff input but rather suggest that changes may have to be done in phases, or a fundraiser may be needed to boost the budget.

After exploring solutions to a particular issue, choose the one idea that you feel has the best chance of working. Give the children time to adjust to the change before deciding if it worked. Do not throw away the list that you generated; it will serve as a resource for new ideas if your first choice does not succeed. Do not be upset if the first idea does not work. With a little flexibility and creativity, you will find what works best for your program.

SHARING THIS BOOK WITH YOUR STAFF

This book can help guide your staff as a source of ideas and solutions when they look critically at their program space for changes to make in the environment. Activities are provided at the end of each chapter to help your staff focus on specific aspects of designing a quality afterschool environment. Having staff read a chapter prior to completing the activities will provide them with information on how to do (or work on) the activities successfully. As you continue to read the book, you will find that it discusses many different areas in an afterschool program, from suggesting materials and equipment, to helping the staff understand their role, to supporting child development needs. Staff can use this information as a catalyst for creating an exciting learning environment. Here are additional ways to use the book with staff:

- Provide each staff member with a copy of the book, and as a group go chapter by chapter to provide in-depth professional development for staff.
- During staff meetings, choose the information in one section as a conversation starter, a training module, or a springboard to generate solutions for areas that need to be addressed.
- Use the information about multiple intelligences, learning domains, and temperaments in chapter 4 to help staff understand how children react to certain situations and events.
- Using the questions and activities at the end of all chapters, have staff work together to answer the questions, reflect as a group on the existing program, and develop a plan for change.
- Download the book's questionnaires from www.redleafpress.org so staff can evaluate your existing program and create a welcoming environment in which children want to stay, play, and learn.

Activities and Questions

Use these activities and questions to determine how informed the program administrator and staff are about the issues addressed in this chapter.

1. Do you have a written job description for all employees? How do you communicate job expectations to employees? How often do you review job descriptions?

2. Do you have a QRIS in your state for school-age programs? If so, what are the benefits of participating in this system?

3. Does your state offer an accreditation process for school-age programs? If yes, what are the benefits and challenges to achieving accreditation?

4. How do you use community resources in your program?

5. Does your state require school-age programs to be licensed to operate? Is your program required to be licensed? If yes, do you have a copy of these regulations, and do you have your license displayed?

6. How often do you observe your staff and program space? How do you document these observations? How do you determine with whom to share the information gained during an observation? How do you communicate the results of the observation to staff?

7. What assistance and training are provided to staff about observation skills and various observation tools?

8. How do you include staff in decisions about changes in program policies, procedures, and environment?

9. What are some ways you stretch your budget to make changes in the environment or provide training for staff?

CHAPTER 3

Creating Safe Environments

IN HIS BOOK *Caring Spaces, Learning Places: Children's Environments That Work*, early childhood expert Jim Greenman writes that there is nothing more important than creating a healthy, safe setting that promotes a warm, personal, and challenging program (2005). This notion transfers easily to school-age programs, as parents, educators, and staff in recreational programs agree that promoting children's health and safety is their foremost priority when creating a caring environment. In fact, parent surveys on out-of-home care indicate this is one of parents' most important considerations when selecting a program for their children (Layzer, Goodson, and Brown-Lyons 2007).

Safety is broadly defined as being free from danger, risk, and injury. Danger, risk, and injury include both physical and emotional harm. Keeping children safe and healthy while in your care is a huge responsibility. Accomplishing this is a balancing act between establishing careful protectors, reducing hazards, and still keeping the environment challenging and fun. Remember: safety is more than just adding or removing items from the environment. It is how the elements in the school-age environment are used by children of varying ages and abilities. A jigsaw is not dangerous when not in use, nor are swings, hammers, or knives. A loft or high platforms are challenging yet usable for older children but dangerous or harmful for younger ones.

By the time children reach school age, they have more or less mastered control of their motor skills. Now they find more thrills and spills through spontaneous activities, often leaving adults shaking their heads. Nevertheless, there are many ways of guarding and guiding children in a stimulating yet safe environment. It is critical to reduce both the occurrence as well as the potential for physical or emotional harm while children are in a school-age program. Anita Olds (2001) contends that when the environment reduces the number of potentially harmful factors, children relax and interact more creatively with their surroundings. Both staff and children can be alert for potentially harmful or hazardous situations. When in doubt about a

Photo 3.1

An exciting school-age environment such as this combines children's needs and interests in a hazard-free but challenging environment. All furniture and materials are well maintained to ensure children are kept safe, healthy, and secure.

safety issue, check with your state licensing agency and your health and fire departments.

In every way possible, school-age children need to receive the message that they are safe, valued, capable, and special to the adults in their lives. All staff members have a responsibility to let children know they can feel safe and secure in your program. While each program is unique in size, location, budget, and number and needs of children, creating a feeling of safety and well-being must be a top priority for all programs.

Physical Safety

School-age children understand about rough play, injuries, and dangerous situations. Talk with children about safety while using equipment both indoors and outside. Get them involved in setting up safety rules and consequences for not complying with these. Have them take responsibility for controlling their environment and keeping it safe. Post and review rules often to ensure all children understand what they mean.

Generally speaking, conducting scheduled safety evaluations is the ideal first step to creating a safe environment. The frequency of the evaluations or any inspection process is driven by regulatory agencies or guidelines. For instance, it is a good practice to inspect your playground daily before children are allowed to use it, while an evaluation of fire extinguishers is done annually. Check with your local licensure, building, or permit department for rules and regulations for your area. In addition, contact the National Program for Playground Safety about playground safety, and consult the Americans with Disability Act (ADA) for requirements to ensure your program is readily accessible to and usable by individuals with disabilities.

INDOOR SAFETY

Watch children at play in indoor places and the need for safe places and protection is compelling. They are adventurous and take risks. They use materials creatively and often not for their intended purpose. Their activity level is typically high with little regard for personal space or personal safety. They need and deserve a place free from hazardous materials or situations that could cause injury. By knowing and following basic principles of indoor safety, you can ensure your indoor program will be a safe and healthy environment for everyone.

Manufacturing safety guidelines for children's furniture are limited to cribs, bunk beds, high chairs, and some materials used in construction and in finishes. The U.S. government has no set standards to regulate the manufacturing of other children's furniture, such as tables and chairs, shelving units, and cubbies. These pieces of furniture come in all styles and are made from many different materials. Sturdiness is a major consideration, since we know school-age children use furniture in all kinds of unintended and creative ways. When evaluating the safety of toys, materials, and equipment for your program, consider the following:

- **Age appropriateness:** Materials for children should suit their age and developmental stage. Children should be interested and engaged with the materials and activity areas; if materials are too easy, they become boring, and if too hard, they become frustrating and potentially hazardous. Keep older children's things in a space designated for them. When in doubt, look at the suggested age on children's materials. These will guide you on what is safe for children of all ages.

- **Safety and size:** The basic guide is the smaller the child, the larger the toy should be. The key aspect to remember about toy safety is that there are no guarantees a toy will be 100 percent safe. Adult supervision is critical to toy safety regardless of the age of the child.
- **Washability:** Cleaning and sanitizing toys and furnishings are critical to keeping children safe and healthy. Look at tags on cloth toys, rugs, and pillows to be sure they are safe to machine wash and do not need to be dry-cleaned. Dry-cleaning solvents can be a source of headaches, dizziness, nausea, and eye and skin irritation for children and adults (Kamrin 2001).
- **Sturdiness and safe construction:** Furniture needs to be sturdy. In addition, avoid poorly made toys with pieces that can be pulled off and swallowed, such as buttons, wheels, stickers, or labels. Do not buy toys with moving parts that can pinch, scratch, or trap parts of a child's body. If you have toys or playthings with strings or cords, keep these shorter than twelve inches to avoid strangulation hazards.
- **Nontoxicity:** Surfaces should be lickable and likable. The Consumer Product Safety Commission (CPSC) maintains guidelines on acceptable materials for toy manufacturers. Millions of toys have been recalled worldwide because of dangerous levels of lead or other potential hazards to children. Access the complete listing of recalled toys and other items used by or with children on the Consumer Product Safety Commission website at www.cpsc.gov/cpscpub/prerel/category/toy.html.

FIRE SAFETY

Fire safety is governed by guidelines set by building codes and structural requirements. Know and follow the rules. Each state has its own fire and safety requirements, so check and follow these carefully. You should consider licensure regulations and building codes as your primary sources of fire safety guidance.

The National Fire Protection Association (NFPA) is the world's leading advocate for fire prevention and public safety. They regularly update safety recommendations in the publication *NFPA 101: Life Safety Code*. The 2012 edition provides extensive guidelines for facilities that have children in group care, including schools, churches, family child care homes, and school-age program facilities. Whether your program is housed in dedicated space or shared space, this guidance applies to you. One useful recommendation relates to the amount of wall space you cover with child-prepared artwork and teaching or display materials: if your building does not have a sprinkler system, do not

Photo 3.2

The ceiling drape and droplights lower the ceiling and soften the overall feeling of the environment. Use flame-retardant fabric and lead-free paint as safety precautions throughout program space.

cover more than 20 percent of a wall. If your building does have a sprinkler system, do not cover more than 50 percent of a wall (NFPA 2011). In addition to reducing the risk of fire from these flammable materials, you will keep wall displays from overwhelming and distracting children and reduce the visual clutter of the environment.

Check the fabric content of furniture upholstery, drapes, valances, and even pillows in your environment. Most fabrics or fibers will burn, but some are naturally more resistant to fire than others. You can find fabric composition on the manufacturers' "Do Not Remove" tags attached to items covered in fabric. Check your local fire codes for specific regulations on what fabrics can and cannot be used in your program. Basically, there are three ratings for fabrics or fibers:

These furniture slipcovers and pillowcases are easy to remove, clean, and replace to keep the environment looking and smelling fresh.

- Fire-resistant fabrics or fibers have been treated to minimize the spread of flames.
- Fireproof or flameproof fabrics literally will not burn. To be labeled "flameproof," the Federal Trade Commission requires 100 percent of the fibers in a fabric to be fireproof.
- Flame-retardant fabrics resist or retard the spreading of flames. These fabrics are either naturally flame retardant or have had special finishes applied to them.

(Interior Mall 2013)

Photo 3.3

OUTDOOR SAFETY

Children have a special connection with the outdoors. Learning in outdoor environments can take place through exploration, creativity, and physical exercise. A safe outdoor environment is more than sturdy playground equipment. It is a space where children are allowed to run, yell, jump, and climb as much as they can. It is a place where children can connect with nature while staying safe from natural harm such as poisonous plants or animals. When you create a rich and complex outdoor environment geared to the children's ages and development, you are well on your way to connecting children with nature.

So that you can take full advantage of the values of outdoor play, you need to carefully evaluate the safety of your outdoor environment. An exciting but safe outside environment is a vital part of any afterschool program and an extension of your indoor learning environment. Does it invite and support children's play, fitness, and discovery without threat of injury? Your outdoor environment should be made up of safe places that are challenging but not hazardous. Children will see a challenge, but a hazard of that activity may not be apparent to them.

Safe playground equipment and adult supervision are extremely important, but this is only half of the equation. In addition, children must know how to be safe and act responsibly on a playground. While children of all ages benefit from opportunities to take risks and test their skills, they also need to be taught how to avoid injuries by using play equipment properly. Posted rules for safe outdoor play along with careful staff supervision and guidance will discourage activities such as sliding headfirst, standing on swings, and climbing up slides. Review the outdoor rules daily, because children forget and new children enter your program regularly. This enables all children to learn the rules and allows them to take responsibility for their own choices. With good planning and close supervision, outdoor environments stretch children's muscles and their learning.

According to the Nemours Foundation (2013), a nonprofit children's health organization, types of equipment that are not safe for school-age outdoor play spaces include the following:

- animal figure swings
- glider swings that hold more than one child at a time
- swinging ropes that can fray, unravel, or form a noose (any kind of rope attached to play equipment poses a strangulation hazard, so never let a child tie jump ropes or leashes onto the equipment)
- exercise rings (as used in gymnastics) and trapeze bars
- monkey bars (as a stand-alone climbing structure)
- trampolines

KEY FACTORS IN PLAYGROUND SAFETY

- close and continual supervision
- proper ground surface and adequate fall zones
- design and spacing of equipment
- regular inspection and maintenance of equipment

SAFETY CHECKLISTS

The indoor and outdoor safety checklists that follow will help you evaluate the safety of your facility (these checklists are available to download and print at www.redleafpress.org). Think of these as minimal compliance guidelines. Add other items to this list based on issues raised by aspects of your program, such as location, ages, or special needs of children, age of

Photo 3.4

Keep protective safety gear close to areas where it is needed, visible, and easily accessible for children to use.

the building, and parental input. Assign at least one staff member to act as the lead safety inspector, but instruct all staff to be alert and report potential hazards. In addition, school-age children are very alert and aware of their surroundings. Capitalize on this by asking them to be health and safety inspectors. The children may prove to be your best detectives. Make this a fun experience with checklists, safety gloves, goggles, flashlights, and magnifiers. When anyone finds problems, remove them, fix them, or safeguard children from them immediately.

Indoor Safety Checklist

1. All locations in the environment are free of clutter, debris, and chipped and broken material.

2. All furniture is in good repair (no sharp edges, splinters, broken or cracked parts, or chipped paint).

Photo 3.5

Like race car drivers, children need crash helmets anytime they are in a wheeled vehicle. Ensure helmets and all safety gear are kept in good condition.

3. All wheeled items have a locking lever or fold-up wheels to keep furniture secured in place.

4. Extension cords and electrical wires are not frayed and do not lay or hang in program spaces where they may cause injury to staff or children.

5. Locations for children are free of potentially harmful materials, such as cleaning solvents, flammable materials, chemicals, medications, instruments with sharp edges or points, and any items marked "Keep out of reach of children" or "To be used by children only with close adult supervision."

6. Floors and rugs are clean, in good repair, and do not pose a tripping hazard.

Photo 3.6

Children must wear protective gear, and staff must monitor high-risk activities carefully.

Photo 3.7

Photo 3.8

Fire extinguishers and smoke and carbon monoxide detectors should be located throughout the program space and checked periodically.

7. Indoor climbing apparatuses, lofts, or platforms over thirty-six inches in height have adequate fall zone protection under and around them, such as padding, mats, or other solid material in sufficient amount to prevent injuries from falls.

8. Steps or stairs with three or more treads have sturdy railings or handrails and nonslip treads.

9. Emergency exit procedures are posted in a location easily seen by children and adults.

10. Emergency evacuation plans are known by children and practiced on a routine basis.

11. Points of egress are clearly marked, and exit zones are free of clutter.

12. Exit door signs, emergency strobe lights, smoke and carbon monoxide detectors, and audible emergency systems are in good working order.

13. Toys, games, and other materials used by children are intact, free of splinters and loose parts, and work properly.

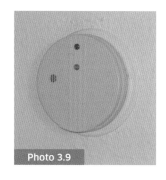
Photo 3.9

14. Fire extinguishers, automatic sprinkler system, panic hardware, and closed-circuit monitoring system (if any) are working properly.

Photo 3.10

Outdoor Safety Checklist

1. Play equipment is free of loose and sharp parts, frayed rope and cables, splinters, broken and cracked material, and chipped paint.

2. Play equipment is securely anchored in the ground.

Select safety devices that have both sound and light detection to ensure anyone with a vision or hearing disability is alerted to a potentially harmful situation.

3. Metal equipment is free of rust; wooden equipment is free of splinters, rough surfaces, and broken pieces.

4. No tripping hazards or protrusions are present in the play area or sidewalks.

5. All outdoor areas are free of animal feces, broken glass, poisonous plants, standing water, and other potentially harmful debris.

6. Adequate fall zone protection is around and under all play equipment as outlined in the Public Playground Safety Handbook (access at www.cpsc.gov).

7. Fences around the play area (if present) are in good repair and free of broken pieces.

This outdoor play space is open yet supportive of a variety of imaginative play possibilities. Check all areas regularly to ensure they are safe for children's use.
Photo 3.11

Health and Hygiene

Healthy children and staff require a healthy place to work and play. Mention of "sick buildings" floods the news. While there are many reasons facilities are unhealthy, this section focuses on key issues for programs that care for children. Incorporating health and hygiene practices into your environment helps convey your concern for the well-being of the children, and it gives families peace of mind to know your commitment.

HAND WASHING

Instilling healthy habits in school-agers is a work in progress. Younger school-age children know they should wash their hands frequently but often find other activities more engaging and a higher priority. Nevertheless, the American Academy of Pediatrics (AAP) says that hand washing is the number one way to reduce the spread of germs and diseases (2006).

Having toilets and hand-washing facilities easily accessible to all children is essential. While specific guidelines for the number of toilets and sinks required for school-age programs are not well defined, general guidelines are based on the maximum allowable occupancy of each facility.

Ensure children and staff regularly review appropriate hand-washing techniques. Post hand-washing signs in restrooms and above sinks to give children visual reminders of what they should do. (Your local health department may require hand-washing signs to be posted.) Remember: children's hands burn easily; keep water temperature at 120 degrees Fahrenheit or less. Ensure children have access to soap, paper towels, and toilet paper.

Photo 3.12

Providing soap, paper towels for children to use independently, and an alcohol-based hand sanitizer to be used with adult guidance is a first step in keeping children clean and healthy.

A soft toy and favorite blanket from home help young children slow down, rest, and relax during a busy day or when they are not feeling well. All materials need to be cleaned and sanitized regularly to keep children healthy.

ILL CHILD AREA

Provide an ill child area in your program. This helps keep all children healthy by reducing the spread of contagious conditions. This place for children to lie down when they are injured or not feeling well should be quiet, separated from other children, and within the line of sight of a staff member. Ideally, this space should be

Photo 3.13

close to a restroom and have lighting that can be dimmed, good ventilation, and cleanable finishes on furniture and floors.

FOOD PREPARATION AND REGULATIONS

If your program prepares or serves food, review food handlers' regulations provided by your local health department and any agency that licenses your program. Typically, the U.S. Department of Agriculture (USDA) requires a separate sink in the kitchen or food service area (USDA 2009). All food products must be stored and prepared within strict regulations to ensure sanitary and healthful foods are served. A place for children to eat apart from activities is recommended. A separate area will not only keep your environment clean and sanitary but will also provide a place for children to hang out with friends while eating healthy meals or snacks. The area where children eat should be sanitized before and after each use. Check with your local health department and licensing agency to determine the acceptable sanitizing methods for your program.

Photo 3.14

All areas where food is prepared, served, or eaten need to be kept clean according to licensure and health guidelines. Solid surface furniture tops and flooring such as these are easiest to keep clean and sanitized.

LEAD IN MATERIALS AND WATER

Because a high percentage of toys, games, and furniture are manufactured in countries that lack strict U.S. inspection and quality assurance procedures, numerous items have been recalled due to lead paint and poor construction. You can access the complete listing of recalled toys and other items used by or with children on the Consumer Product Safety Commission website at www.cpsc.gov/cpscpub/prerel/category/toy.html, and you can sign up to receive recall updates on children's products at www.cpsc.gov/cpsclist.aspx. This is a no-cost and fast way to ensure materials meet safety standards for lead and other safety concerns. Buildings constructed before 1978 were painted with lead-based paint. If your facility was built before 1978, have the paint tested for lead. While this type of paint is harmful, the threat is minimal as long as it is not chipped or peeling.

Consuming drinking water can sometimes contribute to elevated blood-lead levels. The Environmental Protection Agency (EPA 2012) has estimated that between 10 and 20 percent of a child's total lead exposure can potentially be attributed to lead-contaminated water. Afterschool programs, schools, and child care centers are important places to check for lead-contaminated water because of children's regular attendance in these facilities. All drinking water, except that coming from private wells, is treated before it reaches program sites to remove any lead present in the water at its source. However, lead can still leach into drinking water from certain types of plumbing materials, especially from lead pipes.

AIR QUALITY

A healthy environment with good indoor air quality and a comfortable temperature contributes to both physical and psychological health. Unhealthy air is particularly a threat to children's respiratory health because their lungs and immune systems are developing, but is also a risk for adults. The number of Americans who suffer from allergies and asthma increases each year. These problems are so significant that in 2008 the EPA listed indoor air quality as a major environmental health concern (2008). What can you do to keep good, clean air in your school-age environment?

In shared-space facilities, talk to the facility maintenance personnel to determine what is already being done to address air quality in the building. In spaces you have control over, either run exhaust fans or adjust the heating ventilation and air-conditioning (HVAC) system settings to keep fresh air circulating throughout your program. Even better, keep windows open slightly from the top. Individual room thermostats that allow for different temperatures are ideal. Active play areas will need to be kept at lower temperatures, while higher temperatures are more comfortable in areas where children are involved in quiet activities.

Asbestos-containing materials are very common in buildings constructed or remodeled before the 1970s. Asbestos is a health hazard when it crumbles and releases particles into the air. Fortunately, most individuals exposed to small amounts of asbestos do not develop asbestos-related health problems. However, there is no known safe level of exposure, so all exposure to asbestos should be avoided. If you suspect asbestos exposure or are remodeling an older building, hire an accredited asbestos professional to evaluate your building.

The following suggestions will help you reduce airborne pollutants and germs in your program environment:

- Choose washable rather than dry-clean-only upholstery and window fabrics.
- Reduce the amount of carpeting and increase use of resilient floors, such as tile, linoleum, or laminates.
- Clean air ducts regularly.
- Replace furnace or air-conditioning unit filters regularly. It is best to follow the manufacturer's recommendations for cleaning and changing filters.
- Vacuum all floors, and replace vacuum bags regularly according to use, health, or safety standards or manufacturer's guidelines.
- Steam clean or wash rugs, carpets, floors, and outdoor play equipment after all pesticide treatments.
- Use fans to help dry floor covering completely to prevent mold.

In addition, look for the following potential sources of pollutants in your school-age program—and remember, fresh air will help clear the airborne toxins given off by these sources:

- wet or damp carpets or rugs, which can be sources of mold and mildew
- radon
- pets with feathers, fur, or hair
- overspray or residue of pesticides used inside or outdoors
- dust
- cockroaches or other insects
- products that emit an odor while drying (such as paint, cleaning solvents, air fresheners)
- products made using formaldehyde (such as pressed wood furniture, fabrics, glue, sunblock)
- vehicle exhaust that enters the building
- aerosol sprays
  (Boise 2010)

Photo 3.15

This program ensures fresh air flows into its building by leaving top windows open for air exchange without creating a draft on the children.

Photo 3.16

This two-color seamless flooring defines space and adds a color splash to the environment. Durable and easy-to-clean surfaces are a must-have, especially in high traffic areas.

Safety in the Interpersonal Environment

Safety by definition means freedom from danger. Feelings of vulnerability are personal and vary according to our perception of the threat of harm from something or someone. While each child reacts or relates differently to danger, young children and children with disabilities may have more unexplained or hard-to-understand fears of physical or emotional harm. The bottom line is that all children and staff must feel safe whatever they are doing or wherever they are in a school-age setting. This is achieved through structured programming and clear limits while still encouraging discovery and adventure. Danger is often among the first things children mention when talking about their concerns about being away from their home. According to the report *A Child's Place: Why Environment Matters to Children* by Green Alliance and DEMOS, children ages ten and eleven in Europe named the following dangers, in order of frequency and emphasis:

- traffic
- strangers/criminals
- being lost
- bullying
- trains
- terrorism

(Thomas and Thompson 2004)

HELPING CHILDREN TO FEEL SECURE

A feeling of security and well-being comes as much from caring adults as it does from a protective physical environment. While the physical environment is kept safe through compliance with safety guidelines, helping children feel emotionally secure is achieved through constant and careful staff supervision. Children need to feel free from the threat of harsh disciplinary methods, poor peer relationships, embarrassment, and humiliation. If left unaddressed by staff, embarrassment and humiliation can escalate to bullying behaviors. It's your job to know what the children are doing and to keep them feeling safe and protected at all times. (For more on bullying, see chapter 6.)

Regardless of where your program is located—inner city or farming community, shared space or a building of your own—children's needs for security are the same. When all three dimensions of the environment (physical, temporal, and interpersonal) are met, you have created a place where children feel safe and learn best.

Photo 3.17

Large, uncovered glass panels between this room and the hallway provide light and allow staff to monitor children's activities and location. All windows in areas that children use should be either shatterproof or covered with protective film.

In large part, how children are kept safe and secure depends on your facility. If you are in a shared space, decisions about a security system may be determined by others; however, it is the responsibility of staff to understand the system and how to operate it should an emergency arise. If your program operates in dedicated space, the building itself dictates your safety procedures. Ideally, the building has only one point of entry for children, families, and visitors. This does not mean there is only one means of egress from the facility for emergency purposes, but it does limit how individuals arrive and depart. Other measures to ensure children feel safe include the following:

- a no-bully policy taught by staff, understood by all children, communicated to families, and strictly enforced
- a staff member present at the entry point throughout the hours of program operation to monitor arrivals and departures
- adequate lighting both inside and outside the entry point
- closed-circuit television (CCTV) monitor system to record and store images of all individuals entering, remaining in, and departing your program
- alarms on locked doors or emergency exits loud enough to be heard in a variety of locations in the facility
- secured windows or door panels to discourage vandalism or potential break-ins

This program has installed closed-circuit cameras and recording equipment throughout its facility as an accountability tool. These help staff monitor children as they move from place to place.

- established and enforced procedures for individuals dropping off and picking up children, such as computerized sign-in/sign-out codes, swipe cards for entry into program space, photo ID cards, or at a minimum policies on the authorization of people dropping off and picking up children
- procedures for addressing emergencies or dangerous situations reviewed and practiced by children and staff
- appropriate level of supervision depending on children's age and risk of activities
- an accountability system in place and functioning well to ensure the location of all children is known by staff at all times

ACCOUNTABILITY SYSTEMS

To ensure safety of children at all times and in all places, set up an accountability system—a procedure for tracking the exact location of children at any given time. An accountability system should be developed whether your program is in dedicated or shared space. An accountability system teaches children to be responsible for themselves while having choices in activities and location in the program. Children use the system to report where they are as they move from place to place. Staff members monitor the children's location to ensure they are accurately reporting their whereabouts. Families appreciate that the system helps them locate their child in your program space; this also helps them feel welcome and included in your program.

So that staff know how many children are in care at any given time, children must be signed in and out of the program daily. Locating this area near the entrance to your program will serve as a visual reminder for families to follow this policy.

The accountability system you develop will vary in design, approach, and implementation based on the size and location of your program space. To design an accountability system for your program, follow these steps:

1. Determine what activity areas will be available for children.
2. Assign staff to each location available to the children.
3. Based on your staffing, determine how many children will be allowed in each area.
4. Decide how you want to communicate the location of each child.

This last step is the crux of your accountability system.

Most programs use a sign-in and sign-out system so they know who is in attendance. Using this system can provide the staff with an accurate count of children in the program from moment to moment. If you choose to use this system, it is essential that a staff member monitor the sign-in and sign-out sheet so staff know exactly the number of children in the program at any given time. Some programs use walkie-talkies in conjunction with the sign-in and sign-out system to enable staff members in different areas to communicate with each other and to ensure the proper staff-child ratio is maintained.

Accountability Boards

Some programs use accountability boards to track the location of children and staff. This two-part system includes a locator board and home boards. The locator board is placed at the entrance to the program. This board tells parents where to find their children in the program space.

Photo 3.20

Home boards are placed in each home base area in your program—the room that each child reports to upon entering the program. Most programs have a maximum group size that is established by the afterschool licensing agency, an accrediting organization, or the program itself. Because of the maximum group size, even small programs can have more than one home base in the program space. Each group of children should have a separate home board.

Both the home and locator boards list the areas available to the children and the maximum number of children in a space based on the staff-child ratio outlined by your afterschool licensing agency or accrediting organization. Sometimes the size of the space, the available equipment, or type of activity limits the number of children in an activity space. In addition, each board has a name card for each child and each staff member. Children and staff alike are responsible for moving their name to indicate their current location in the available areas. The boards must be placed at a height that allows children to see and easily move their name from place to place.

Include a separate section on the locator board for each home group. Color coding groups or using some identifying image such as a geometric shape or stickers to indicate different groups of children enables families,

Photo 3.21

Creative signs and multiple languages help children feel valued and allow them to choose their own activities or places to go.

This master accountability board is centrally located and color-coded with available choices for the children.

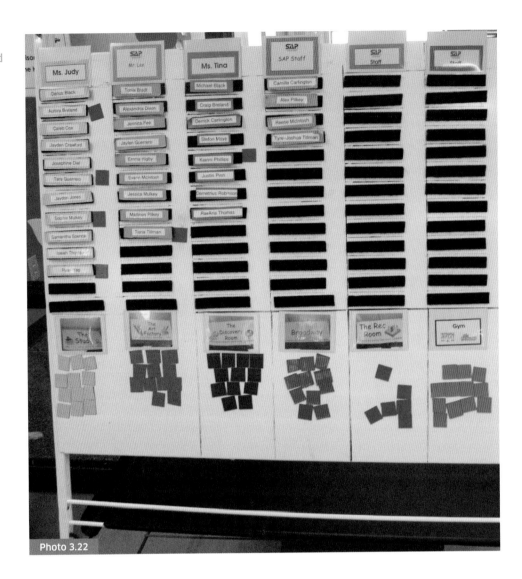

Photo 3.22

staff, and children to find whom they are seeking. The larger your program, the more helpful it is to break the home groups into subsections. Without this labeling, it can be a frustrating process to find a child out of a hundred names on the locator board. This system allows both the family and staff person to know where the child is at any given time.

This system works like this: when children enter the program, they place their names in their home base sections on the locator board; they then report directly to their home base and place their names on the home boards to indicate they are in attendance. When they are ready to move to another activity space, they move their name cards to their destinations on their home boards and then go to the locator board and move their name cards from home base to the new destination. Then they go to their chosen activities. These actions repeat each time they move to a new location. When children leave for the day, they sign out and return their name cards to where they are stored when children are not present.

Tips for a Successful Accountability Board System

- Clearly identify all areas on the locator board to which children have access.
- Print labels for each room or activity area and a name card for each child and staff in large, easy-to-read letters that can be seen from several feet away.
- Ensure children's name cards are durable and easy to replace or make when new children enroll in your program. Use materials such as laminated card stock or magnetic business cards, and add a small photo of each child.
- If there are names left in activity areas at the end of the day, give these to the staff responsible for those children. It should be their responsibility to teach and reinforce the use of the accountability system.

Accountability in Limited Space

Many programs with multiple spaces use a walkie-talkie system to track where children are and how many children are in each space. Programs that have access to only one indoor space and one outdoor space can create a simplified version of the accountability system outlined in the previous section. This version has three locations on an accountability board, which is placed in the main program space. The three choices are bathroom, main program space, and outdoors.

Helping Everyone Understand an Accountability System

For an accountability system to work effectively, training is critical. Make sure everyone—children, families, and staff—understand the importance of recording the location of children at all times. Stress to families and staff the value of letting children account for themselves rather than doing it for them. As you introduce the new system, integrate it slowly into your program. Expect children to make mistakes at first. It takes time to make it work smoothly.

Once children understand the workings of the system, discuss the consequences of not using it correctly. (For more information on consequences, see Rules and Consequences in chapter 5.) Include staff, children, and parents in the discussion. Allow children to help set the consequences. Together with the children, decide what constitutes a reminder, a warning, a note home, or as a last resort a restriction from certain activity areas. Then post the consequences next to the accountability system to serve as a visual reminder. Include an explanation of the accountability system, including the consequences for infractions, in the family and staff handbooks. Families will appreciate that the system helps them locate their child in the program space. In addition to the convenience for them, it also helps them feel welcome and included in the program environment.

Activities and Questions

These activities and questions examine the procedures and policies that create a safe environment for children in your program.

1. Do you use an indoor and outdoor safety checklist? How often is this completed? Who is responsible for completing the checklist? When problems are found, how do you get them corrected?

2. Look at the indoor and outdoor safety checklists in this chapter, and compare them to your checklists. What is missing on your checklist? What additional items are included on your checklists that are specific to your program?

3. Do you have an emergency evacuation plan? Where is it posted?

4. How do you keep track of where the children are at all times?

5. Check all fabrics, furniture, drapes, and pillows in your program to determine what is fire resistant, fireproof, or fire retardant.

6. What is your policy for sick children? Where is your space for ill children located? Is it easily supervised? Is there a place for them to sit or lie down?

7. For children with chronic illnesses or allergies, do you have a list of items that might trigger an episode? Compile a list of known triggers and survey your environment to see if any of these triggers exist.

8. What are your policies for safety or evacuation drills? What drills do you conduct? How often are these conducted? How do you document these drills?

9. What security systems are in place in your program?

CHAPTER 4

Understanding the Total Child: The Foundation of Environmental Design

HAVE YOU EVER GONE INTO A STORE or a museum or tried to read a book only to find it did not fit you? Advertising and marketing researchers are in a never-ending search to ensure they meet the needs of customers and the general public. So too should a school-age environment reflect the interests, abilities, and needs of the children enrolled there. When staff members are consistently observing and planning with children in the pivotal position, they create exciting and challenging environments. Remember that the children are the customers and need to feel a sense of belonging. All children are unique and come to your program with individualized sets of skills, interests, abilities, and knowledge. Likewise, children learn in many ways. What makes children so unique and special?

Psychologists have developed a number of ways to help understand and assess the inherent traits and learning styles of school-age children. This chapter presents a brief look into brain research, multiple intelligences, learning domains, and temperament. This background on child development should help you understand your observations of children, which are essential to designing a quality school-age environment.

Brain Research and Multiple Intelligences

The brain is much like a bank. It stores experiences children have early in their lives, then pays dividends later in their lives. When babies are born, their brains are highly disorganized with chaotic activity. Little of what infants experience makes sense to them. Yet over time, they begin making connections between what is going on. These connections, or the more accurate term *wiring*, enable them to learn. The more wiring or connections created, the greater the learning possibilities. Because childen's surroundings and inter-actions affect their experiences, the environment we provide has a critical impact on their brain development and learning. The more exposure we give them to various kinds of learning, then repeat the learning in various ways, the more efficient their brains will become.

By definition, intelligence is the ability to learn, understand, or deal with new or trying situations. School-age children need and deserve a stimulating and challenging environment to support their growth and learning. Develop-mental psychologist and neuropsychologist Howard Gardner developed the theory of multiple intelligences—which he called "many frames of minds"—to help us understand the process of learning. This concept is highly significant to the school-age environment. Gardner contends that several brain systems make up children's intelligences, all of which function separately. He believes that being smart is more than correctly answering questions on an IQ test and that success in life is not determined solely by our IQ scores. Gardner has looked at ways of being a successful learner in areas not covered on an IQ test. Thomas Armstrong (2009), in his work on human development and multiple intelligences, notes that what is included in the environment affects learn-ing for all kinds of learners. Armstrong says that the arrangement, schedule, interactions, and materials included in children's settings must be designed to activate and support learning success in all of their intelligences.

What are the eight intelligences Gardner identified? How can your pro-gram environment support these intelligences? The following chart includes eight identified intelligences. The various categories of intelligences have been separated out only for the purpose of looking at their unique features and how to use them effectively in a school-age environment. Remember that chil-dren and adults possess all intelligences in unique ways, with skills at varying levels. Gardner maintains that with practice, a supportive environment, time and encouragement, everyone can develop all their intelligences to an adequate level of competency (Arm-strong 2009).

Journals provide a place for children to draw, communi-cate feelings, and write creatively.

Providing open-ended art options for children encourages creativity.

Games such as checkers help teach logical-mathematical skills to children. They learn to take turns and to understand cause and effect and how to use strategies to win the game.

Motion and movement allow children time to experience music in a new way.

Planting, weeding, and harvesting plants can establish an understanding of nature.

Providing instruments for children to play can open new possibilities for them.

Engaging with others in group play or building activities helps children to build friendships and to develop effective communication and problem-solving skills.

Multiple Intelligence Supports

GARDNER'S INTELLIGENCES	DESCRIPTION	PHYSICAL ENVIRONMENT SUPPORTS	TEMPORAL ENVIRONMENT SUPPORTS	INTERPERSONAL ENVIRONMENT SUPPORTS
Verbal-Linguistic	"word smart" enjoys writing, journaling, reading, communicating with others may find learning multiple languages easy	library areas, writing center, and media resources (talking books, earphones, etc.) displays of children's projects	rules and consequences posted in simple terms word paddles/small whiteboards with simple directions for transitions and/or assisting children scheduled time for brainstorming and problem solving lesson plans with opportunities for dramatic productions	positive, enabling relationships with each child a place to talk through problems and develop conflict resolution time to brainstorm and problem solve encouragement for children's dramatic productions and written projects
Logical-Mathematical	"logic smart" enjoys and performs analytical and mathematical activities easily and accurately	math and science/discovery activities construction areas with math resources, problem-solving games, experiments, and construction materials individual and group reasoning activities	sustained, uninterrupted time for problem solving and science experimentation predictable routines and rituals	offering group analysis and logical deduction activities promoting construction projects large- or small-group science experiments adult-led dialogue and guided dialogue for problem solving and logical reasoning cooperative brain teaser activities
Visual-Spatial	"picture smart" can make sense of the physical world visually likes to draw, paint, and be involved in visual arts activities	art, visual media, and visual-thinking areas maps and graphs picture or photo galleries	opportunities to create and display children's work scheduled time for an art or photography club	encouraging and supporting children to create involving children in group projects, such as designing sets and costumes for dramatic productions or painting murals encouraging participation in art, photography, and other creative activities
Bodily-Kinesthetic	"body smart" able to use the whole body (fine- and large-motor skills) for problem solving and creative pursuits.	areas and equipment for physical and creative development tactile-learning or hands-on resources (clay, blocks, and materials of varying textures)	scheduled opportunities to move around rules that help children learn to use and control their bodies lesson plans that include hands-on learning and manipulatives	giving permission to have the body in motion during homework or other quiet times using hand gestures and body or sign language to give directions/redirection encouraging participation in group or individual athletic events

Multiple Intelligence Supports

GARDNER'S INTELLIGENCES	DESCRIPTION	PHYSICAL ENVIRONMENT SUPPORTS	TEMPORAL ENVIRONMENT SUPPORTS	INTERPERSONAL ENVIRONMENT SUPPORTS
Musical	"music smart" enjoys making or listening to music may find playing an instrument, singing, or reading music fun and easy	music performance or listening areas with instruments or recorded music musical environment with background music or soft environmental sounds	using chimes, songs, or other musical tones to signal transitions activities introducing a variety of music, such as attending concerts or musicals guessing games drawing or painting while listening to music	group choral or instrumental music activities dancing or aerobics to music opportunities to create and showcase musical efforts inviting musicians (family members or other guests) to perform or share their instruments
Intrapersonal	"self-smart" often prefers being or working alone more than with others	areas for individual activities (lofts, semi-enclosed small spaces, or study carrels) computer with high-interest programming for one child	scheduled time to be alone or get away individual learning activities that grow self-esteem self-paced learning opportunities such as assisting staff or other children games with more than one winner scheduling individualized activities such as yoga	giving permission to be alone or separated from group activities encouraging children to take charge of own behavior opportunities to share emotions with a staff member one-to-one
Interpersonal	"people smart" enjoys being and working with a group most of the time	areas and resources for group activities (comfortable furniture, lofts, tables and chairs) social area with group games, projects, and activities	scheduled time for group discussions and cooperative learning group or team games such as Red Light–Green Light, tag, badminton	peer or adult-led group opportunities opportunities for children to take on leadership roles peer sharing cooperative groups
Naturalistic	"nature smart" loves to learn about, be in, and care for natural surroundings, including living things, the earth, the universe, and beyond	living things to grow and care for (plants and pets) natural outdoor areas a variety of related models, manipulative, and active learning opportunities in science recycle bins	opportunities to connect with nature and to care for pets or plants holding indoor activities outside scheduling time for ecology or nature club	opportunities to perform plays and skits and read poems about nature involved in adult-led group nature hikes, walks, and short camping trips participates in ecology or nature club activities

(Armstrong 2009)

Learning Domains

Researchers and medical experts have mapped out the typical progression of children's development starting at birth. Sometimes the areas of development are referred to as *learning domains* and include benchmark skill sets in the specific areas according to the child's age. In basic terms, *domain* simply means "category." Children learn and then master skills in each of five learning domains; a mastered skill is referred to as a *developmental milestone*. Doctors, families, and educators keep track of children's development (and developmental milestones) over a period of time. For instance, when they have learned all the basic locomotor movements of skipping, hopping, jumping, and so on, they have mastered these skills and have met developmental milestones in the physical-motor domain. Their failure to reach a developmental milestone within a given time frame is cause for concern and for watchful attention to their progress.

Environmentalists believe that children's learning and behavior are influenced primarily by their surroundings (physical, temporal, and interpersonal), whereas other theorists believe children's learning is shaped mostly by their genetic makeup. Some people refer to the debate about the relative importance of these two developmental influences as "nature versus nurture." Regardless of what we believe about what influences a child's development, we cannot control many of these factors. At the same time, we can do many things to support total child development in all areas.

Separating learning into domains helps us observe and evaluate how children think, feel, act, and learn. While all domains present unique parameters of learning, we must understand that learning is not isolated by domains but rather occurs across these categories. All five domains are interconnected, and the optimal learning environment must support whole child learning. Ideal environments integrate several domains at the same time. For example, when children are involved in a soccer game, they are developing skills in all learning domains in an integrated way.

By understanding that all five domains work together for total child learning, we can better plan a supportive and challenging learning environment for all children. So what are the five developmental learning domains? What elements in the environment support the total child development associated with each domain? The following chart summarizes the five learning domains and how you can support them in your program.

Learning Domain Supports

DOMAIN	DESCRIPTION	PHYSICAL ENVIRONMENTAL SUPPORTS	TEMPORAL ENVIRONMENTAL SUPPORTS	INTERPERSONAL ENVIRONMENTAL SUPPORTS
social-emotional	sensing and managing internal feelings, values, enthusiasms, motivations, and attitudes responses to events and the environment feelings about self and others and about events in the environment highly correlated with how children learn	gathering areas for small- and large-group activities resources to help each child be successful, such as a variety of reading materials and computer programs at various levels of difficulty	planned cooperative play or project activities fair and appropriate rules, consequences, and limits	supportive adult involvement and guidance to promote cooperation rather than competition among children adults modeling acceptable ways to deal with situations and express emotions
physical-motor (or psychomotor)	developing and coordinating muscles for specific purposes and skills locomotor movements (walking, galloping, skipping, jumping, running, sliding) nonlocomotor movements (swimming, twisting, stretching) fine-motor skills (dexterity, manipulation of tools with the hands)	places for indoor and outdoor movement activity equipment for physical skills development hand-operated devices, such as musical instruments, calculators, abaci, puzzles, and woodworking tools	scheduled time for routine practice, guided practice, and self-improvement of physical skills	opportunities for non-competitive individual or team activities staff guidance or modeling to help children master skills
cognitive	developing intellectual skills ranges from a simple recall or recognition of facts or concepts to creating, applying, and evaluating information	resources that stimulate higher-level thinking and problem solving brain teasers games with rules determined by the children building materials that require creative strategy	planned experiences to support lifelong learning and success for children of all ages and abilities	staff guidance in making connections between previous experiences and new information problem-solving strategies freedom to make informed decisions encouraging children's natural instinct to discover, question, think, and apply their knowledge to new learning experiences

Learning Domain Supports

DOMAIN	DESCRIPTION	PHYSICAL ENVIRONMENTAL SUPPORTS	TEMPORAL ENVIRONMENTAL SUPPORTS	INTERPERSONAL ENVIRONMENTAL SUPPORTS
language and communication	expressing and sharing ideas and feelings with others through language and communication skills both verbal (speaking, writing) and nonverbal (gestures, facial expressions, body language, drawing) learning in all other domains dependent on a child's acquisition of communication skills	resources that promote healthy verbal interactions peace table to resolve children's conflicts puppets or marionettes speaker's corner for presenting opinion pieces walkie-talkies	opportunities for speaking, acting, presenting written work opportunities or acceptance of self-talk or thinking out loud	staff who listen as well as talk with (not at) children discussions about current issues and events and learn acceptance of various opinions
creativity and self-expression	self-expression, creating imaginatively, and thinking independently willingness to try new approaches, take risks, and find new answers to problems.	resources that promote new ways of thinking or doing science experiments "retold" fairy tales abstract art or sculptures displays of children's creative projects	sustained periods of time for imaginative play time for project work self-reflection or introspection	staff-supported opportunities to be imaginative group activities bouncing ideas off each other encouragement by adults to use stimulating materials

Temperament

Often the words *personality* and *temperament* are used interchangeably, but they have different meanings. *Temperament* is defined as how an individual interacts with and reacts to others and the environment. Each person is born with a certain temperament. *Personality* is a combination of life experiences and temperament.

A long-term study in the 1950s looked at how temperament influences a children's ability to make adjustments throughout their lives (Thomas, Chess, and Birch 1968). The study examined nine behavior characteristics: activity level, regularity of sleeping and eating patterns, adaptability, intensity of emotion, mood, distractibility, persistence, attention span, and sensory sensitivity. Today the list is commonly reduced to three categories: flexible (easy or adaptable), feisty (difficult), and fearful (slow to warm up or cautious). Some individuals are a combination of these three categories. As with all things, each category has both strengths and weaknesses.

Watch school-age children as they arrive at your program and enter into activities. Some children enter slowly and cautiously, while others burst through the door, finding or creating their niche immediately. Some are fearful and reluctant to try anything, while others are feisty and go headlong into anything with a feeling they will do well. And still others are flexible, willing to be accommodating and not easily angered. A child's temperament is an innate characteristic that affects how he reacts to and responds to the environment and interacts with the people in the environment. By the time a child arrives in your school-age program, his temperament is fairly well defined and apparent to all around him.

The following chart looks at these three types of children's temperaments and how they influence your school-age environment. The chart also presents some strategies to help you be flexible enough to swing with each temperament. Remember that children's usual behavior can change if they experience a change in their access to nutritious snacks and meals or to the amount of daily sleep.

Temperament Supports

TEMPERAMENT	DESCRIPTION	PHYSICAL ENVIRONMENT SUPPORTS	TEMPORAL ENVIRONMENT SUPPORTS	INTERPERSONAL ENVIRONMENT SUPPORTS
fearful	mostly inactive and fussy; more hesitant, cautious, and shy than their peers negative reaction to new foods, people, places; reaction becomes more positive with continuous exposure retreats from conflict gives up when faced with a challenge may need more time during transitions than others thrives when the environment (including routines, schedule, staff, and the physical setting) remains constant	quiet places for relaxation with books, soft furniture, and pillows independent play activities, such as puzzles, creative art, journal writing, and listening to music	consistent schedules in all program spaces advance notice of schedule changes time to practice routines	allowing children to watch before they participate in activities

Temperament Supports

TEMPERAMENT	DESCRIPTION	PHYSICAL ENVIRONMENT SUPPORTS	TEMPORAL ENVIRONMENT SUPPORTS	INTERPERSONAL ENVIRONMENT SUPPORTS
flexible	easygoing, optimistic, happy, predictable, calm adjusts easily to environmental factors and even radical changes copes with loud noises, bright lights, food textures although flexible, often resent not having things go their way tends to have very deep feelings but show little outward emotion	a variety of activities and games that span the abilities of the children puzzles with a variety of pieces books that span from no words to chapter books games of different skill levels, such as checkers, chess, or Go Fish	planned activities and areas that develop communication and problem-solving skills establish a conflict resolution process time for the staff to engage children in conversation opportunities for role-playing difficult situations	small- or large-group leadership opportunities opportunities to lead a game by giving directions to other children mentoring program where older children help younger children
feisty	high-activity (but not hyperactive), inquisitive, even intense distracted by loud noises, bright lights, food textures fearful of new situations and people jumps right in, often creates conflict persistent when faced with a challenge often predisposed to disruptive or aggressive behavior, exhibited in temper tantrums, excessive fussiness, or loud outbursts function well with a patient, consistent approach to clearly explained boundaries	places and activities that allow children to be in motion and engaged dance area for moving to a variety of music open gym for activities such as basketball, volleyball, running, and relay games places to exercise regularly outside activities at least thirty minutes per day, weather permitting	plan activities that build conflict resolution, problem-solving, and communication skills time to process the child's conflicts and problem solve alternative but acceptable solutions	participation in group activities offering both challenges and skill building acknowledgment of attempts and successes of the child's skills adult's patience

Fearful: These children may need a slower pace and require additional time and encouragement to finish a task or even clean up. They often need to watch an activity for a while before trying it, because they want to succeed and fear failing. If fearful children are forced to join the group without an adjust-

Even if an activity looks like fun, fearful children will sit on the sidelines and watch until they feel they can participate successfully.

ment time, their shyness will become worse. If given enough time, they can become happy members of the group.

Flexible: Do not forget the easy-going children just because they are so compliant and accommodating. They need you to periodically recognize and acknowledge their cooperative and accepting behavior. Monitor flexible children closely, setting aside time to talk with them about their frustrations and things that bother them. They will not start the conversation, but they will share their feelings if you initiate the communication. By helping them develop good communications skills, you will enable them to take a stand when it is really important for them to do so.

The flexible child will do whatever she is asked even if it is something she does not want to do.

Feisty: Keeping rules strictly enforced and maintaining an organized environment will definitely help these children react appropriately. Making sure children understand the safety rules will help them do specific activities safely. Prepare these children for transitions and changes in schedules by making them aware of changes as soon as possible. Often adults do not understand this temperament and view these children in a negative light. Your patience and consistent approach with feisty children will result in a positive

adjustment and a happy environment for all. Feisty or high-activity children who investigate the environment and instigate situations need opportunities to burn off energy safely and with close adult supervision.

The feisty child loves challenges and will keep trying a given task until it is mastered.

When working with children of various temperaments, your approach as the adult determines the ultimate outcome. When you identify children who are challenging, remember these tips:

- Put yourself in their place. How do they see this situation?
- Be considerate and caring: be a wallflower when you observe, look, and listen without interrupting children's play. Make notes about the physical environment as well as the verbal and nonverbal cues.
- When in doubt, ask yourself, *What is it that the children want or are trying to tell me?* Engage them in conversations to make sure of what they want. When you know what they want, then ask yourself, *Is what I am providing meeting that need?*
- Understand your own temperament and your feelings about a situation (your hot spots or blind spots). Ask yourself, *Are they determining how I am responding to the situation?*
- Look beyond the behavior to the emotion or reason behind the action.
- Once an adaptation is made, reevaluate to see how well your change has worked for the children. Be open to trying more than one change.

Remember, a flower does not reach its full potential overnight. It takes watering, weeding, and lots of sun. Children are no different. We shower them with support by providing for their needs, we determine what is appropriate by weeding out behaviors that are unacceptable, and we surround them with rays of encouragement and understanding. With these things, children can reach their full potential.

The Power of Observation

For years, researchers and educators debated how to identify the basic components that best support children's learning needs. Eventually they reached the consensus that no one-size-fits-all answer exists. Instead, the key to supporting children is regular observations. So much of what is included in the learning environment relates to children's individual personalities, temperaments, and learning styles. For this reason, the children in your program are the foundation, or driving force, of the design for your program environment. Through individual observations, you will get to know the children and learn about their needs and interests. Only then can you design a physical, temporal, and interpersonal environment that works. Observation will help you design and adapt your environment to the abilities, interests, and ages of the children you serve.

Whether you are aware of it or not, observations are something you do every day. They may be as simple as noticing that children who could not button their shirts in dramatic play now accomplish this without help. Or you may notice that children are not visiting an area of the room and realize that you need to make changes. Observations need not be lengthy or formal to be useful. School-age programs can have so much happening all at once that often observations are spontaneous and quick. The point is to record what you see and hear. Write down your observations to document areas that are working well, how children are engaging in particular areas, and areas that need to be improved. Effective observations follow these steps:

Step 1: Observe. Write only what you see or hear, *not* your feelings, reactions, or opinions. Avoid using value statements and words such as "I feel" and "I think." Write down how children are interacting with each other and with adults. Note what activities children are engaged in. Record the toys, equipment, and materials they are using. Likewise, note any people, areas, activities, and equipment with which the children are not engaged. Here are examples: "Tommy built a tower with the wood blocks that was three feet tall." "Sally and Kirsten had a disagreement, and both worked out a solution at the Peace Table." Notice that these statements are not judgments and do not assign value but rather state simple facts.

Step 2: Reflect. Review and think about your observation notes. You may find it helpful to sort them into categories, perhaps by program area or by type of action needed to improve the overall environment, whether physical, temporal, or interpersonal. Do not forget to consider any notes about materials or people the children were not engaged with; these may signify that something is not working well. As you reflect on your observations, ask yourself some questions:

- What interactions did I observe between the children? With materials? With staff present?
- What types of children's behaviors did I observe?
- What areas did children visit? How long did they stay there?
- What skills have children recently mastered, shown interest in, or been struggling with?
- What areas of the environment need to be redesigned or updated?

Step 3: Plan. With your combined observations and reflections, figure out exactly what you can do to improve your program environment to ensure you are offering an exciting environment that contributes to the children's learning. What can you do to support growth in the children's physical, emotional, and social development as well as to promote learning experiences throughout the environment? Your plans should include changes to the physical, temporal, and interpersonal environments. Develop an action plan with timelines, and note who will be responsible for enacting each change.

Step 4: Do. Implement your plans. These actions include making changes to the physical environment, engaging children in activities, and interacting with them to ensure they feel at home in the environment.

Some observations need to be planned in advance and shared with colleagues, supervisors, or families. These observations include developmental screenings done to identify special needs, learning delays, medical problems, or behavioral issues.

Observational information helps you evaluate the effectiveness of activities, schedules, routines, transitions, rules, and consequences. When you incorporate both spontaneous and scheduled observations into your program, they will open your eyes to the effectiveness of your environment. The next several chapters address the three environmental dimensions in greater detail. As you delve into each of these realms, you will continue to use observations as your guiding light:

- Observations are based on *daily activities*.
- Daily activities and what is included in the environment are based on *planning*.
- Planning is based on *reflection* and careful thought.
- Reflection is based on *observations*.

PLANNING VS. DOING
Remember that *plan* and *do* are two different words. One looks good on paper (planning), and the other looks great in your program space (doing). Children grow and learn when you *do* all the wonderful and well-thought-out ideas you have planned for. If something doesn't work as planned, look at other options for change and implement those.

Activities and Questions

These activities and questions are designed to help you examine your under-standing of multiple intelligences, learning domains, and temperament and how your program environment supports the variety of ways children learn.

1. Use your enrollment list to determine who is feisty, flexible, or fearful; then note where these children play most often. Revise or redesign places to interest and challenge children with each of these temperaments.

2. Look at your program space and lesson plans. List the areas and activities that meet each of the five learning domains. Does each area of the environment support learning for all five domains?

3. If your program is designed to promote only one or two learning domains—for example, it is a remedial or tutorial program, sports or athletic program, or creative arts program—how do you weave the other learning domains into the environment?

4. Based on what you know about Gardner's theory of multiple intelligences, does your environment support children in all eight areas? What can you change or add to the environment to further children's learning in these areas?

5. Based on your observations of children in your program, are your activities, schedules, and physical environment appropriate for the ages and abilities of the children in your program? What would you like to replace or remove from your program? What would you like to add?

CHAPTER 5

The Temporal Environment: Establishing Predictability and Expectations

SCHOOL-AGE CHILDREN are industrious and competitive. They have longer attention spans than preschoolers. Their constant movement and changing interests, however, can be challenging at times. The whirling mass of energy that school-age children bring may even leave you feeling overwhelmed. You may long for children to come in quietly and go from one area to the other and let peace and quiet prevail, but the reality is that children have been sitting most of the day. The last thing they want after school is to sit even more. Or after laboring over lesson plans, you may be disheartened to discover the children are no longer interested in the activity. That was "so last week," the children say. These issues come under the scope of the temporal environment.

The temporal environment addresses how school-age children spend their time while in your program. Programs that provide outlets for children's energy and enthusiasm will go a long way toward maximizing their potential and minimizing challenges. Keeping your finger on the pulse of what the children are interested in and quickly integrating that information in the lesson plans can smooth the way to child engagement and staff satisfaction. To appeal to children's individual needs, interests, learning styles, and temperaments, the ideal temporal environment provides a balance between activities that are quiet and loud, small-group and large-group, and staff-directed and self-directed. Some programs choose a theme to guide them in developing individual activities to include in their weekly lesson plans. Your observations and children's interest surveys will provide ideas for engaging thematic activities that support the children's learning. Planning activities with specific outcomes in mind helps you design lesson plans that meet the needs of all children.

The temporal environment includes the planning of activities, schedules, and routines. It also establishes behavior expectations with rules and consequences that help children learn the importance of moderating their own behavior to fit appropriately in the context of the school-age program community. Engaging the children in the process of setting rules and consequences facilitates their understanding of what the rules mean and what is expected of them. Because they helped create the rules, children seldom argue about the consequences when they break them. The daily rhythms of the temporal environment provide predictability and rules that make behavioral expectations clear. These structural supports help school-age children learn to self-regulate the choices they make for their own activities and behavior.

The checklist A Day in the Life of Your Temporal Environment is designed to help you reflect on your temporal environment. Take time to look realistically at your temporal environment and truthfully answer the questions. (The checklist is also available at www.redleafpress.org for downloading and printing.)

Lesson Plans, Schedules, Transitions, and Routines

Four items are necessary when designing the temporal environment: lesson (or activity) plans, schedules, transitions, and routines. While each of these is separate, they work hand in hand. For example, you might need to change the schedule on a given day because an activity in one area takes longer than planned and the next activity needs to either shift its location or start time, which necessitates a change in the routine. Both the schedule and the lesson plans should include time for transitions and routines. The amount of time will vary with the type of planned transition or routine. Keeping flexible and understanding how different aspects of the temporal environment affect the overall flow of the program will help the program run smoothly. Intentional planning keeps the needs and interests of each child in mind, which results in a learning environment that will support each child in some way. Smooth transitions create a temporal environment in which time flows from one activity to another without disruption.

A Day in the Life of Your Temporal Environment

LESSON PLANS

1. Weekly lessons plans outline daily activities for each program area.

2. Lesson plans provide a variety of activities that meet the individual needs of the children.

3. Learning outcomes are noted for each activity on the lesson plan.

4. Lesson plans are posted for families and staff.

5. Staff use the lesson plan to guide them as they place books in program areas, gather art supplies, and rotate materials.

6. Lesson plans are reviewed to determine which activities were successful and which were not.

SCHEDULES

1. Schedules outline the large blocks of time and have both words and pictures.

2. Schedules are reviewed regularly, and the times associated with each block are changed as the need arises.

3. Staff are flexible in following the schedule when a teachable moment occurs or children need more time to complete a project.

4. Children are notified when the schedule will be changed before the change occurs.

TRANSITIONS

1. Transitions are smooth and allow minimal waiting for children.

2. Whenever possible, children are allowed to transition from one activity to another independently.

3. Minimal transitions of the entire group occur.

4. Systems are in place that allow staff and families to know where the children are at all times.

5. Children are told when transitions will occur before they occur.

ROUTINES

1. Routines are taught and reinforced daily.

2. Pictures are used to explain routines such as snacktime, hand washing, and cleaning up.

3. Expectations are discussed when introducing routines and before children begin a routine.

Encourage school-age children to give input about the daily schedule, field trips, and activity choices. A program that children want to come to is a program that includes children in the planning of activities and events. Their input in planning helps ensure their participation in activities. Ask the children what they are interested in or would like to know more about. Give them an interest survey to help identify those areas. Conduct these surveys several times a year. See appendix A for two interest surveys you can reproduce for use in your program. (These surveys are also available to download and print at www.redleafpress.org.) One is geared to children who are nonreaders, emergent readers, and English as a Second Language (ESL) readers. This survey has pictures for each area so that children can just check a box to communicate their interests. The second survey is geared to fluent readers and older children and asks open-ended questions that allow children to elaborate on their interests in a variety of areas. Getting the input of the children creates a win-win situation. The children feel their opinions are important to the adult, and the adult can use this information to create environments that interest them.

FADS
Research children's fads before incorporating them into your plans to be sure all aspects are appropriate for your program.

LESSON PLANS

Whether you call them lesson or activity plans, these critical tools describe how each program area will be used and what materials will be offered. An intentional outline of activities should be created anew regularly—usually each week. Most programs find it beneficial to create weekly rather than monthly lesson plans so that they can change activities quickly when children become uninterested in a specific area or an activity needs to be modified to be more appropriate for the children. Monthly plans may keep staff locked into scheduled activities for the entire month regardless of the interests or needs of the children. In addition, weekly plans allow you to develop activities that can span several days. This gives children time to build skills, explore, and experiment. Their attention spans are long enough to take on multiday projects, such as making things out of papier-mâché, knitting, building race cars from cardboard boxes, and building sets for a play. Weekly plans allow you to extend a project into the next week if more time is needed or to change the focus of a project when the children are interested in other aspects of the topic or they have lost interest sooner than you anticipated. When you include long-term projects in your lesson plans, you help school-age children understand that some things take more time to complete.

Lesson plans help staff members focus on keeping the environment exciting for children. Look at your lesson plans at the start of each program day to help visualize your role. Try to imagine how all parts of the environment will

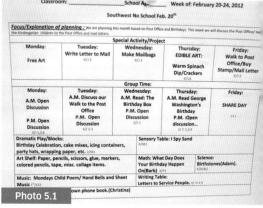

Photo 5.1

Written lesson plans should be posted so that children and adults know what is happening throughout the program day.

fit together to both interest children and keep them learning. An added benefit of lesson plans is that they allow the program to maintain continuity even
when a staff member is absent. A detailed lesson plan coupled with adding
needed materials in advance throughout your program space will enable substitute staff to provide consistency in the activities for that week.

Float and Sink Activity

In creating lesson plans, draw inspiration from the interests of the children. For example, children in one school-age program were curious
about the principle of float and sink. This started a project that lasted
for three weeks. The first week, staff began by discussing what floats
and what sinks. Children were given time to guess what would float and
what would sink. Their predictions and the results were charted as the
children tested each item. When a bowling ball was tested, all the children thought it would sink. When it floated, they discussed why they
thought this happened.

Extending on this activity, during week two the children used aluminum foil to make vessels they thought would float. Each boat was tested,
and the children were able to make modifications if their boat did not
float. Once all creations floated, the children were asked in the third
week to predict how many penny nails their creations could hold without sinking. The children tested their predictions, while the staff asked
open-ended questions to help the children analyze how the boats were
sitting in the water and what needed to be done to keep a boat from tip-
ping over in the water.

Photo 5.2

Photo 5.3

Photo 5.4

Left: Charting and photographs provide visual reminders of children's predictions and document the process. Middle: Taking the information gained from
predicting and testing, children extend their learning by designing, testing, and
modifying a structure until it floats. Right: Once the structure floats, adding
weight further expands children's understanding of structural design, weight
distribution, and balance.

Lesson plans describe how each activity relates to a given outcome or theme. The float and sink activity, for example, was listed under science on the lesson plan. The description simply stated, "Children will look at a list of items and work independently to decide if a certain object will sink or float." The outcome: "Children engage in the scientific process of predicting, testing, recording, and analyzing." In preparation, two tubs of water were set up in the sensory area. A list of books that deal with things that float was placed in both the book and sensory areas of the program and was also included in the literacy section of the lesson plan. In the sensory area, the staff encouraged children to test items they found in the program or brought from home to see if they sank or floated. The following week, the lesson plan took this science activity a step further by incorporating what the children had learned the previous week. The lesson plan read, "Using aluminum foil, allow the children to create a vessel that will float: build, test, rebuild, and retest." In addition to the books in the literacy area, a word wall was created with the words *vessel, ballast, keel, buoyancy*, and *density*. Children were encouraged to add to this list daily. During the third week, the science activity was to estimate how many penny nails each child's boat would hold before sinking. Children were asked to predict the outcome, test their predictions, record the outcome, modify the conditions, and retest. Using weekly plans allowed the staff to plan according to the children's interest or lack of engagement.

Competition and mastery are ingrained in most school-age children. In the float and sink example, the children gained mastery by repeatedly experimenting to discover what would float. They reinforced their mastery by comparing the items that floated, looking for commonalities, and listing items on charts. The children used the knowledge they had gained from this process to create their own vessels. Again they used information gained from trial and error to reshape their vessels until they floated. The next challenge came from asking, *How many penny nails will your boat hold?* This challenge satisfied the children's need for competition, as they created and reshaped their vessels to hold the most penny nails. Setting up the sensory area so that children could experiment independently over several days met the emotional needs of children who would not try anything new in a large group until they had had time to master it. Other children could jump in and try that same task, confident they would have the skills to complete it at an acceptable level.

While school-age children enjoy competition, try to create lesson plans that allow them to compete with themselves rather than with other children. For example using the float and sink activity, children could experiment and record findings about their boats, trying to add more penny nails each day, rather than competing and comparing their efforts to what their peers had done. Encourage noncompetitive games when children play as a group. When you plan opportunities for all children to be successful regardless of their ability, you create a well-balanced program to support each child's individual needs. When planning activities or themes, consider the following questions:

- What will be the learning outcomes?
- What books will be displayed in the reading area and other areas around the room?
- What books will be read aloud by staff or older children to younger children?
- What materials and activities will be available in each area?
- What long-range projects will be offered?
- What activities will be available inside?
- What outside activities will be offered for both quiet and active options?
- What field trips or guest speakers will be planned?
- How can the indoor and outdoor space be set up to support the learning outcomes?
- What is the alternative plan if an activity has to be changed due to inclement weather, inability to use the indoor space, or staffing?
- How can the planned activity be adapted to ensure success for children of all ages and abilities?

Post your lesson plans so they are easily seen by families and visitors, who can then see you are purposefully planning with the children and the learning outcomes in mind. In addition, by letting families know what is happening during the children's time at your program, you give them topics for conversation and opportunities to explore extended learning with their children.

Observe how your lesson plans go. No matter how carefully you plan, you must remain flexible and ready to make changes to the environment according to the interests and needs of the children. Record notes that address the following questions:

- How well did the activity work?
- What adaptations were made?
- How well did the children receive the planned activity?
- What would you add next time to the area to support or extend the learning outcome?
- What other changes would you make if you repeat the activity?

Your notes will provide you with important information to improve your lesson plans in the future. In addition, your notes will offer ideas to support or extend the learning potential in future lesson plans.

SCHEDULES

While a lesson plan describes what activities will be offered each day, a schedule is a sequence of events that happen each day. The same sequence repeats daily. The schedule's consistency and reliability let children know what will happen next. Its predictability helps children feel safe. *Guiding Children's Social Development and Learning* notes, "The daily schedule or routine supports children's ability to act autonomously" (Kostelnik et al. 2011, 274). Freedom to move from one activity or area to another offers the child autonomy to explore areas of interest or to choose something new to explore in a safe environment purposefully designed to encourage learning through exploration. Allowing children to choose what they will do and which area they will visit gives them choices within the preset limits of the temporal environment—the schedule, the planned activity, the materials provided, and the program rules.

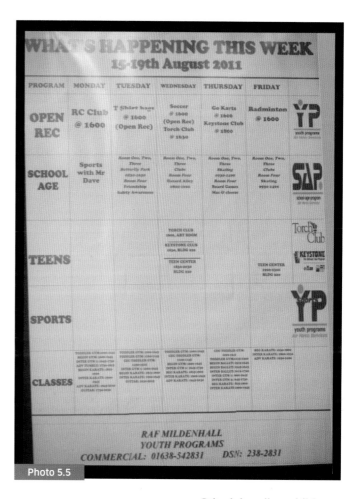

Photo 5.5

Schedules allow children and adults to know when each segment of the program occurs.

To create a schedule, first look at the major components of the program day. These components might include arrival, group announcements, snack, activity choices, outside play, homework, clubs, and departure. Each component needs to be assigned a time frame. Times set for each of the components will vary based on the number of components you have, the hours your program is in operation, and the children's ability to become engaged in the activities.

Next, consider what things you are required to do, such as thirty minutes of outside or large-motor activities. Then look at time constraints, such as sharing the gym. If your time slot for the gym is from 4:00 to 4:30 p.m., then on the schedule your large-motor time will be from 4:00 to 4:30 p.m. The time slots should be viewed as guidelines, because sometimes children become so engaged that a teachable moment occurs, and rather than transition them to a new topic, you should use that time to extend the learning. For instance, if the children continue to ask questions or show interest in how vinegar and baking soda interact past the end of the time for that activity, consider sliding the time of the next activity for a few minutes. Schedules need to function on "kid time" as much (or more) than "clock time." Some programs include a disclaimer on their posted schedule indicating that times are approximate, based on the children's interest and learning needs. Nevertheless, while teachable moments offer wonderful opportunities to connect children's interest with real learning, you should stay within the broad strokes of your schedule. You do not want children to miss out on other learning opportunities offered through a variety of intentional activities.

If this is your first time developing a schedule or if the program length has changed, you may have to live with the schedule you develop for a few weeks to assess how it is working and then revamp it as needed. During observations, see how the schedule is being followed:

- Do the staff have to rush through activities because there is not enough time?
- Is there too much time and not enough content to fill the time slot?
- Are children transitioning to activities or locations that are not on the schedule?

If you answer *yes* to any of these questions, then the schedule should be changed to reflect what actually happens in the program.

Make a visual display of the schedule using both pictures and words. This enables nonreaders and children with limited English skills to understand the information. Post the schedule to communicate clearly to children, families, visitors, and substitute staff that the program has a predictable schedule and things happen at the same time every day. By informing children of when and where they will move, you eliminate some challenges. Posting the schedule allows families to go directly to the correct activity space when picking up their child. It also helps families determine the best time for pick up so their child will not miss a favorite activity.

Whenever you need to make a change to the schedule, notify children as soon as they enter the program space so they have time to adjust to the change. For example, if your schedule offers free choice inside, be sure to let children know if you cannot offer going to the gym as an option on a given day.

The three sample program schedules included here are intended as generic guidelines for breaking a program day into time blocks. Develop your own schedule to fit your program mission, your number of program areas, and your number of children and staff. The following list will guide you as you design your own daily schedule:

- Involve children and parents. Ask about their interests, needs, and suggestions. Meet with them regularly to see how the schedule is working.
- Plan a variety of activities: divide the time into active and passive activities and into large-group, small-group as well as individual activities.
- Provide children with choices within time slots.
- Keep times flexible.
- Have backup plans: have alternate plans to accommodate the weather or changes in the availability of space, materials, or staff. Keep a folder of alternative activities or a box of alternate materials in an accessible place for when the schedule is not working or a sudden change is needed.

The following are examples of schedules that were developed by various programs based on their children's needs and organizational mission.

DAILY SUMMER SCHEDULE

M W F	0500	Program opens and choice of activities available ("early bird" breakfast snack available upon arrival)
T Th	0600	Program opens and choice of activities available ("early bird" breakfast snack available upon arrival)
	0700–0800	Breakfast buffet available
	0800–0830	Morning blitz (all children)
	0830–1130	Clubs (children's choice)
	0930–1030	Morning snack available
	1130–1230	Lunch and children's choice of quiet activity or rest
	1230–1630	Clubs (children's choice)
	1530–1630	Afternoon snack available
	1630–1700	Camp adventure closing (all children)
	1700–1800	Choice of activities and good-byes

SCHOOL-AGE DAILY SCHEDULE

6:00-8:00 a.m. – Arrival/breakfast/free choice
(phonemic awareness, word recognition, and fluency K)

7:45 a.m. – Breakfast over/clean up table

8:00 a.m. – Group time K-6
(communication: oral and visual K-6)

8:15-8:30 a.m. – Outside play
(earth and earth and space sciences/geography 1)

8:30 a.m. – Board bus for school
(citizenship rights and responsibilities K-6)

8:30-9:15 a.m. – Kindergarten children continue to arrive/
breakfast snack/free choice
(economics K)

9:15-9:30 a.m. – Group with p.m. kindergarten children
(reading process: concepts of print, comprehension strategies, and
self-monitoring strategies/acquisition of vocabulary: literary
text/research/communication: oral and visual)

9:30-10:00 a.m. – Arts and crafts with p.m. kindergarten children
(citizenship rights and responsibilities/people in societies)

10:00-11:00 a.m. – Free choice/small-group games and activities
(geography/scientific ways of knowing/physical sciences/data analysis and
probability/mathematical processes/geometry and spatial sense)

11:00-11:30 a.m. – Set up lunch/outdoor play
(social studies skills and methods/people in societies)

11:30 a.m.-12:15 p.m. – Lunchtime with kindergarten children
(acquisition of vocabulary/communication: oral and visual/citizenship rights
and responsibilities)

SCHOOL-AGE DAILY SCHEDULE

12:15–12:45 p.m. – Group time/outdoor play
(reading process: concepts of print, comprehension strategies, and
self-monitoring strategies/acquisition of vocabulary: literary
text/research/communication: oral and visual/social studies skills
and methods/people in societies)

12:45–1:30 p.m. – Free choice
(economics K)

1:30–1:45 p.m. – Group with a.m. kindergarten children
(reading process: concepts of print, comprehension strategies, and
self-monitoring strategies/acquisition of vocabulary: literary
text/research/communication: oral and visual)

1:45–2:15 p.m. – Arts and crafts with a.m. kindergarten children
(citizenship rights and responsibilities/people in societies)

2:15–3:15 p.m. – Free choice/small-group games and activities
(geography/scientific ways of knowing/physical sciences/data analysis
and probability/mathematical processes/geometry and spatial sense)

3:15–3:45 p.m. – Set up snack/outdoor play
(social studies skills and methods/people in societies)

3:45–4:15 p.m. – Children arrive from buses/outdoor playtime
(geography 1/scientific ways of knowing 2/earth and space
sciences 3/physical sciences 4)

4:15–4:30 p.m. – Group with all children /snacktime
(communication: oral and visual K–4/government K–4)

4:30–5: 30 p.m. – Homework/free choice/small-group play
(social studies skills and methods K/scientific inquiry 1/numbers, number
sense, and operations 2/physical sciences 3/geometry and spatial sense 4)

5:30–5:45 p.m. – Clean up room and move to front room with Kathy

5:45–6:00 p.m. – Kathy's room/children leave

DAILY SCHEDULE CONSIDERATIONS

BEFORE-SCHOOL TIME

1. Breakfast or "early bird" breakfast snack available when children arrive
2. "Start My Day" activities
    -   Fun and active
    -   Finishing homework
    -   Hang-out time (with friends and/or staff)
3. Transition time to school
4. "Heigh-Ho, Heigh-Ho, Off to School We Go"

AFTERSCHOOL TIME

1. Snack or grab-and-go snack available when children arrive
2. Post special events/activities for children to read as they arrive.
3. Hang-out time
    -   Indoors: can have only some areas open
    -   Outdoors: all open for active playtime (can be a short amount of time)
    -   At least one-third staff available just to talk to children
4. Group/teams time
    -   Only if or as needed for specific purpose—for example, additional information about
        o   special activity
        o   visitor
        o   upcoming event or project
        o   children's input for planning activities, menus, etc.
    -   Keep these short and interesting to the children.
    -   Spread these groups throughout the facility.
5. Choices! (This should be the largest amount of time in your schedule.)
    -   Homework time (only for those children needing this!)
    -   Clubs
    -   Special activities/events
    -   Projects
        o   Finished in a day
        o   Long-term
        o   Service-community
        o   Computers and technology
    -   Outdoor time (at least 30 minutes per 3 hours)
6. "Headed home" time
    -   Cleanup
    -   Light snack (optional and not a group time)
    -   At least one staff should be available to hang out with the kids now.

TRANSITIONS

Your schedule includes a number of transitions, during which children move from one block of time to another, from one activity to another, or from one space to another. As anyone who works with children knows, transitions can be difficult for them. The more you can avoid group transitions with school-age children, the better. Too often, large-group transitions bring out negative interactions between children and between adults and children. Group transition issues include increased conversations and noise, children's unwillingness to leave their current activity, and confusion about how to behave. If an adult wants children to be quiet during this time, a power struggle can occur between the adult and children. If children are not engaged while waiting, negative behaviors result.

You can help make transitions successful by allowing children to transition individually, either by following a child leader or by choosing to initiate their own transition. Planning transitions and being flexible and realistic about them will help minimize challenges and reduce inappropriate or unsafe behavior of the children. For example, keep the children who are ready and waiting to transition engaged with a song, a riddle, a story, or guessing games until the whole group is ready. These techniques minimize the chatter and negative behaviors because the children are involved in a planned activity rather than looking for something to do while they wait.

Another technique is to transition a portion of the children to the next activity area as soon as they are ready. For example, if you have 30 children and 2 staff, have one staff member take the first 15 children lined up to the next activity, while the other staff member stays and takes the remaining 15 when they are ready. Some children will be ready sooner than others, because some children disengage from an activity quickly while others lag behind. With planning and practice, transitions that must be made with a group can go smoothly.

Tips for Smooth Transitions

- During daily arrival and departure, greet the child and family members by name.
- Develop a consistent schedule.
- Announce unpredictable changes in schedule.
- Post the schedule in multiple locations.
- Clearly define activities that are accessible to children.
- Allow children to choose what they want to do.
- Warn children three to five minutes before a change will take place.
- Rotate to each group, telling children of the upcoming change.

ROUTINES

A routine is a sequence that gives children a consistent process to follow. Whereas a schedule is a sequence in time, a routine is a sequence in procedure. The procedure may relate to an event, such as the arrival of a guest, washing hands before lunch, or hanging up their coats when entering your program space. For instance, while snacktime is scheduled, what we do in snacktime is a routine. Unlike schedules, routines also outline behavioral expectations. Children learn to depend on routines because they are predictable. Children know what to expect and how to act in each given area that has established routines. When routines are consistent, children feel safe and successful.

Some routines will need to be explained and practiced, such as proper hand washing. Often getting the children to wash their hands or ineffective hand washing can be a stumbling block, so teaching children why washing their hands is so important can encourage compliance. You may find that a child does not understand a routine or is unfamiliar with how the routine is done in your program. Placing pictures of proper washing procedures above sinks can serve as a reminder for children when they wash their hands.

Establishing snack routines that allow children to sit together while taking responsibility to pour their own drinks and clean up after themselves sets clear expectations about their role in the snack area and says staff believe they are capable of completing the task without adult help.

Photo 5.6

This technique is also helpful for younger children or those with special needs. You can help them learn routines by providing visual cues, photos, or sign language pictures that illustrate what is expected in small, sequential steps. Explaining and practicing routines help children understand what is expected while encouraging self-help skills, such as cleaning up after they have eaten snack. Following routines helps children develop responsibility and a sense of ownership in the afterschool program and increases their successful participation.

During snacktime, the routine for children might look something like this:

1. Wash hands.
2. Come to the snack area.
3. Pick up snack and drink.
4. Take snack and drink to the table.
5. Sit at a place with a napkin.
6. Eat snack.
7. Clean up space at table.
8. Throw away garbage.
9. Wash hands.
10. Go to next activity.

Also, the staff in charge of snack have a routine of setting out food and drink, placing napkins at places around the table, washing each vacated space, and placing a new napkin down for the next child.

Remember that all school-age children can do things for themselves, depending on their age and abilities. Some modifications, such as small pitchers and materials that are easily accessible, may be needed for children to complete these tasks independently. Some children take longer to learn routines or struggle to follow a schedule, but with your patience and help, they will become successful. They are capable of pouring their own drinks, serving their own snacks, getting out materials, and cleaning up after themselves. Routines give children opportunities to practice life skills.

Rules and Consequences

Rules are all around us. They guide our lives. Some define individual expectations, while others are written into laws, and still others reflect cultural norms. Rules we live with include obeying speed limits, paying for items we want to have, and practicing social etiquette, such as using a tissue for a runny nose, flushing and washing hands after using the toilet. Children do not come equipped with the knowledge of how to act, listen, and respond appropriately to every situation. We must teach them. They need adults to equip them with a toolbox of skills that help them learn the rules, control impulses, make appropriate choices, problem solve, negotiate, be respectful, and collaborate in a group. Learning the need for rules and the importance of following them and becoming aware of natural consequences are large parts of the

Photo 5.7

Post rules as reminders to children about what is expected from them when in the program.

successful development of children's social competency. With every success, children gain confidence, and they feel valued in the group. When children try but are not successful, the adult should remind them of the rules and consequences so they will learn from their experiences.

An accepted rule of nature is that for every action, there is an equal and opposite reaction. In other words, our actions generate consequences (or reactions). Some of these consequences are natural; others are logical.

A natural consequence occurs when action is or is not taken; typically this consequence does not include another person's involvement. For instance, if a child falls down, his body will be injured according to the intensity of his movement. If children do not eat, they get hungry. Children learn rather quickly and on their own about natural consequences—though adults still must be alert to keep children from harm. You have an obligation to keep children safe and secure at all times.

A logical consequence makes a connection between a behavior and the resulting disciplinary action. If children use markers to draw on walls, a logical consequence is to have them clean the marks off or not use markers until they understand why this is unacceptable behavior. The consequences for breaking a rule make sense to children when they understand a logical link to the rule. Children need positive guidance to help them take responsibility

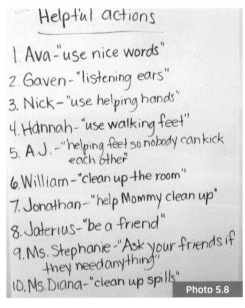

Helpful actions

1. Ava – "use nice words"
2. Gaven – "listening ears"
3. Nick – "use helping hands"
4. Hannah – "use walking feet"
5. A.J. – "helping feet so nobody can kick each other"
6. William – "clean up the room"
7. Jonathan – "help Mommy clean up"
8. Jaterius – "be a friend"
9. Ms. Stephanie – "Ask your friends if they need anything"
10. Ms. Diana – "clean up spills"

Photo 5.8

White Room Class Rules

1. Use helping hands.
2. Use helpful words.
3. Use walking feet.
4. Use listening ears.
5. Use inside voices.
6. Have fun!

Photo 5.9

Left: Having children define words used in your rules helps everyone understand what the words mean.

Right: Once the children and staff have developed the rules, having children sign the rules helps them remember they agreed to follow the rules.

for themselves. When they fail to be responsible, logical consequences that are fair and applied consistently help them learn from their mistakes and ultimately act in appropriate ways.

By developing rules in your program, you will support many social skills in children. Some programs have general rules that guide children throughout all of the program spaces and post more specific rules in areas where they are needed or make sense. For example, outside rules remind children of appropriate outdoor behavior, including the freedom to run and use loud voices. Indoor rules remind children of appropriate indoor behavior, such as walking rather than running and the proper use of a computer. Other programs have only one rule, which they pose as a question to encourage children to think for themselves: *Is it safe?*

To make your program rules most effective, include children in the process of setting the rules and establishing fair consequences for breaking the rules. While this process may be time-consuming, it offers a number of benefits:

1. Staff become more aware of children's ideas of what is and is not appropriate in the program.

2. Children come to a consensus about what a rule means, giving them a shared understanding of the rule. Being part of this process makes children feel valued.

3. Children gain a sense of ownership and belonging, which helps them to make responsible choices and to be accountable for their own actions.

CHILDREN'S BUY-IN
Give children a sense of ownership and belonging by allowing them to help create their environment and establish rules and consequences that govern program space.

4. Children who are involved in making rules and creating consequences know them and tend to follow them more consistently.

5. People do not often argue with their own rules or the consequences for not following them.

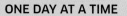

ONE DAY AT A TIME
Remember that each day children are in your program is a new start without any carryover of previous problems from their last time in your program.

Ultimately, develop rules and consequences that are needed for the safety and the administration of your program. Rules work best when children help create them and reach a consensus about the meaning of a rule. Engage children in a dialogue about the rule you would like them to consider. For example, a collaborative process might begin by asking an open-ended question like, *What do you think might happen if we run inside the program space?* or *Why do you need to wear goggles while you are working with tools?* Open-ended questions such as these can help the children come to their own conclusion that rules are needed. The discussion helps them understand why running inside might be unsafe—they might run into a table, trip on toys or other children on the floor, or get hurt or hurt someone else. By helping children connect the dots and understand the consequences of their behavior, both natural and logical, you link cause and effect.

One of the biggest pitfalls for staff is assuming that children know how to make appropriate choices in every situation. What children are allowed to do at home, in school, or playing outside may be different from what they can do in your program space. Remember, when children do not know the name of a crayon, we do not punish them for not knowing but rather teach them its name. Your first goal is to help the children understand what acceptable behavior is and is not. For instance, if the games are being misused for the first time, explain your expectations and the rules for caring for the games. If a second infraction occurs, the consequence may be losing the privilege of playing those games. Children will start to link the rule with appropriate behaviors and understand the consequences of choosing not to follow the rules.

Just as getting children's buy-in is critical in developing rules, so it is equally important to have them help craft the consequences. This can be done as a group, in one-on-one conversations, or by having them write (or draw) their suggestions. Often the consequences generated by children will be far harsher than those of the staff.

The best option is to prevent a behavior from occurring. If you see children about to make inappropriate choices, warn them by saying, "Make a different choice." Alerting them that they are about to make poor choices allows them to correct their behavior before it occurs.

If they continue to make poor choices, try the following steps to defuse the situation and help them understand the infraction and the result of their choices:

Step 1: Remain calm. Privately remind the children of the rule. Ensure that they understand the rule and why breaking it is not acceptable. Discuss this with them. Then have them explain to you why their choice was inappropriate. This will help you know whether they understand the rule and if they know what would have been a better choice.

Step 2: If you or the children need time to cool off, let them take a break in an area without distractions or activities to think about their behavior before starting step 1. Tell them to let you know when they are ready to talk.

Step 3: Acknowledge the children's behavior, frustration, or aggression, but firmly insist this stop. Once you have finished talking, if you feel the children still cannot rejoin the group, redirect them to a new location.

Step 4: If the behavior is unsafe for themselves or others in the program, have a meeting to discuss further strategies to support the children who are having difficulties making appropriate choices. This meeting should include the children involved, their families, and staff who work with the children.

Tips for Creating Rules and Logical Consequences

- Use positive and clear language. State what children are to do, not what they are not to do. If you are reluctant to use this strategy, try picturing a rule that says, "Don't stand on the chair." Visualizing the negative is very difficult, so children visualize what they can, which is standing on the chair. If your rule says, "Your feet remain on the floor," children can picture themselves standing on the floor. Avoid using terms with vague or various meanings. Rules such as "Be nice" or "Share" can be interpreted in vastly different ways.
- Use pictures and words to show how to follow the rule.
- Limit the number of rules—a maximum of five is recommended.
- When a rule needs a consequence, state it clearly along with the rule.
- Post rules and consequences where children can see them. Be sure to post specific rules in areas that need them, such as the computer space, large-motor area, outside, and restrooms.
- Review rules and consequences regularly with children. They often forget.
- Above all, enforce the rules consistently—at all times and places and with all children.

Activities and Questions

Use these activities and questions to determine how to best support and encourage growth of children's social competency skills.

1. Do you use lesson plans for your program activities? If so, how often is your lesson plan created? If not, list the areas in your program and what is planned for each area. Once this is done, you will have created your first basic lesson plan.

2. For which program areas do you make intentional lesson plans each week? What other areas could you include in your planning? If lesson plans are not used, how do staff plan learning experiences appropriate for all children?

3. How are lesson plans shared among staff? With children? Families? Visitors?

4. How do you evaluate and document the effectiveness of your lesson plans?

5. How do you include each area in the program schedule? How consistently do staff follow the schedule? What changes can you make to the schedule to reflect how the day's activities actually occur?

6. How do you communicate the schedule to staff? To children? To families? To visitors?

7. Does your schedule use pictures and words? If not, redesign your schedule to include both words and pictures.

8. How consistently do staff follow the written schedule? What changes can you make to the schedule so it reflects how the day's activities actually occur?

9. Do you use an interest survey (see appendix A)? If so, how often do you give the interest survey to the children? If not, meet with the children and ask them what they are interested in or would like more information about. Add to this additional ideas you think they might find interesting.

10. What do you do with the results of interest surveys? If you do not use the results, how could you use them in your program?

11. List the routines that the children follow every day. Then list the children who are having a difficult time with these routines. What activities can you plan to help those children master those routines?

12. How do or can you involve children in creating your rules?

13. When are rules reviewed with children?

14. What would be the benefit of having rules in both words and pictures?

15. Review how your program's rules and consequences are worded. Reword any rules that are written in the negative, using positive language instead.

16. What process do you use to create consequences for not following the rules? How are the children reminded of consequences?

17. Where are your rules and consequences posted? List the areas that need specific rules, such as computer space, high-risk activities areas, and outdoors. Are rules posted in those areas where children can see and review them easily? If not, engage the children in a discussion to create specific rules; then post the rules in the area to which they apply.

18. What long-term projects have you planned for the children enrolled? What are the learning goals for each of the areas in your room?

CHAPTER 6

The Interpersonal Environment: Facilitating Social Competence

THE INTERPERSONAL ENVIRONMENT encompasses two main areas. This chapter discusses one of these areas: teaching children the social skills they need to be able to interact with others in a way that benefits both themselves and others. Chapter 7 discusses the other area: creating a welcoming place in which everyone feels comfortable.

As you might guess, the interpersonal environment involves relationships and interactions between people. Facilitating smooth interactions can be a challenge, especially with children. They are in the process of developing skills in social competence that help them interact with others in socially acceptable ways. Supporting social skill development is an important element of the interpersonal environment in an afterschool program. The good news is that you can do this no matter what limitations you face in your physical environment.

School-age children need your guidance and supervision in social competency. Your relationship with them is different from that of a schoolteacher. You are more of a mentor, which puts you in an ideal position to help children develop social competence. But school-age children are also at a developmental stage during which friends become very important. As they develop strong peer relationships, they become less dependent on interactions with adults. Your role, then, needs to be that of a supporter, motivator, supplier, and facilitator of activities that foster social competency. A key to fulfilling this role is observation. By observing how children interact with others in your program, you will learn what social competence skills they need to work on. Once you have identified these missing skills, the next step is to intentionally plan activities, opportunities, and materials they can use to learn and practice appropriate social skills.

This dramatic play area encourages children to become involved in pretend play during which they can try on different roles or personalities and develop new skills too.

Photo 6.1

A safe and accepting environment offers children many opportunities to build a foundation in social competency in the short term as well as for their lifetime. By teaching and providing opportunities for children to practice social skills, such as responsibility, acceptance, and communication, you help them learn how to respond to situations in a way that solves problems rather than creating or worsening them. These are skills they will use throughout their lives.

The following checklist will help you evaluate how effective your program's interpersonal environment is. Reflecting on these points will give you an insight into the positive aspects and the challenges in your interpersonal environment.

A Day in the Life of Your Interpersonal Environment

SOCIAL COMPETENCE

1. There are comfortable, quiet spaces where children can talk and work side by side.

2. The environment is safe and free from physical hazards, bullying, and name calling.

3. Rules and consequences are posted and equally enforced.

4. A conflict resolution center is located in your program.

5. Activities are planned that help children learn how to make good choices.

6. Free choice play is available each day.

7. Jobs are available for children to develop self-help skills and ownership in the program.

8. Clear instructions are given about how jobs are to be completed, enabling the children to be successful.

9. Multiday projects are planned regularly.

10. Open-ended art projects are planned to encourage creativity.

11. Art materials are available to children daily.

12. Higher-level thinking materials are included in the program.

13. Activities are planned to help children learn to cope with difficult situations.

14. Staff plan role-playing situations that help children understand how to communicate effectively.

15. The staff refrain from using endearments in place of children's given names.

1. Children and families are not discriminated against for any reason.

2. Staff encourage families to share their cultural celebrations and traditions.

3. The program uses a variety of communication systems to inform families about policies and events.

4. The program has a means to obtain input from children and families.

Principles of Social Competence

According to the National Association of School Psychologists (NASP), "The extent to which children and adolescents possess good social skills can influence their academic performance, behavior, social and family relationships, and involvement in extracurricular activities" (2002). We use social skills every day as we work and interact with other people. What are the behaviors that define this skill set? Jim Ollhoff and Laurie Ollhoff, specialists in education and social psychology in school-age care settings, have identified seven social skill clusters children need to be socially competent (Ollhoff and Ollhoff 2004):

1. community building
2. control
3. confidence
4. curiosity
5. coping
6. communication
7. conflict resolution

THE SEVEN Cs
When planning activities to develop and strengthen social skills, keep in mind the seven Cs of social competence.

While each of the seven clusters has different aspects, they are all interwoven and crucial in helping children become successful when interacting with others around them. Effective environmental design provides the foundation for building these seven clusters of skills.

COMMUNITY BUILDING

Community building relates to children's ability to make friends, work in a group, cooperate, and feel empathy. As children feel valued, develop ownership, and understand their role in the program, a community develops. How the environment is designed plays a large role in creating a sense of community. A safe, nonjudgmental community environment encourages children to try new roles, practice social skills, investigate new areas of interest, and use trial and error to make sense of the world around them.

When designing an environment to encourage community building, provide comfortable spaces where children can talk or work side by side and collaborate to create group events and celebrations. Quiet places, such as a book area or a gathering place with soft furniture, provide areas for children to talk and catch up with friends. This casual environment helps children learn how to make friends and develop an understanding of how others feel. Art and homework areas that are equipped with tables and chairs allow children to work side by side, which helps foster collaboration and peer mentoring. A construction area with plenty of floor space provides children with enough room to either create individualized structures or collaborate on a joint structure. Opportunities for children to work together, learn to cooperate, and develop empathy for their peers are the keys to building community.

Photo 6.2

As children work side by side to create this Lego structure, they learn how to problem solve, cooperate, and collaborate on its construction. These are hallmark skills in creating a sense of community within the afterschool program and throughout life.

CONTROL

Control is composed of self-discipline, responsibility, and conscience. In a safe community, children are able to learn coping skills that allow them to develop self-control or self-regulation. The safe community helps build children's confidence that they can make good choices. Look for ways to include children in setting rules and consequences so that they know what the behavior expectations are in your program. Provide children with a quiet place where they can get themselves under control when things seem to overwhelm them. Teach them ways to de-stress and to think before they speak. Provide opportunities for them to role-play situations that help them understand others' feelings.

Help children take responsibility for their actions. If they take something out, then it is their responsibility to put it back. When they have finished an art project or snack, they are responsible for cleaning it up. They may not clean it up to your standards; however, with practice they will improve not only their cleaning skills but also their self-discipline and responsibility.

CONFIDENCE

Confidence is feeling capable and having positive self-esteem. You help children feel that they matter when you call them by name, engage them in conversation about their school day or weekend, and encourage their input when appropriate. Creating jobs and encouraging children to do their assigned jobs sends the message that you believe they are capable of completing the job successfully and independently. Develop jobs such as snack helper, homework aide, art helper, and transition helper so the children can begin to take ownership of the program space. Help ensure their success by making sure they know what the job entails, and provide guidance for those who have never done a specific job before. Real-life lessons about employment and pay teach children responsibility, confidence, and positive work ethics. This confidence, coupled with good communication and conflict resolution skills, equips children to get their needs met in acceptable ways.

BUILDING CONFIDENCE

One afterschool program set up a jobs board and asked the children to sign up for a job they thought they would like to do. Once all the jobs were filled, children went to an in-service training so they knew what their job entailed. Those who took care of snack were instructed on food-handling guidelines, where the snacks were kept, and how and when to wear gloves. Those who answered the phone were given a script, and they practiced exactly what they were to say on the phone. The art helpers, who replenished the art supplies when they were getting low, were told where the art supplies were and how to place them in the containers.

A middle-school program took program jobs one step further and had the children apply for each job. At interviews that simulated real job interviews, the children were asked why they wanted to do the job and what skills they brought to the job. The children then met together and were asked how they wanted to be paid. They decided on a piece of candy for each day they completed their job. On Friday they received their paycheck, and they turned it in for their pay. The children were surprised to discover that for a five-day job they received three pieces of candy; the missing two pieces of candy represented the taxes.

CURIOSITY

Curiosity drives children's love of adventure and play and their intrinsic desire to learn. Creating an environment where children feel safe and are encouraged to learn sparks their curiosity about the world around them and establishes a love of learning. Encourage children's curiosity with open-ended art projects that provide opportunities for children to be creative and with science projects in which children can see how things work or experience a different outcome and find out why it did not work exactly like their peer's project. Through this process of trial and error, children become intrigued with learning. Only when adults label children's efforts a failure do children believe they cannot do something.

Materials that challenge children also fuel their curiosity and love of learning. Strategy games (chess, checkers, Connect Four), mind benders, and logic puzzles help children use the knowledge they currently have while developing problem-solving techniques to solve unfamiliar problems. These games and activities challenge them to develop an understanding of game strategy and logic, which are higher-level thinking skills that inspire continued learning and curiosity.

Photo 6.3

These paintings created by the children to depict their favorite things are displayed in a prominent location, which sends the message that their work is respected and valued.

COPING

Coping is the child's ability to deal with stress, crisis, and anger. Create opportunities for children to learn how to de-stress by including quiet places that allow them to relax and unwind. Equip quiet places with materials for a variety of relaxing activities, such as a basket of books, writing and drawing materials, and earphones for listening to pre-screened music. Providing children with activities such as photography or painting not only teaches coping skills but also may open the door to a life-long hobby. Role-playing difficult situations helps children learn how to deal with anger, resolve conflicts, and react appropriately to stress and crisis.

COMMUNICATION

Communication comprises listening, expressing feelings appropriately, and assertiveness. Often children come to an afterschool program with a variety of acceptable and unacceptable communication skills. Perhaps you have heard a child declare, "But I am allowed to say that at home." Setting clear behavior expectations for your program allows you to respond to that statement with, "In our program, that language is not acceptable."

Observe children's verbal interactions with peers and adults to determine what skills they have. Actively teach children to listen and to use appropriate words when they talk. Role-playing and giving children the proper words to use are two ways to help children practice good communication. Listening to others can be a challenge for children when they really want you to know how they feel. In this situation, have the person who is speaking hold an object, such as a stuffed bear, a ball, or a Frisbee, to alert the other children that they must listen. The adult, as the role model, should also hold the object when speaking. When the next child wants to speak, the object is passed to that person. These visual reminders can make a big difference in establishing good listening skills. Remind younger children that this activity is for teaching them good listening skills and it is not always necessary to hold on to an object when they want to talk with each other.

CONFLICT RESOLUTION

Conflict resolution includes negotiation skills, ability to generate resolution strategies, and dislike for violence. Establish a no-bullying policy and a conflict resolution process to give children a non-aggressive, constructive way to solve problems. Equip the environment with materials and activities that allow for skill building. For example, set up a peace table, and include an outline that suggests ways the children can handle conflicts. Create a listening center where two children can go to talk, solve problems, or just regroup and de-stress. Provide opportunities for peer mentoring, during

Creating a clearly labeled space and providing materials for conflict resolution helps children know where to go when problems arise.

which children help each other learn appropriate ways to resolve their problems. One program asked children who were struggling with conflict resolution themselves to be peer mentors. In helping other children learn how to work through their problems in a peaceful way, their own conflict resolution skills improved.

Creating a Supportive Social Environment

Quality school-age programs encourage children to choose from a variety of social learning opportunities. Some of these opportunities are child-initiated, while others are adult-led. Children's social skills and overall development flourish when they can interact freely with adults and peers in a safe and nurturing environment with carefully selected choices of activities, materials, and experiences. Children make mistakes—we all do. They do not always accurately follow directions or have the appropriate words to express themselves. They often need to repeat an activity to understand it or get it right. When you encourage learning rather than judging the children for not saying the right thing or completing the task "correctly," you set up a nonjudgmental environment where children feel valued and accepted.

Photo 6.5

Encourage social interaction in your after-school program by providing spaces in the environment and time in the daily schedule for children to gather with peers, make friends, and have conversations. Help children build social skills by encouraging problem solving and appropriate communication. The process of working through differences with their peers shows children that there is more than one viewpoint and more than one way to do something. Remember that you are a role model as you interact with others throughout the program day. Children are watching and observing acceptable ways to handle situations. When they see you compromising and working well with other adults, they are more likely to feel that the environment is emotionally safe for everyone.

Both the adults in the environment and the environment itself play a part in facilitating social competency. Adults set the tone and the expectations for children in your program. Staff members choose activities, furniture, and games that support the development of social skills. Adults are the glue that holds all the pieces of the afterschool environment together. When observing children's interactions with others, ask yourself the following five questions.

1. Does the environment provide areas where children can work independently or with a group? Ideally, programs should provide a mix of program spaces that allow children to quietly sit and read a book, do homework, talk to friends, or listen to prescreened music along with areas where they can

Photos of the children and their families in collage frames provide a connection between the program and families. Creating homey places where children can gather and relax encourages conversation and provides time to make friends.

play group games, work together on a project, play board games, or conduct long-term projects. Children's interests and needs change from day to day; providing this variety of spaces will increase engagement and opportunities for children to choose something that meets their needs on any given day.

2. Are there places in the room where children can gather and just talk? These places can be easily created with a blanket under a tree during outside play or inside with a few floor pillows, a soft couch, or an impromptu tent made by draping a sheet over two easels. After a long day at school, children need time to de-stress, chill out, or calm their minds and just relax while chatting with friends. Providing these spaces where children can regroup sends a message that it is okay to stop and relax and that they do not always have to be on the run. Let them take time to smell the roses and enjoy being children.

3. Can children choose to display their artwork, or do staff choose which artwork is displayed? Children put much time and creativity into their artwork, so it is important that they have a space to display it if they choose to do so. Sometimes children would rather take their artwork home than display it in the program space. At other times, however, they want to know that their work is worthy of displaying, and they need places to do just that. Designating a bulletin board or providing an empty display case so children can self-select their artwork is a wonderful way to show them they are valued. Some programs have each family bring in a picture frame for their child. Children are allowed to put any artwork or photos they choose into the frame and change it as often as they like. These frames are placed around the program space, much as you would do in your own home. Some programs create an art gallery and place all the picture frames on one wall or a table close to the family center. Display art projects such as sculptures, sewing, woodworking, or jewelry on tables or bookcases or in display cases for everyone to enjoy.

4. Do staff members listen to children and seem interested in what they have to say? In the hustle and bustle of the program day, you are approached by many children wanting to talk. When they want to engage you in conversation and talk about their day, they may be looking to you to determine how they should handle a situation. It often takes just a moment to make children feel they are heard. If you are in the middle of something, hold their hand and explain that you really want to listen and you will hold their hand until you have finished what you are doing. When you are ready, get on eye level with them and listen. Be in the moment with them.

Snacktime is also a great opportunity to have conversations with children. As you sit with the children at snack, find out about their day, ask how the test went, what they did over the weekend, or how the game was on Saturday. Asking questions gives children practice with two-way conversation and listening and lets them know you are interested in what is going on in their lives and that you have been paying attention to what they say. This is yet another way to help the children feel that they belong and are valued.

5. Does the lesson plan include intentional teaching of social skills? Assuming that all children have the same level of social skills will send you down a bumpy path. Saying "please" when requesting something and "thank you" when receiving something might seem like something all children know, yet that is not the case. Your observations and interactions with children provide clues to what needs to be taught. Assess what the children need to know to make them competent in a skill, and then teach them what they need to know. If the children do not clean up after themselves, adjust the environment so they can do that effectively, for example, by placing pictures and words where materials go on the shelves or by moving the trash can closer to the snack area for easy cleanup. If children need to problem solve, role-play situations that have been troubling and engage the group in developing appropriate solutions.

Bullying

As part of creating a supportive environment, all staff need to be on the lookout for bullying. Bullying is a learned behavior. Children learn how to bully by watching older children, adults, and media such as television, videos, and screen games. Bullying hurts in many ways: physical, verbal, social, and psychological. Children who are victims of bullying tend to show more signs of anxiety, depression, and insecurity when compared with nonbullied children (Harvard Health Publications 2009). Bullying is an ever-growing problem. More children seem to be resorting to verbal and physical violence to get what they want. Sometimes we forget that some children do not have appropriate social skills or feel insecure. These shortcomings can make children targets of bullying.

Every school-age program should have a bullying policy in place. The policy should be spelled out in the family and staff handbooks. Equally important is to address the root of bullying, which can be the lack of appropriate social skills. We want all children to have the ability to get their needs met in socially acceptable ways; bullying should never be acceptable. You may have heard from a child, "But my dad said to hit him." Helping children understand that your program is a place where all children are safe and bullying is not acceptable helps define the expectations for their behavior. Sometimes just identifying what is a bullying behavior and role-playing can provide children with other ways to get their needs met. Verbal bullying is often the unseen bullying in programs, so you should discuss name calling and how this might make someone feel. There is no magic wand to erase bullying; it takes time, patience, empathy, dedication, education, and clear behavior expectations. School-age program staff have both the opportunity and responsibility to change children's aggressive and hurtful behaviors to ones of respect and acceptance. You can start by instituting a no-bullying policy.

Tips to Ensure Your No-Bullying Policy Is Effective

Here are ways to make your no-bullying policy a vital part of teaching children social competency:

- Communicate and enforce a policy of no tolerance for any type of bullying. Staff must administer the policy systematically and without exception to be effective. Children need to know that what is written in the policy is enforced daily, by all staff, and in all locations. No exceptions.
- Discuss and review the policy with children often. Plan discussions about what bullying is so all children have the same definition and understand it is unacceptable. Practice with the children what to do if they become the target of a bully. Some programs have children sign the no-bullying policy and promise to adhere to it.
- Ensure children are aware of the reporting procedure if they witness bullying or they are victims. (Consider having a "Bully Box" where children can place anonymous reports of bullying incidents.)
- Remind children of the difference between "telling" and "tattling." "Telling" is needed when the tellers believe there is a situation that could be harmful or dangerous to themselves or others. "Tattling" is when the tellers are angry, want attention, or want to get someone else in trouble.
- Review and help children practice skills to problem solve difficult situations and to negotiate or work toward conflict resolution.
- Systematically enforce the consequences for bullying.

Publicize the no-bullying policy by posting it throughout the program and including it on your website and in the staff and family handbooks. Be sure to have adequate supervision throughout the program space to enforce the policy. Staff should be constantly on the lookout for any type of bullying or potentially hurtful situation.

Managing Conflict

Creating an environment that provides ample supplies, games, materials, and activities will minimize the conflicts that occur when there are not enough materials for the number of children served. Provide enough space for activities so that children can move freely without disrupting others at play.

When you observe a conflict, note where it happened, what it was about, and how it was resolved. Remember, there is always a story before the story. In other words, you saw only one part of the interaction: the conflict. You need to know what happened beforehand—the story that led up to the conflict. If you assume that what you saw was the entire incident, you are doing a disservice to all the children involved. Your role is to guide a conversation between the parties in a conflict by asking each child to tell you what happened. Children should speak one at a time while the others listen. Use "I" messages such as "I can see you are upset," or "Use your words and tell me what happened." Help children see how the others feel and why they are upset to help the children develop empathy. Ask them how to solve this problem. If the children agree on a solution, your role as a facilitator is finished, even if you feel the solution is not fair.

Creating a conflict resolution center will provide a place away from other children to quietly solve problems. Teach the children how to use this center to solve a conflict, and use role play to reinforce the lesson. You will need to revisit this process with the entire group several times throughout the year as well as when new children enter the program. To make this center an independent learning area, equip it with the tools children need to be successful:

CHILDREN AS PROBLEM SOLVERS
Include the children in problem solving to reach solutions. This is a perfect opportunity for them to practice coping and conflict resolution skills.

- books on feelings
- puppets to help children act out their situation or talk freely with each other when they cannot or will not express themselves verbally
- pencils, markers, crayons, and paper to write or draw the situation or express their feelings
- a list that enumerates the problem-solving process:
  1. Cool down.
  2. Tell your story.
  3. Listen to others.
  4. Find a solution.
  5. Get adult help if needed.
- an object that the child who is talking can hold as an outward sign that others should be listening
- a list of phrases and "I" statements to help children who do not have the words they need to solve the problem appropriately, such as "I get so mad when . . ." or "I just wanted to . . ." or "Maybe we can . . ."
- posted rules for the center, such as "Use quiet voices and listening ears"

Let the children know that you are a resource for them if they cannot solve a problem. That means you will be there to help them through the process but not to solve the problem for them.

Addressing Problem Behavior

Often children act inappropriately because they do not have good social skills. They may not know what words to say to get their needs met, so they resort to hitting, name calling, and fighting to get what they want. Do not judge children by their age or size when thinking about what they should know. Have you ever caught yourself saying, "But he is eight, he should know better"? This type of assumption can set up a child to fail, because you have already decided what he should know. Regardless of their age, children may not know appropriate words or alternate ways to handle a situation. Children know only what they have learned from the significant adults in their lives about how to handle situations, and these strategies are not always appropriate.

You can help children understand why you are requesting that they choose other words or different behaviors by explaining that your afterschool program is a safe place and certain words and behaviors are not acceptable. Once you have helped children process an inappropriate event, talk about other ways to handle the situation and other words they could have used. This gives them tools to use when similar situations arise in the future. The following story is an example of how, with sensitive guidance, staff can help develop children's social skills through real-life situations.

EMOTIONS AFFECT BEHAVIOR

The behavior of a child in a military school-age program changed very suddenly from cooperative and happy to aggressive and acting out. Staff observed her carefully for a couple days, noticing she mentioned death and war constantly. After talking quietly and privately with the child, the staff learned that her mother was to be deployed within days. The child misunderstood the word *deployed*, confusing it with *deceased*. She was confused and afraid. What would happen to her mother? Through careful and sensitive discussion with the child and her mother, the staff were able to help the child work through this issue, and her behavioral problems were resolved.

The Role of the Adult

School-age staff have a critical role in the development of children's social competency. Observation and anticipation are keys to identifying the social skills that children possess and those that need to be taught and practiced. As you observe the children in your care and see them getting ready to make an inappropriate choice, give them an opportunity to make a different choice. By saying, "Make a different choice," you let them know that what they are about to do is not acceptable in your program, and you allow them to take control of their behavior and make other choices that are more appropriate. While not all children will take the hint in the beginning, if you use this process consistently, they will learn to make different choices. By allowing children to make different choices, you send the message that you believe they can come up with an appropriate choice. Sometimes all children need to regulate themselves is the knowledge that someone believes in their ability to choose appropriately.

You support—or hinder—children's social skills every day in ways you may not even be aware of. Staff members in school-age programs serve as tour guides in the learning environments, taking children from place to place, giving them exciting information about where they are, and encouraging them to revisit these places often. Your positive and enthusiastic interactions with children, colleagues, and families are very important. Without this element in your environment, children's growth in social competency will be limited. To ensure that children are supported, understand the impact that you have on them. In addition to setting up your environment to facilitate social competency, monitor your own behavior by using the following tips as a guide:

- Be a good role model.
- Be a good mentor and teacher.
- Be open-minded.
- Build children up; do not tear them down.
- Tell children simply and clearly what you mean.
- Accept children for who they are—do not try to make them into someone you think they should be.

Be a good role model. Children take their cues from you. How they act, talk, listen, or feel about themselves comes from watching you and your reactions to different situations. When you listen to them, your colleagues, families, or supervisor, they learn that communicating is as much about listening as it is about talking. School-age children learn not only by listening to what you

Photo 6.6

Staff members' positive interactions with children support children's sense of self and help them understand the need for good social skills.

say but also by watching how you act. Be consistent in all you do to mold children's social competency.

Be a good mentor and teacher. When children's behavior or demeanor changes, be there to help them. You will find that each child's challenges are different. Some children struggle with their homework, while others struggle with their friends. It is important to guide children in problem solving, negotiating, working to consensus (or at least a peaceful compromise), and cooperation. Give the problem back to the children, and ask how they can solve the situation, all the while listening to them as you guide them to practice all facets of communication.

Be open-minded. When facilitating a conflict between children, remember that you often see only one part of the interaction. Ask them open-ended questions to reveal what happened before you noticed the conflict. This allows children to feel they are being heard when they describe from their point of view how the conflict started and why it happened. Remember: there is always a story before the story.

Build children up; do not tear them down. Give guidance that nurtures children's sense of self-worth by acknowledging their efforts, not just their successes. Treat each child fairly; remember that each child is unique, and our guidance must reflect their individuality. Some children need a little more of our time, patience, and understanding as they work through problematic situations, while other children are quick to tell you they get it and are able to resolve their issues more quickly. Adapting your guidance to children's needs will support their efforts to resolve conflicts. Effective guidance is not "one size fits all."

Tell children simply and clearly what you mean. Use clear directions and redirection so children do not scratch their heads trying to figure out what you were trying to tell them.

Above all, accept children for who they are. While all children follow a typical progression of growth and development, individuals develop with their own sequence and timeline based in part on the variety of social systems to which they are exposed. These include, for example, home, church, schools, school-age programs, sports, dance, scouting, and music instruction. Within these various social systems, children learn how to interact with others in their own way, with a wonderful inner spirit unique to each of them. Nurturing their specialness supports their learning and self-confidence.

The Value of Play

Play is a natural activity in which children make sense of the world around them, often while interacting with others. During play, children act out daily activities, such as cooking or caring for a pet, and take on roles, such as mom, dad, or a sibling. Many times, children act out the same situation over and over, trying different ways to handle situations. Instead of the process, they practice and internalize valuable social skills, including self-regulation and how to get their needs met in a socially acceptable way. Mastery of social skills happens when children connect with play-based activities, peers, and materials that keep them involved for long periods of time. This learning process may be one reason why play is considered an essential part of the development of the whole child. In fact, play is so important to children's overall development that the United Nations High Commission for Human Rights recognizes it as a birthright for every child around the world (United Nations 1989). Yet we live in a world where children feel pressure to buckle down and work. Some children no longer have opportunities for play, even though play promotes learning through meaningful, real-life situations that are exciting and interesting.

Your program can play a critical role in promoting play in children's lives. Recognize play as a foundation for their learning and provide avenues to encourage play-based learning. As you plan schedules for your temporal environment, make sure you are providing time for children to play. Through play, they will practice and build social as well as cognitive, language, and physical skills. Through play, children also learn coping, negotiation, problem solving, and decision making.

Negotiation, problem solving, and communication occur during play as children talk about how to play a game, who is going first, or how to stack their blocks so they do not fall down. Taking turns and learning how to handle disappointment during play helps children develop appropriate coping skills. They learn how to communicate when they are working together to make a marble tower, plan a party, or make sets for a dramatic production. Play can provide children with an opportunity to be creative when they dance to different types of music or create new games from old ones. Through play, a group of children can learn to collaborate and

SOME OF THE SOCIAL SKILLS LEARNED THROUGH PLAY
- negotiation
- problem solving
- coping
- decision making
- communication
- creativity
- collaboration
- self-regulation

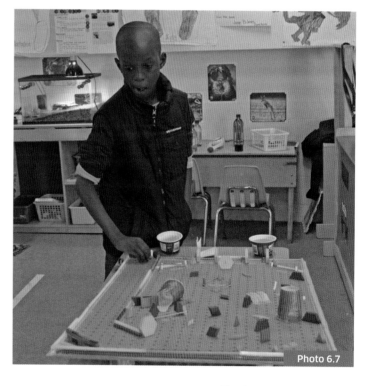

Photo 6.7

Allowing children to experiment with cause and effect as they design and redesign their pinball game provides opportunity for problem solving and promotes learning through play.

find creative solutions to a problem, such as how to climb a tree without falling or how to mix baking soda and vinegar together without smelling like a pickle. When children are given a chance to think outside the box, their problem-solving and creative solutions can amaze you.

Play is where children learn to self-regulate their behavior. This behavior includes such things as waiting for their turn, willingly helping someone else, and cleaning up without being asked. It also includes taking on a role and staying in it. As children play, they learn the give and take of interacting in a relationship or within the rules of a game or play theme. Dramatic play is an obvious example of this; if children are playing restaurant, one person cannot be both the customer and the chef.

Play is also a fun way to teach skills that support self-regulation. For example, for children to participate successfully in a ball game, they need to know the rules for what is expected of them on the field and off. Your role is to explain the rules of the game so that children can understand them. Asking them to repeat the rules can demonstrate whether they were listening, but it does not demonstrate their understanding. For that, children need to practice various scenarios, such as when you are considered safe on a base. Once children master an understanding of the game's rules, they can make appropriate choices for their behavior.

To support play, you may also need to teach game skills, such as catching a ball with a baseball glove. Teaching these skills helps ensure success.

Here is an example of how this works: have a child throw the ball up and catch it. Once that is mastered, invite another child or a group of children to participate. Have the children form two parallel lines approximately five feet apart, each of them facing someone in the other line. Have the children toss the ball back and forth between the two lines. When that distance is mastered, have them move back a step and try again.

TIPS TO SUPPORT PLAY IN YOUR SCHOOL-AGE PROGRAM

- Schedule uninterrupted and sustained periods of time daily for child-initiated play.
- Provide suitable spaces and materials to encourage and facilitate play.
- Advocate play as an avenue to learning through your program policies. Include information about the benefits of play in your handbooks, on your website, and in newsletters.

Right: Allowing children to use the dramatic play area to act out a birthday party provides an opportunity to re-create a real-life event.

Photo 6.8

Activities and Questions

Use these activities and questions to help you explore how your environment encourages the building of appropriate social skills. The answers to these questions will help you define areas of strength and areas that need some improvements.

1. How often do children have access to free play each day?

2. How do you handle conflict in your program? Review your program's step-by-step guidelines (or develop them).

3. How are all staff members involved in your program's conflict resolution process?

4. What training have staff received about tolerance and antibullying in the past six months?

5. Do children have opportunities to have a job/role in the program?

6. In what ways do staff role model tolerance and respect?

7. What activities have you planned in the past month that intentionally teach children tolerance, acceptance, and antibullying?

8. How do you determine what are inappropriate behaviors, materials, and interactions in your program? How is that information communicated to children, staff, and families?

9. Make a list of the seven Cs of social skills, and describe how your environment, planning, and intentional teaching support each social skill.

CHAPTER 7

The Interpersonal Environment: Ensuring Everyone Is Welcomed

SCHOOL-AGE CHILDREN are turned on—or off—to places very quickly. It is almost like they have special sensors that tell them, "I like it here!" or "How can I get out of here?" In all kinds of ways, the environment can shape children's responses either positively or negatively. Children have difficulty quantifying these feelings, but when they feel comfortable and welcomed, they want to stay. Likewise, an accepting interpersonal environment creates an atmosphere in which staff love to work and families and other stakeholders feel welcome. This chapter looks at the various components that help both children and adults feel welcome in your program—regardless of their race, ethnicity, nationality, religion, socioeconomic status, age, sexual orientation, or disability. A welcoming environment creates a supportive community where children feel accepted for who they are and for what abilities they have without judgment or criticism. Just think: Wouldn't that be a place you would like to be?

To evaluate how your school-age program makes participants feel, first consider your own experiences in various places. Think about a time when you were in a place where you felt uncomfortable or undervalued. Maybe you felt ignored, or nothing was of interest to you, or you did not know anyone. Maybe you could not put your finger on it, but you just did not like the way the space made you feel.

You can design a welcoming environment for your school-age program no matter what your resources. If you share your space or have a restricted budget, you may think you cannot improve the feel of your program. Think again. Perhaps the most important component of a welcoming atmosphere is the attitude of your program's administrators and staff. Regardless of your title—teacher, caregiver, staff, administrator, or provider—you, as the adult in the environment, are the agent of change. Friendly and open communication is critical. The manner in which you address and engage coworkers, children, families, and others is infectious. Make sure you are modeling the image you want to create. You set both the tone and the example. Others will follow your lead. The welcoming environment you create encourages school-age children to

- feel good about themselves,
- celebrate their families' unique characteristics,
- learn that people can be different yet still have much in common, and
- be respectful of others who are different from them.

Fostering these values helps children grow up to be respectful and accepting adults.

As you intentionally design your welcoming environment, pay attention to the temporal environment. Tailor lessons, activities, and events to let all children, regardless of their ages, abilities, and limitations, participate and experience success. A predictable schedule, routines, clear expectations, and consistent staffing help the children in your program feel safe, which in turn makes them feel comfortable, secure, and welcome. By supporting each child's uniqueness, your environment promotes a sense of well-being and comfort for everyone. A welcoming environment helps each child become an active, successful learner and encourages children to interact with each other. The following components are key to a welcoming interpersonal environment:

- welcoming all stakeholders
- engaging in two-way communication
- accommodating individual needs
- embracing diversity
- cultivating openness
- teaching tolerance and respect
- building community

The sections that follow address each of these components, explaining why they are important and how to design your school-age program's interpersonal environment to support each of them. As you begin the process of designing a welcoming environment, evaluate your program using the How Welcoming Is Your Program Environment? checklist and questions as a guide. (The checklist is also available at www.redleafpress.org for downloading and printing.)

How Welcoming Is Your Program Environment?

ENGAGING IN TWO-WAY COMMUNICATION

1. Are families and children greeted as they enter and leave the program?

2. Do families provide information about their child's likes, dislikes, health issues, and individual needs?

3. Are families asked to share their family celebrations, culture, and traditions?

4. Is regular written communication given to families and community organizations?

5. Is written material stated simply and easy to read (at or below a fifth-grade reading level)?

6. Is written material translated for families whose first language is not English?

7. Is there a suggestion box placed in the program so parents can give input about the program?

8. Are children asked what interests they would like to explore and what activities they would like included in the program?

9. Are staff available to schedule conferences with parents so information about their children can be shared?

ACCOMMODATING INDIVIDUAL NEEDS

1. Is input from families requested and used to educate staff about the children and to design an environment that supports their identified needs?

2. Are materials accessible and developmentally appropriate?

3. Do materials reflect the interest and diversity of the children enrolled?

4. Are adaptive materials available for the children who need them?

5. Do staff encourage children to use all materials? Is the environment arranged so children can use all materials regardless of their gender, race, abilities, or limitations?

6. Can all children access materials independently?

7. Is the environment free of barriers?

8. Are pathways clear of obstructions and wide enough to accommodate mobility aides for children who need them?

9. Does program space provide other physical supports, such as adequate lighting and appropriate signage to define spaces?

10. Can children choose whether to participate in group activities?

11. Does the environment include places for children to feel comfortable being alone?

EMBRACING DIVERSITY

1. Are families asked to share their culture, and are they included in program activities that celebrate diversity?

2. Do all materials (wall displays, books, computer software, toys, and games) show people from diverse groups in positive, nonstereotyped ways?

3. Is the composition of the staff reflective of the demographics of the greater community by gender, age, ethnicity, and culture?

CULTIVATING OPENNESS

1. Do program staff make it a priority to respect and value differences among people?

2. Do staff model an accepting and respectful attitude?

3. Do staff encourage families to share information, food, language, and history of their culture?

4. Do materials and learning opportunities support an open, antibiased worldview by including pictures, books, activities, field trips, and speakers that expose the children to cultures from the world at large?

TEACHING TOLERANCE AND RESPECT

1. Do all staff members exhibit zero tolerance for teasing, bullying, and other negative child-to-child interactions including but not limited to discrimination of race, religion, culture, gender, abilities, limitations, family unit, sexual orientation, or appearance?

2. Do lesson (or activity) plans teach nonbullying techniques, socially acceptable communication skills, and respectful interactions for all?

BUILDING COMMUNITY

1. Are children involved in the planning of the program environment and activities?

2. Do staff provide opportunities for children to engage in peer mentoring and multiage activities?

3. Is the children's artwork on display?

4. Do children have assigned jobs to promote ownership in the afterschool program?

One Environment, Many Stakeholders

Creating a welcoming environment includes helping all stakeholders feel comfortable in your afterschool program. A stakeholder is anyone or any group of people who has an effect on your program or who is affected by the program. Your stakeholders include

- children
- families
- program staff
- program administrators
- community organization members
- school personnel

The message from your environment to each person coming through the door should be, "We're glad you're here with us today." This message is especially significant for children, since they spend more time with you than most other stakeholders. In fact, many people think of children as the only stakeholders in a school-age program. Indeed, your primary goal is to meet the needs of children. And meeting children's needs is complex, especially if your program, like many others, is comprised of children representing a variety of ages, ethnicities, abilities, strengths, medical conditions, limitations, and challenges. Because children are your primary stakeholder, you need to consider their needs not only as a group but also as individuals to ensure that each participant feels welcome in your program.

But you have several other stakeholders as well. Welcoming all stakeholders into your program sends a message that they are valued. Encourage them to visit your program and invite them to participate in activities and field trips. Creating opportunities for stakeholders to become involved in your program gives them ownership and can develop lasting community relationships.

The degree to which you incorporate the needs of other stakeholder groups will depend on the dynamics of your particular program. For example, if families represent a wide range of backgrounds—racial, ethnic, educational, economic—you will have more success making all of them feel welcome in your program if you reach out to them in a variety of ways. And they will have an easier time identifying with program staff if the staff reflects the diversity of families in your program and the community.

All stakeholders in your school-age program bring their own perspective and often their own set of concerns. At times these concerns will conflict. Addressing the wide variety of stakeholders, both in your program environment and in the community at large, can pose a difficult challenge. But doing your best to balance the various interests can reap great rewards. One way to get input from all stakeholders is to create an advisory board. The advisory board provides an open avenue for stakeholders to bring up concerns, make suggestions, and give feedback to improve your environment and programming. Include staff, parents, children, and community members on your advisory board. When all stakeholders believe their opinion counts, they feel a greater sense of unity and common purpose.

The Importance of Communication

Respectful communication sets the tone for a welcoming interpersonal environment. Two-way communication is essential in creating effective relationships with children, families, staff, and community stakeholders. You set a welcoming tone by greeting children and family members by name. This helps them feel they matter, and it shows visitors that you care. When you listen attentively while children and family members talk, you show your interest in what they have to say. When you ask families for feedback about the program—and listen to the feedback you receive—they know that you value their opinions. When you offer events such as parenting classes, parents' nights out, game nights, reading events, and potlucks, your program helps support the families of the children you serve. All of these interactions help create an environment in which children and families feel valued and an important part of the program. From watching you interact with others respectfully, children learn to see people for who they are and to not be afraid to reach out to others. Your role as a communicator also goes beyond the general tone you establish through verbal interactions with children and families. It includes written communications such as your handbook, newsletters, and permission slips.

To foster a welcoming interpersonal environment, begin by learning specific details about the children and families in your program and about your colleagues. This knowledge increases your ability to connect on a deeper, more meaningful level. Educate yourself about the unique cultures, family dynamics, abilities, languages, medical conditions, strengths, and challenges of children in your program. Valuable conversations with family members will enable you to design the environment so that each child can participate fully in the program. (See later sections of this chapter for more information on educating yourself and on designing the environment.)

As a communicator, you need to gather and give information. This give-and-take of information is the foundation for establishing a two-way communication system that will help all parties feel valued and accepted. While communication is important with all of your stakeholders, in this chapter we focus on the two biggest groups: children and families.

GATHERING INFORMATION

Gathering information will help you understand the children and families in your program so you will know how to accommodate their needs and help them feel welcome. Often family members can provide you with valuable information about their child, including strategies and suggestions that will allow their child to be successful in your program environment. Children can also provide you with valuable information about how the program can be structured to meet their individual needs. Take time to ask them. Always remember that your program needs to be designed for the children, so who better to tell you what they like to do or what they are interested in than the children themselves? Family members can help you understand their child's fears, interests, limitations and medical needs. Observations can help you determine each child's temperament, learning style, and learning strengths. (See chapters 2 and 4 for more information on observations.) Armed with information from observations, from children, and from families, you can create a personalized environment in which each child feels comfortable.

Both formal and informal methods can be used for obtaining information. Formal methods include information from the various registration forms completed during enrollment and updated annually, observational data, information about child development and medical disorders or handicapping conditions from libraries and professional organizations, and interest surveys filled out by children and by families. If a child has an Individualized Education Program (or Plan) (IEP), make sure you have the family's permission to be a part of the IEP meetings. Your participation will result in consistent support strategies for the child at home, in school, and in your program. Informal methods of gathering information include day-to-day conversations, e-mails, phone calls, and anecdotal notes. Four key topics to inquire about are families' needs and traditions, children's likes and dislikes, health concerns, and any other special needs the child may have.

Know the Families in Your Program

Personalizing a school-age environment to meet the needs of the children in your program begins with learning about them and their families. Children and families come to your program with a variety of life experiences, expectations, and needs. With family dynamics in society changing, you cannot make assumptions about a child's family. Often children live in nontraditional family units, such as ones with only one parent, grandparents, or gay or lesbian parents. Children can experience a variety of events that can affect their behavior or mood, such as a death, divorce, a move to a new neighborhood, and the birth of a sibling. Understanding the families' needs can help you design a program environment that is flexible and respectful of family dynamics, cultures, and traditions. Ongoing dialogue with children and families, combined with your observations of children in the program environment, will enable you to continually evaluate and adapt your environment to meet children's needs.

Ask children and families about their family traditions, holiday celebrations, family members, cultural heritage, language spoken at home, and favorite foods. Some programs choose to present these questions more formally, using a form that asks parents to share information about the family. (Understand that some families choose not to share this information, so this form should be optional.) Also, the form can ask if they would like to share their family heritage or celebrations, and, if so, when would be a good time for them to do so. Searching the library or Internet can provide you with current information about specific cultural celebrations, such as when and how they are celebrated. Observe the children's interests and questions about people. This will tell you what they know and want to know about people from differing backgrounds. All this information can help you intentionally design environment spaces and program activities to reflect the needs of the families while celebrating the diversity of their cultures and traditions.

Photo 7.1

Creating an area to showcase families' cultures and traditions shows respect and acceptance.

Discover Children's Likes and Dislikes

When you know the likes and dislikes of all the children in your program, you can plan an environment they will want to return to each day. Make sure they understand that you will consider everyone's likes and dislikes but that you will not be able to include input from everyone in your program. Some of what children want may be inappropriate to include in your program. When this is the case, tell them why an idea is not acceptable. For example, one program asked the children what they would like on the snack menu. The overwhelming majority of children said chips and salsa, pizza, and sodas. When these suggestions were not accepted, the children were extremely disappointed. Explaining that the program was required to follow certain guidelines when preparing snack helped the children understand why their ideas were not used. But the disappointment could have been avoided if the children had been given the nutritional guidelines before they were asked for snack ideas. Try to anticipate responses, and ask only those questions that will result in answers you are willing to act on.

Also, you can learn a lot about children's likes and dislikes by talking with them. Give children a voice in designing their space and choosing activities, field trips, and community service projects. Not all children will tell you what they like—you will also need to observe and take note of children's likes and dislikes. Watch what areas children visit, listen to their questions about how things work, and observe what books they read.

Including children in the process of community building helps them feel valued, builds their self-confidence, gives them appropriate control over their environment, and develops their empathy and an understanding of the needs of all those in the program. Several times throughout the year, conduct informal or formal surveys of children to gather up-to-date information about their interests (see the children's interest surveys in appendix A). Getting input from the children creates a win-win situation. The children feel their opinions are important to the adults, and the adults can use this information to create environments that interest the children.

To plan successful learning experiences, tune in to children's current interests and needs. Research and give thoughtful consideration to all children's input to ensure their ideas and suggestions are appropriate for your program environment. School-age children like to follow fads. Ask the children to explain a fad and how best to incorporate it in the program. Not all fads will be appropriate for your program. If they are not, explain to the children why they are not appropriate. For example, take the fad of creating bracelets with embroidery floss. This activity sounds easy and simple, but make sure you know if different colors mean different things. If inappropriate meanings are assigned to some colors, rather than eliminating the activity, you could intentionally provide only those colors that have positive meanings and explain to the children that this is a safe, respectful program; it is not a place for being disrespectful to others. Adding fads to your program can meet the interests of the children while becoming a teaching moment for both staff and children.

Photo 7.2

Adding new games and materials chosen by the children establishes ownership. Staff may need to assist the children in playing the game for the first time to increase the children's confidence.

When you follow children's fads and find appropriate ways to include them within your program space, you will keep children interested in coming back. Remember that fads are just that—fads. They come into favor unexpectedly and just as quickly disappear from view.

You may need to put limits on the dollar amount spent on field trips or materials. If you find that what children have suggested is inappropriate or falls outside your budget, then explain to them why their ideas cannot be used so that they know you heard them. Be open to their suggestions or modifications to their ideas; when given a chance, children are great problem solvers. This can start conversations about why certain items cannot be used in the space. With children's input, brainstorm how to raise money to go on the field trip or purchase the requested equipment. Discussions of how much something costs and how to plan for it are great opportunities to provide an understanding of money management.

Research Health Issues

The children in your program may come with a variety of health issues, be they physical, medical, or emotional. Use a Health Care Plan document as part of your registration papers. Requiring this document to be completed by all families at the time of registration and then annually will help you identify any health needs and better inform you of diagnosed health issues, treatment plans, and accommodations or adaptations that families feel their child needs. Check with your local health or licensing department to determine what type of Health Care Plan is used in your area. Some disorders and diseases, such as epilepsy and asthma, have care plans that are specific to the disorder or disease. For specific care plans, check with the national support organization for that condition.

When you work with a child with a health condition, you should talk to the family to get specific information about their child's condition. They will be your best partners as you plan for their child's care. Learning from the family about what the child can and cannot do creates continuity between home and your program and limits stress for the child.

In addition, look to local or national organizations for more information about the disease, disability, or limitation. They provide information and suggested adaptations and supportive materials. Ensure your sources are reliable. Sources such as the American Academy of Pediatrics, American Medical Association, American Cancer Society, and American Lung Association are all good places to start. For example, if a child has been diagnosed with asthma, contact the American Lung Association at 1-800-LUNG USA (1-800-586-4872) for information about asthma, proper administration of medicine, the need for an Asthma Action Plan, and local resources.

By educating yourself about children's diagnosed conditions and available resources, you can avoid giving children unnecessary limits or having unrealistic expectations about their participation. Use the information you learn when setting up the environment or planning activities. You will also find it easier to empathize with the child and family. In so doing, you send the message that you want to create an environment where all children can participate fully and feel valued.

Special Needs

Families may ask to have their children with identified special needs enrolled in your program. The term *special needs* includes children's individual qualities, ranging from learning or physical challenges to giftedness in special areas. For instance, parents may tell you their child has been identified as being gifted in music, math, or art, or you may learn that a child has physical or learning disabilities that need to be addressed.

Having a child with any type of special needs can be a stressor in the family. Some families find it difficult to locate a program that they feel comfortable with and that can meet their child's needs. Families may face additional expenses, such as special classes, supplemental therapies, or special equipment. It is critical for school-age staff to recognize and be sensitive to each family's feelings and to provide encouragement and support for them and their child.

Use the list that follows to guide you in developing a trusting relationship with families and staff from other programs that are providing services to children with special needs and in creating an environment that will help them achieve their potential:

- Get written permission to communicate with staff from other servicing agencies.
- Follow family or Individualized Education Program (or Plan) goals for the children.
- Ask about the children's daily routines.
- Observe and learn about the children's disabilities or giftedness.
- Create lesson plans around what families tell you their children enjoy.
- Invite participation and feedback from families and staff from other servicing agencies.
- Build on the skills and interests the children have.

When looking for ways to adapt the environment for children with special needs, refer to the lists of accommodations in the section in chapter 2 about the Americans with Disabilities Act (ADA).

GIVING INFORMATION

Consistent and timely communication with both children and families is very important to the success of your program. When children know what to expect, they feel safe. Keeping families informed helps them feel included in your program. When children or family members receive information that differs from one staff person to another, they receive mixed messages and may find it hard to trust. Make sure you are communicating the same information as other staff members. Posting written information also helps avoid confusion.

Communicating with Families

TYPES OF COMMUNICATION		DESCRIPTION/PURPOSE
Formal	**Program Handbook for Families**	a written document given to each family explains the program policies, procedures, mission and goals, program philosophy, fees, daily schedule, emergency procedures, and activities offered usually given at family orientation and updated every year
	Family Orientation	a time set aside before the child enters the school-age program to orient new and returning families to the program includes an overview of the program handbook discusses changes in program structure addresses any questions and concerns
	Family Board	a display board placed near the sign-in and sign-out sheet or the family table displays the newsletter, the program handbook, lesson plans, snack menus, information about field trips and other upcoming events, and photos of the children participating in program activities displays information about community resources and events for families and children
	Conferences	scheduled times for families and staff to discuss issues related to a child a regularly scheduled event usually yearly or biannually; may also be scheduled as needed by parent or staff request
	Newsletter	a printed newsletter distributed to all families and other stakeholders and posted on the family board contains information about current and upcoming program events, family reminders, parent education, community outreach activities, and changes in policy or procedures
Informal	**Day to Day**	This opportunity occurs daily when family members pick up and drop off children in your program. Greeting them with a friendly smile and a genuine hello will go a long way to cementing relationships with families. This also provides a time to tell the families what great things their children have done. The staff should limit the negative comments made to families during this time because negative comments about children can be overheard by other families and children. If a serious problem arises, a face-to-face conference can be held for this discussion.
	Phone Calls	Randomly calling parents to talk about their child and the program can be a vehicle to provide positive feedback about their children, ask about their satisfaction with the program, and develop a working relationship with families.
	Notes Home	Sending notes home is a simple way to communicate with families about the great things their children are doing in the program, give details about a field trip, set up a meeting, invite them to a meeting or special event, or ask for help in finding resources or materials.

Communicating Program Information

Post a written set of rules and consequences (created with the children's input), a daily schedule, and lesson plans in your program's family center. In addition, give children verbal reminders of daily activities to ensure they know when and what is available to them.

Provide family members with current program information—the program handbook, newsletter, field trip notices, policy changes—to keep them up-to-date on events, activities, and policies. Posting lesson plans provides families with discussion topics when asking their children about their day. Distributing a weekly or monthly newsletter is a good way to let families know what will be happening in the program. The newsletter is a means to educate families about policies and procedures and to highlight children's accomplishments. In addition, the newsletter can give families information about parenting and about other resources, such as low-cost or free community activities.

Creating a family center provides one place in the program where family members can go to find information. Here you can place schedules, notices of upcoming events, a copy of your newsletter, and information about family-friendly community events. Also, everyone enjoys seeing displays of the children's artwork, photos of the children's families, and photos of children participating in program activities. In addition, the family center is a great place to do some family education by making available your handbook and current articles about health-related issues and child development.

If your program is located in shared space, the family center can be as simple as a trifold board or two that can be stored easily each day. If you are fortunate enough to have dedicated space for your program, you can create a cozy area with comfortable chairs where family members can wait for their children or just relax after a hard day at work.

Translating Communications

When communicating with family members, be sure to use the preferred (first) language of the families. Giving information to families in their first language ensures that they more fully understand the information related to program policies, procedures, and their child. When they provide you with information in their first language, it is more likely to be accurate, giving you a better understanding of their child. Giving parents the opportunity to use their first language also creates a welcoming and accepting environment.

For help with translations, contact local colleges or the local school district. Sometimes foreign language teachers will translate materials for a small fee. Bilingual parents may be able to translate your program informa-

Photo 7.3

Photo 7.4

Photo 7.5

Photo 7.6

Family centers provide one-stop access to program and community information.

Photo 7.7

Photo 7.8

tion. You can purchase software programs that can do the translation for you, but these generally translate word for word and do not include idioms native to a language. Have a bilingual parent read any translation prior to sending it out to ensure the document is readable and effectively communicates the information.

Photo 7.9

Providing a quiet place for adults to wait for children gives them the opportunity to relax and read about program activities.

Accommodating Individual Needs

Exciting, comfortable, and friendly learning environments for school-age children are typically active, happy, and even noisy places. It is not unusual to see a group of children sitting on the floor involved in activities while others are playing or working independently. This is the look of afterschool programs that accommodate all children's needs regardless of gender, ethnicity, abilities, or disabilities. Quality learning environments are flexible and designed around children's needs, skills, and interests. No standard model can be followed, but the common thread in all quality programs is simple: support each child's individuality.

When you accommodate the individual needs of all the children in your program, you enable them to be independent and to develop social, physical, and cognitive skills. Children's successful experiences in your program help them feel good about themselves and establish a sense of belonging, which builds their self-esteem. As their skills and self-confidence grow, so does their success with creating positive relationships. From your observations and the

Photo 7.10

Children read at various levels and have varied interests, so providing a variety of reading materials helps meet the needs of all children.

information you gather both formally and informally about the children in your program, you can design the environment to ensure their successful experiences and support their independence regardless of their ages and abilities.

Your temporal environment can support individual needs when you design activities that ensure success for everyone. For example, when designing and constructing the sets for a play the children have chosen, there are jobs a thirteen-year-old can do and other things a five-year-old can successfully complete. While the thirteen-year-old can draw and construct the sets, the five-year-old may be able to design the cover of the program or paint a small box needed for the set. Each child walks away feeling valued and a part of the overall play experience.

When planning some activities, you may have to teach a skill or make an adaptation to the activity or materials to enable all children to participate. For instance, if the children would like to play basketball but not all of them can dribble a ball, the first thing you will need to teach is how to dribble. Also, you may need to design a smaller court with a lower basket for younger children or those in wheelchairs. Those not wanting to play can keep score, be a line judge, or be cheerleaders. All the children can find their own niches based on their ability or choice.

In addition, various components in your physical environment can adapt to the abilities, interests, and ages of the children you serve. When designing the physical space and purchasing equipment and materials, take into consideration the spectrum of sizes and developmental and physical capabilities of the children in your program. Create an environment that is accessible and supportive to all children, including those with disabilities. For more information about simple accommodations, please refer to the section on the ADA in chapter 2.

As you look at your program, consider the following suggestions to help you design an environment that supports individual needs:

- Make pathways wide enough for wheelchairs and walkers. Include handrails.
- Place toys and materials on open and accessible shelves to support the children's sense of independence.
- Label shelves with pictures and words to help children select and return materials independently.

- Create signs with pictures and words to designate areas of the environment for nonreaders as well as for readers.
- Use color cues to guide children to locations or materials.
- Provide developmentally appropriate materials—including a range of books, games, and puzzles—that span the children's ages, abilities, and interests to ensure successful interactions and learning.
- Equip a crafts center with a variety of scissors: left- and right-handed, blunt and pointed ends.
- Offer reading materials in a variety of formats, including large print and Braille
- Include a chair with armrests or greater back support.
- Post schedules with pictures and words to help both readers and non-readers know the sequence of events.
- Create individual sets of schedule cards to give to children who have memory issues or trouble concentrating. Make a card for each component of the daily schedule and for each transition to a new activity within the schedule. This tactile, hands-on tool helps children keep on task, moving through the schedule independently and on time.
- Purchase large storage units that are configured so that smaller children or a child in a wheelchair can easily reach all shelves.
- Select height-adjustable equipment, such as easels and free-standing basketball hoops so that all ages can use them.
- Install computer software programs that are appropriate for all ages, from beginner reading and math programs to those that will meet the cognitive needs of the oldest children in your program.

OUTDOOR SPACE

When choosing large outside equipment, purchase items suitable for a variety of ages and abilities. You want outdoor play equipment and spaces that are challenging but not hazardous for any child regardless of ability or age. This will allow your program to accommodate any child now or in the future.

Purchasing smaller outside equipment seems to be a simple matter, but you must consider all the children in your program. For example, a variety of sizes and weights of bats are needed for playing baseball. What a ten-year-old can lift and swing is very different from what a five-year-old can use safely. Soccer balls, footballs, and basketballs all come in a variety of sizes. Purchasing one of each size allows all children to play successfully. To help children who have not played basketball or football before, purchase balls with hand placement guides so children learn to hold the ball correctly.

CHILDREN WITH IDENTIFIED DISABILITIES

Specific disabilities of children can affect how space is designed. For example, if you have a child who has mobility issues, take that into consideration as you design traffic patterns in your program space so all children can move independently through it. For accessibility in school-age environments, the ADA includes guidelines to address the following issues for children with identified special needs:

- access to a variety of learning opportunities comparable to those for children without disabilities
- an arrangement of the physical space that allows those with mobility issues to interact with their peers
- passageways and spaces that enable those with special needs to move independently and to freely choose to participate in all activities

Titles II and III of the ADA and Section 504 of the Rehabilitation Act set guidelines for including children with disabilities in child care, which includes school-age programs. The basic provisions needed to adapt the environment are referred to as "reasonable modifications" or "reasonable accommodations," which mean changes made to help children with disabilities reach their potential and participate as fully as children without disabilities. For example, when designing the environment to accommodate a child with visual problems, you may need to provide large-print books and signage, install adequate lighting, and keep the environment free from tripping hazards. You may need to learn sign language and gestures to communicate with a child with hearing problems. If you have a child in a wheelchair, then leave an open space at your art table so the child can wheel up to the table and participate in projects. Children who are not comfortable playing baseball—whether because of a physical limitation or lack of confidence—can be scorekeepers or base umpires so they can participate in the activity at their own comfort levels. (Additional information about the ADA and Rehabilitation Act as well as suggested accommodations for children with disabilities can be found in chapter 2.)

Wide pathways and tables that can be adjusted to accommodate a child's wheelchair help children with disabilities feel included in activities and promote interaction with their friends.

Photo 7.11

Universal Design Principles

Universal design refers to ways to construct buildings, products, and environments with simple accommodations that help everyone, not only individuals with disabilities. It started from the "barrier-free" concept to support greater movement, independence, and success for individuals with disabilities. Facilities built using universal design principles have wide interior doors and hallways, lever handles rather than twisting knobs for opening doors, and light switches with large flat panels rather than small toggle switches. Universal design is a part of everyday living and is all around us. Applying universal design principles to your physical environment can increase the inclusiveness of your interpersonal environment. The "undo" command in most software products that allows computer corrections to be completed with one hand movement and color-contrast dishware with steep sides that assist those with visual and dexterity problems are good examples.

Photo 7.12

Switch plates like the one shown here use universal design principles that are simple to operate for children or individuals with limited hand functioning.

MEETING THE NEEDS OF OLDER CHILDREN

Children ages nine to eighteen need the opportunity to have some control over decisions that affect them. Do not assume you know what they need only to discover later that you are way off base. Take time to listen to the older children in your program. They will tell you all about their needs. Share the planning with them and have them help make changes to the environment.

At times, older school-agers need or choose to be with younger children. However, often they want to separate themselves and look for places where they can gain privacy or just hang out with peers. There are many reasons for this. Their bodies are different from those of younger children—bigger, stronger, and, for lack of a better word, changing. They just feel different from the younger children, may be worried about acceptance by their peer group, and have a need for greater independence.

Providing a separate area for older children helps them feel comfortable and valued for who they are.

Photo 7.13

The environment that worked for them even a few months earlier may be too childish now. They require more thought-provoking games, challenging equipment, and bigger furniture. They enjoy personalizing their own space with posters, artwork, and colors that do not appeal to younger school-agers. The way the environment looks and feels influences the way older children participate in and value their surroundings. With inviting resources and a supportive atmosphere, older children can be successful and feel good about themselves. Interests and hobbies that older children experience in afterschool programs often develop into lifelong pursuits.

Photo 7.14

This sign reminds preteens there is a place just for them—and also for the need to sign in to use this area.

Designate an indoor space just for older children. Options include hallways, stages, or a corner of a large room. What is important is to provide a location that is uniquely theirs. If you are limited in space or room size, consider using portable dividers to designate the older children's place while always maintaining adult supervision as needed or required. Older children can personalize these dividers with art or wall displays of their choice to give this area its own atmosphere. Include areas in the space that encourage them to practice social skills and develop friendships as well as to kick back, relax, and just chill out. Include comfortable furnishings that are easy for the children to move around, such as beanbag chairs, large floor pillows, area rugs, and even baby mattresses covered in colorful fabric.

Also, designate a place in the outdoor space for older children. Furnish it with sturdier and more physically challenging playground structures, equipment to promote large-motor development, and equipment to support individual and team activities.

Encourage cooperation among older children by planning group projects or clubs for children to pursue their personal interests, such as building a pen for the program's pet rabbit, baking cakes for monthly birthday celebrations, or organizing a service project for the local homeless shelter. Give older children time to work together with minimal adult input—but always with appropriate supervision—to encourage a feeling of community and support for each other.

Embracing Diversity

Children are observant. Even in infancy they notice differences in people's skin color. By the time children reach school age, they see differences in people with disabilities and know some people are rich or poor, old or young. They learn from the adults in their lives how to interpret these differences. Help children celebrate the joy of diversity and understand that our world is full of diverse people. When you and your school-age program embrace diversity, you expose children to people, information, images, and experiences that represent a spectrum of gender, race, ethnicity, family structure, religion, sexual orientation, and socioeconomic conditions. This rich diversity alerts children to your program's accepting attitude toward others. Also, they know that you accept them for who they are. This increases their feelings of safety and trust in others. As their awareness of the world grows, children see where they and their families fit in this bigger picture. The positive self-identity they gain helps give children a sense of individual and family pride.

Using the information you gather from families to share some of what makes them unique also builds understanding that we are all more alike than different. For instance, trying different types of food gives children an opportunity to taste foods prepared in new ways. Playing a traditional game helps children understand that children everywhere like to play and that some of the popular games they play originated in another country. Learning a folk song or dance reminds children that everyone enjoys music, even if it sounds or looks different from what they know.

If you have families in your program who have recently moved from another country, invite family members to visit and share something from their culture. Have parents who speak another language come and sing songs, read books, or teach the children a few words in that language. If they are unable to visit, ask them to record the songs, book, or phrases so you can play them for the children. Read the book in English to the children prior to or as the book is being read in the other language so they can hear and make connections between the two languages.

Holidays are perfect opportunities for children and families to share their culture and traditions. This acknowledges the value of children's ethnic or cultural backgrounds. By planning together with families, you can decide which holidays to celebrate and how to create a meaningful environment. For holidays to have value, children must feel a sense of connection with them. Above all, resist creating an overly stimulating environment that does not help children understand the meaning or the value of the holiday. Ask families to bring in memorabilia to display, such as photos of past family celebrations, favorite holiday books, easy holiday recipes or foods, and arts and crafts projects. In addition to helping connect families, these engagement projects

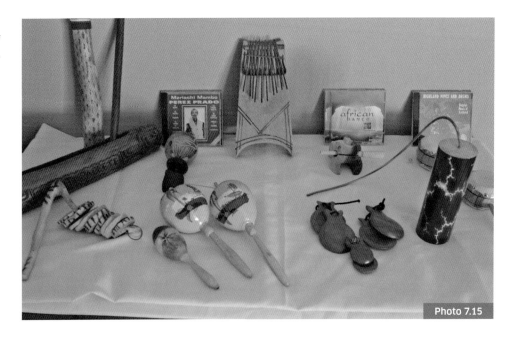

Exposing children to musical instruments from a variety of cultures expands their knowledge of musical instruments and the sounds they make.

Photo 7.15

promote respect and understanding of diverse celebrations for the children. Remember to notify all families of any holiday or cultural celebration activities. The religious or cultural beliefs of some families may make them uncomfortable with some of your program celebrations. Provide alternative activities for children not participating in these celebrations.

An interpersonal and physical environment that embraces diversity includes a variety of resources. Share books about children with special needs, diverse family units, or intergenerational characters to help children see commonalities among people. Also, include folktales, fairy tales, and fables from around the world to celebrate diversity. Add recorded music, instruments, toy foods, empty clean boxes of ethnic foods, and cooking and eating utensils from many cultures.

If your program families are a homogenous group, creating opportunities for children to experience the diversity of the world at large encourages acceptance and respect. Avoid creating a tourist approach environment with posters from foreign countries, Native American feather headdresses, or sombreros in the dramatic play area. None of these stereotypes help children connect themselves with people from other cultures. Help children get an in-depth look at a given culture by immersing them in all aspects: look at photographs, listen to and learn some of the language, sing songs, listen to music, read stories, taste food, try on clothing, and learn games from that country. Think of it this way: looking out a plane window and seeing a country while flying overhead is very different from landing in that country, walking around, talking to people, tasting the food, learning the history, and visiting the sites. Through an exciting and well-planned school-age environment, you can come much closer to providing the latter for the children.

Cultivating Openness

Variety is the spice of life. School-age programs are as diverse as the children, families, and staff in them. All families want safe, quality care for their children. The more exposure children get to a wide variety of people, the more they develop an appreciation and acceptance of those who are different from themselves. In an environment that embraces diversity, children often quite naturally develop an attitude of openness to other people, places, and experiences, thus creating a safe place for everyone. Fostering an interpersonal environment that makes everyone feel included and welcome may even broaden the worldview of families in your program. The variety of influences that surround children every day builds their acceptance of others, regardless of who they are. You can help cultivate the children's understanding and respect for likenesses and differences in other people. Your acceptance, respect, and interactions with diverse people provide children with a model of openness, curiosity, and tolerance.

Sometimes it is very difficult to understand someone else's culture. While cultures around the world share many similarities, each one has unique characteristics. Most people are eager to share their culture. They are pleased when you show an interest and ask them respectful questions. The curiosity you exhibit can teach children openness to other cultures that lasts a lifetime. A man from Honduras once mentioned that the most difficult American custom for him to get used to was opening gifts as soon as they were given. In Honduras, that is considered very disrespectful; it sends the message that the present is more important than the person. Helping children learn about each culture's traditions is key to teaching them a respectful attitude.

Photo 7.16

Inviting families to share information about themselves helps children and their families feel included in the program.

Some families struggle to find appropriate care for a child with a special need—perhaps a child who is considered gifted or who has a medical condition or disability. For families that face unique challenges in finding school-age care that meets their needs, a welcoming and inclusive environment signals to them that they have finally found a place where they can feel at home. Accommodating children with special needs shows children how to be open and inclusive regardless of a person's limitations.

Take every opportunity to give children honest information about fairness, prejudice, biases, and cultural issues. Invite guests, speakers, and prominent community members to share stories about their culture, ethnicity, gender, age, disability, or even sexual orientation. Ask them to talk frankly about their challenges and successes. When you bring in outside speakers, inform parents about the topic of the presentation. Some parents may choose to remove their children from the program during that presentation. If so, you will need to have an alternate activity or location for these children.

The list that follows includes suggestions for ways to celebrate diversity and cultivate openness in your interpersonal environment. How and what you choose to include in your program to support openness and embrace diversity will depend greatly on the information you have gathered from families, the children themselves, and the greater community around you.

- Post photographs that look like the children and families you serve.
- Display "all about town" photos showing people in your neighborhood, community, city, or state in nonstereotypic ways—for example, a female doctor, a male preschool teacher, or an older female bus driver.
- Display pictures of daily life—homes, cities, typical activities of children and families—in foreign countries (especially those with significance to the children in your program).
- Exhibit an art print from a famous artist that depicts a landscape or region different from where you and the children live.
- Ask family members for recipes you can make and serve at snack or mealtime.
- Purchase books and ask a librarian for books about a variety of other cultures. Display books with the covers showing because children often choose a book based on the cover rather than the content.
- Collect books in different languages—especially those spoken by children enrolled in the program. Include some written in a dual-language format to help nonnative English speakers learn to read independently.
- Supply your art area with construction paper, crayons, pencils, and markers in a variety of skin tone colors so children can draw themselves as they see themselves.
- Include child-sized costumes or dolls in traditional clothing from around the world in your drama or dramatic play area.
- Provide multicultural family and intergenerational figures and dolls, and small toy animals from areas other than your own.
- Research where common games like hopscotch, soccer, football, and dice originated, and share this information with the children.
- Provide a variety of items from nature, such as rocks, seashells, and sand, and display photos of plants and bodies of water that are from the local area and the geographical area of the children's families.
- Stock your math area with abaci, marbles, games, and decks of playing cards from foreign countries.

Teaching Tolerance

School-age children are often quick to judge others who look, dress, eat, or talk differently. This can lead to teasing, finger-pointing, or even bullying of peers, all of which are hurtful and harmful for children of any age. To support a welcoming interpersonal environment that helps children cultivate greater tolerance for others, include lessons and activities focused on acceptance and respect for everyone. For example, they can learn that people who ride in wheelchairs do so not because they do not want to walk but rather because they cannot walk.

When flare-ups among children occur, as they often do, all staff members should stress the importance of mutual respect and help children understand that each person is unique, with varying opinions, beliefs, and ways of doing things. (See chapter 6 for more information on bullying and managing conflict among children.) Activities, learning opportunities, and materials that celebrate diversity send the message that your program is accepting of all children. This helps children feel connected to—and tolerant of—others in the program community. Creating temporal, physical, and interpersonal environments that are sensitive to each child's needs provides a supportive framework. When children feel accepted and valued for who they are, they have an easier time tolerating others.

LEARNING TO BE OPEN, TOLERANT, AND RESPECTFUL

At a school-age program that enrolled both typically developing children and children with special needs, three boys played Monopoly together. One of the boys was in a wheelchair. He could not talk and had very limited motor skills. The other two boys were typically developing second graders. The boy in the wheelchair was actively involved in the game, and he was winning. He had more houses and hotels on the Monopoly board than either of the other two boys. One boy rolled the dice for him, while the other one moved his token around the board.

"Do you want to buy Park Place?" one of the boys asked. Both boys watched the child in the wheelchair, who appeared to give no verbal reply or hand gesture that could be considered an answer. Yet in unison the other two boys agreed he did not want to buy Park Place. How did they know this?

After the game, when the boys were cleaning up, an observer asked one of them, "How did you know he didn't want to buy Park Place?"

"Oh, that's easy," he said. "He blinks once for 'yes' and twice for 'no.'" This activity provided these boys with an opportunity to see people different from themselves for their potential and not for their problems.

Building Community

Building a sense of community in your program is a process of developing ownership and engagement among the children and families. Most school-agers come to your program already understanding what community is. They generally know their family structure, such as who their siblings, parents, grandparents, and extended family members are. School-agers may know where they live and what their parents do for a living. Additionally, they know who they like and can trust. The family is the first community in which a child is involved. Children understand their role and the role of others in the family, and this sets the tone for how they react in other community-based groups.

You can capitalize on children's awareness of their responsibility to others. Staff must help children understand what is acceptable and expected of them while in the program. Help them make good choices, and hold them responsible for the choices they make. One way to support children's success is by giving them program jobs with clear expectations. Encourage children's input, listen to what they have to say, and do what you say you will do. All of these approaches build children's sense of personal responsibility and help them learn to trust others. Combined, these ingredients cultivate a sense of community that will enrich your program's interpersonal environment. (See chapter 6 for more information on how to build children's social competency.)

A great way to foster a sense of community and ownership among school-age children is to involve them in decisions about your program's physical environment. Ask them for suggestions as you redesign. In shared space, where the environment needs to be re-created each day, ask the children to help set up the space. Keep the environment new and exciting by allowing the children to make adjustments, add materials, and choose games of interest to them. Displaying pictures, artwork, and posters that children have either made or chosen personalizes the environment and promotes their sense of belonging in the program. In shared space, use core boards and trifold boards to display posters, artwork, and family pictures so that you can store them easily at the end of each day.

Your temporal environment can also support a sense of community among school-age children. Group activities, projects, clubs, and field trips all help school-age children connect with their peers. You can encourage a multiage community of children by scheduling a specific time and place for older children to connect with younger ones if they choose. For example, older children can assist younger ones in learning a new game or activity, help with mentoring activities, or simply hang out with them. When planning activities, start by looking at ways older children can support younger children both socially and academically. Have a younger child read to an older one. Have older children provide homework help to the younger children. Let the older children help with physical skills, such as shooting a basket, dribbling a soccer ball, or learning how to swing a bat. These activities give the older children roles that make them feel valued and capable.

School-age children like to participate in projects that have a purpose. Community service projects provide children with an opportunity to give back to the community in which they live. This participation connects them to the larger community and builds community in your program as they work together on the project. In multiaged school-age programs, carefully choose and plan service projects that allow children of all ages to participate on some level.

COMMUNITY SERVICE

One school-age program looked for a community service project that the children could do at the program's site, because transportation was not possible. Once a week during the summer, the children made lunches for a homeless shelter in their community. So that all children could participate, tasks were divided into three parts: sandwich making, packing, and delivering. The older school-agers made the sandwiches, and the younger children placed fruit and chips in bags or placed bags in coolers. Once lunches were completed, the children loaded the coolers into wagons, and together with the staff, all children walked to the homeless shelter and delivered the lunches. Having the children hand out the lunches showed them that their efforts made a difference in their community.

Photo 7.17

Engaging in community service projects helps children know they can make a difference in the lives of others.

Photo 7.18

Providing a place for families to put suggestions gives them ownership in the program and a sense that they are valued.

Community building begins with sharing information. A family board creates a consistent place to share information with families about their children's activities, opportunities for parent involvement, and where to find further information about the program and the community.

Give families a sense of belonging in program space by setting up a comfortable and welcoming area for adults near the entrance. Include adult chairs, a suggestion box, program materials, and photos. Help families feel even more connection to your program by encouraging them to share pictures and information for a display board. You can use the materials they submit to create a photo collage of the children and families, their homes, members of their extended families, family celebrations, and customs.

Display a world map, and indicate the cultural origin of each family and each staff member. A fun project for families is a family heritage quilt (or mural) with a square made by each family with fabric or memorabilia significant to them. As new families come into your program, they can make and add their own square. Another idea that encourages families to connect with one another is a basket that contains family items that share their heritage, culture, traditions, or celebrations. Display these baskets together as a group, and encourage children, families, and visitors to look through the collections to achieve a better understanding of the diversity in your program.

Offer events such as parenting classes, parents' nights out, game nights, reading events, and potlucks. Set up a basket where family members can place unwanted coupons and take coupons they can use. The more opportunities you provide for families to get to know and help each other, the more you foster a sense of community in your program. Just as involvement of families in their children's education helps improve student performance, likewise involvement of families in your afterschool program helps children feel connected to a community.

Photo 7.19

Activities and Questions

Use the following activities and questions to identify welcoming elements in your school-age program.

1. Think about a child in your program who has a special need such as a medical condition, learning disability, or physical disability. How would you approach the family to learn more about the child's need?

2. Thinking again about a child with a special need, make a list of all changes you can make to the physical or temporal environment to help this child be successful or reach full potential.

3. Given the physical layout of your program space, what special place or space can you create or redesign for your older children (ages nine and older)? What input will you ask from them, and how will you use it to personalize this area?

4. What special events or activities could you plan to encourage families to share their cultural, religious, or ethnic heritage throughout the year? How would you incorporate this into lesson plans to prevent a tourist approach, as described in this chapter?

5. Consider how your present physical environment supports the needs and interest of children enrolled in your program. How does your temporal environment help children learn tolerance and promote acceptance of peers? What changes are needed?

6. What do you do to welcome all stakeholders in your program?

7. Where is your family information located? List what materials are available in the family center. How often are the materials in this center updated? What changes do you need to make to your family center?

8. How does the program feel when you enter? Does it feel welcoming? Are parents and children greeted by name when they enter the program? Are the family members given the opportunity to provide feedback about the program?

9. When issues around tolerance flare up, how do you handle them? Write down activities and direct teaching that you do to encourage tolerance among children.

10. What community service projects have you planned or carried out for older children? What others would be appropriate to include?

CHAPTER 8

The Physical Environment: Arranging Spaces

THE PHYSICAL ENVIRONMENT in your school-age program includes several components, some of which may be more obvious than others. The physical environment includes

- overall program space;
- floor plan, or arrangement of all of the areas in the space;
- lighting plan, colors, textures, sounds, and smells; and
- specific materials and equipment found in each area of your program.

This chapter focuses on your overall program space and the arrangement of areas in that space to facilitate a smooth flow of people and activities. Chapter 9 addresses the physical elements that appeal to the senses, and chapter 10 suggests how to equip each area in your program to promote children's learning. As you read about the physical environment, think about which aspects of your program space need attention:

Children need a place to store their personal belongings safely when they are not needed.

- Do you need a complete makeover—a redesign—of the physical space to improve the overall organization and flow and to help children be independent learners?
- Is a new area needed to support children's interests and their learning?
- Would changes to lighting, textural aspects, or color improve the aesthetics of the physical environment and support children's learning?
- Would refreshing and rearranging the materials in an area be enough to meet the children's needs and interests?

Photo 8.1

School-age programs typically include a variety of areas to stimulate or generate activities for the children. These areas may be referred to as *learning centers, activity areas, stations,* or *corners.* In this book we use the word *area* to describe the sections of the room or program space dedicated to specific learning activities. Some programs have only one large room for all these different areas; others have a separate room for each one. Regardless of the name, size, or location of these areas, afterschool environments need to provide a variety of options from which children can choose. This enables your physical environment to change with the children's varying activity levels, interests, and moods. When you divide your physical environment into various areas to support different functions or learning skills, the children engage more deeply and ultimately have the opportunity to learn more. All areas do not need to be the same size or have the same furnishings or

Right: This cart serves many purposes, from storage of food service items to displaying the daily menu. Multiuse furniture is essential in programs with limited floor or storage space.

Photo 8.2

Standard-sized furniture and functioning appliances give this dramatic play area a sense of realism and usefulness. It can be used for cooking projects or even food preparation if needed.

Photo 8.3

Photo 8.4

resources. For example, areas that support quiet activities can be small and cozy, while active play areas require large open spaces and hard floor surfaces. Some areas may support only one type of play or function while other areas may be appropriate for a variety of purposes. When your program space is organized so that each area has a well-defined function, you will have less congestion, possibly less aggression, greater interaction of the children with materials and each other, and greater freedom for children to be independent. All these benefits give staff more time and children a safe, engaging environment.

No standard model exists for arranging a school-age program's physical environment, but it must be well-defined, organized, and purposeful. While all indoor physical environments have the same basic architectural features of walls, floors, windows, plumbing, electricity, and climate control, like children, each is unique in size and even personality. Your program's goals, budget, and facility size dictate much of what you can do, but most importantly, your observations of the children themselves must guide your decisions about what to include or change in the physical environment.

Left: This program has clustered materials and defined a play center to support children's imaginative play by selecting materials carefully and displaying them on open shelving around the area rug.

Photo 8.5

This organized area provides a quiet place for study, homework, or working together on a project.

Arrange areas in locations according to their intended purpose. This science area is placed near open windows to keep plants growing and the children's gardening efforts successful.

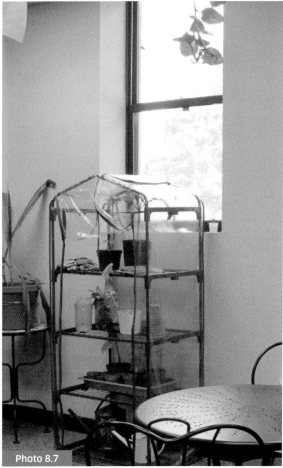

Photo 8.7

Photo 8.6

Small, comfortable areas remind children to slow down or sit down for a while to enjoy a book, rest, or hang out with a friend.

Evaluating Your *Current* Physical Environment

As you consider the design of your program space, think about what messages your physical environment sends to each child. Remember that good physical spaces create a sense of well-being in children that promotes their social skills and interpersonal and intellectual growth. Children should want to come to your program. Consider the following list of messages in an ideal physical environment for school-age children as goals for your program:

- You belong here.
- You can trust all adults in this place.
- You can be independent and do many exciting things that help you learn.
- You can get away and be by yourself or be with just your friends.
- There is a place where you can be away from younger children.
- There is a place where you can choose to be with your brother or sister.
- This is a safe place to explore and try out your ideas.
- Materials are available to you, and you can use whatever you like.

- You know where things are, and they are always in the same place.
- This is a happy place that helps you learn new things.
- Somebody knows you and what you like to do and can help you at any time.

Consider reviewing the items on this list with the children. For each item, you could ask the children to make a drawing that shows how they interpret the goal. Then post the statement from the list along with children's drawings to help you visualize how children interpret these goals in your program environment.

School-age children love to move freely (and rapidly) from place to place. They move more like hummingbirds than arrows. They use their whole body to zigzag through the environment, looking for someplace that interests them. When too many children congregate in too little space, they react like clouds in a stormy sky. When they get too close or collide, the friction causes restless or aggressive behavior. If this happens frequently in your program, you may wonder where all your program space has gone. Look to your licensing agency for guidance on the recommended minimum amount of floor space (or square footage) per school-age child. Expert opinions vary greatly on this important environmental component. Nevertheless, there are some general physical needs that must be met no matter the size or type of facility you have.

The feeling of a program begins when the front door is opened. This entry area welcomes everyone with comfortable furnishings and décor.

Photo 8.8

Photo 8.9

Overhead fluorescent lights can be softened with the use of floor and table lamps and a warm, natural wall color. Children's artwork adds a personal feeling to this gathering area.

Photo 8.10

The arrangement of program areas combines natural and artificial light to keep the environment open, ease children's eye strain, and promote greater well-being too.

The arrangement of the physical environment plays a key role in school-age children's behavior and affects how they feel—positively or negatively—while in your program. When your physical environment is poorly arranged, the children let you know. They tell and show you readily when they are bored or do not like what is in the environment. Look for repeated patterns in behavior, including lack of involvement. Most children have days or times during a day when they need staff guidance or redirection to keep them following the rules. However, when you routinely observe a pattern of inappropriate behavior in a variety of settings or during various times of the day, these are signs that your environment is a contributing factor.

Taking a close look at your physical space is critical and can be done in several ways. Observation and documentation provide the foundation to determine if and when a program area needs to be changed, updated, or moved to a new location. Note how many children use the area and what they do in that area. Having children sign in and out of an area may help you determine its usage. This form of documentation is especially useful if you have limited staff and are unable to routinely take time to observe. If observing usage is possible, be sure to observe at different times of the day and different days of the week. Children in the morning program may be interested in different activities and materials from those in the afternoon program. You may find more children are interested in active play when the weather is good but need more cozy places when it is cold or dreary.

As you observe an area, ask yourself, *What happens here?* Completing the Environmental Planning Worksheet in appendix B (or print from www.redleafpress.org)—which is an evaluation tool for getting input from members of a team or committee—and identifying the successful and the problem areas in your program will help you develop a strategy to answer this question. Problematic areas may be an entire room or a small space or alcove in a room. Before making any modification to an area, make sure children understand what to do in that area or how to play a game. If you observe that a child is not visiting an area, try to understand why. Look at what consumable materials have been used or are needed.

The following checklist is designed to help you evaluate your physical environment. Use it and the other checklists in this book to help you determine not only what is not working but also what is working well. Your answers will provide insight into your physical, temporal, and interpersonal environments. You can also use one of the formal environmental assessment tools listed in appendix C.

Basic Requirements for a School-Age Program's Physical Environment

Does your program meet all of the following basic requirements for your physical space?

- an entrance or gathering area for children and families as they arrive or depart
- enough space for children to move freely and independently within and between program areas
- storage for children's, staff's, and activity materials
- toileting facilities
- areas for active and quiet play without children disturbing each other
- space for large- and small-group activities
- a variety of activities taking place simultaneously in separate, well-defined locations

Warning Signs in the Physical Environment

Review the following list to help you recognize signs that your program's physical environment is not functioning well. Use it to help you observe the children's behavior, their interactions, the physical arrangement in your program space, and what is or should be included in your program play areas.

Do the children in your program exhibit any of the following negative behaviors?

- consistently running inside
- wandering around looking for something to do
- remaining uninvolved and unable to stick with an activity
- appearing bored or telling you they are bored
- avoiding activities or not going into some play areas
- fighting over toys and materials
- using materials, games, and books destructively or inappropriately
- shouting from one area to another
- crawling under tables or on furniture
- resisting cleanup
- consistently depending on adults for the things they need

List each negative behavior you observed on a separate sheet of paper; then look for patterns by answering these questions:

- Where did the behavior take place?
- At what time or times during the day did it happen?
- On which days over the course of a week did it happen?
- Who was involved?

Look for other clues that your physical environment is lacking:

- Are the same materials out day after day?
- Are there cozy areas where children can get away and be by themselves?
- Are materials organized and displayed attractively?
- How many displays are on the walls? What is the purpose of each display?
- Are wall displays hung at or above the children's eye level?
- Do displays include the children's work?

Evaluate the traffic patterns, level of activity, and noise in your environment:

- Is there a visual indicator or boundary to define each area?
- Do children know what is to happen in each area?
- Are children distracted from activities by too much noise or visual clutter, or by peers?
- Can children move easily and independently from place to place?
- Are there visual reminders of the number of children who can participate in each area?

Think about which program areas function well and which do not. Step back and think critically and objectively about how each area in your program is actually used:

- How much play or project work happens in an area?
- What ages or number of children use each area at one time?
- Do older children have a separate place to get away?
- Can one or two children hang out in an easily supervised quiet place?
- Are any areas unused or underused?

Photo 8.11

Photo 8.12

Photo 8.13

Photo 8.11: Unused materials take up space that could be used by children. Clutter and disorganization can be obstacles to children's learning.

Photo 8.12: A ceiling drape of loosely woven fabric allows artificial and natural light to filter through and helps define the space. In facilities with fire suppression systems, it is necessary to keep anything hung from ceilings away from sprinkler heads according to manufacturer's or safety guidelines.

Photo 8.13: Posting a clear visual sign of how many children can be in a specific area allows children to move independently and see if there is space for them to play in that area.

Mapping the Physical Environment

Once you have thoroughly evaluated your overall space and identified the strengths and the problem areas, you are ready to start the fun part: making plans to rearrange the environment. When dividing and organizing your program space, you want an arrangement that can adapt to changing needs, ages, and numbers of children enrolled in your program. Additionally, the physical environment must be able to change with the seasons, holiday celebrations, community events, extenuating circumstances, and family needs. You might want to have flexible play areas that can be switched between inside and outside when the weather changes quickly. Have containers of books, bins of blocks or building materials, and even musical instruments and dance materials available to use inside and outside. When your enrollment of older children increases, the arrangement of your physical environment needs to change to fit them—from the scale of the furniture to the space between areas so they have room to move independently and competently.

It is important to remember that children will let you know when your physical environment is effective and functioning well. If the space in your homework area is too small and restricts the number of children who can use it, you need to expand it. When children do not gravitate to the science or discovery area, you should look at its features and change the materials or the location or reduce its size. When the physical arrangement works well, the children are eager to participate and accomplish the tasks that are in line with your program goals and philosophy (Greenman 2005).

WEBBING YOUR PROGRAM

A useful preliminary step in mapping your space is to use a webbing process. Draw a circle in the middle of a blank piece of paper and write, "The Children," in it. Everything you do, from wall displays to window treatments, relates to these two words—*the children*. Now, draw spokes coming from the circle and write goals you have for the children, such as improved grades at school, more cooperative attitude, greater respect for peers, encouraging creativity. Once you have named the goals, continue a step further by adding what program areas will support each goal and what materials and activities will need to be added to that area to achieve the goal. For example, if one of your goals for the children is improved social skills, your physical environment supports could include a comfortable, quiet place for children to hang out alone or with their friends. In that space you may want a sofa, soft floor pillows, music, age-appropriate magazines, and card games.

The webbing process is much like setting out for a trip and mapping how you are going to reach your destination. We can get to a place only when we know how to get there. When completed, your web will indicate what goals you have for the children and how the arrangement of the physical environment will support them as learners. The webbing process is not limited to just the physical environment; it can be used to help you develop your temporal and interpersonal environments too.

This web shows the content areas that need to be included when webbing.

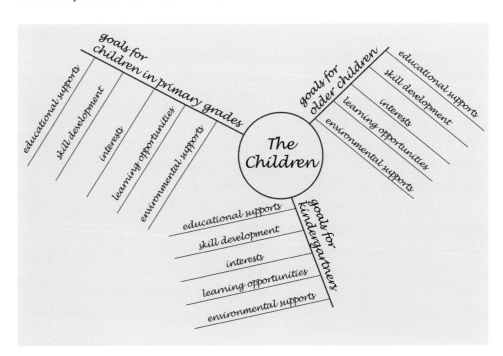

LAYING OUT YOUR PHYSICAL SPACE

Once the webbing activity is finished and staff have identified their goals for the physical environments and how essential needs of the children are met, use the following steps and the graph paper found in appendix D to help you create an organized and effective arrangement of space. You will need at least one sheet of graph paper for each room or area in your program. Here is what you will do on paper before you make any changes in the room:

Step 1: Measure the entire program space.

Step 2: Draw the overall space.

Step 3: Define immovable elements.

Step 4: Determine where to place each area.

Step 5: Evaluate each area and the space arrangement as a whole.

Step 1: Measure the Entire Program Space

Use a tape measure to record the length and width from wall to wall on the graph paper. Be sure the entire length of your tape measure is parallel to the floor. Use your measurements for Step 2.

Step 2: Draw the Overall Space

Copy the graph paper found in appendix D, and then sketch the dimensions of the room on it. Use one piece of graph paper for each room if you have more than one room used by the children. Each half-inch square represents one foot (twelve inches) in the room. If you have one large room, you may find it helpful to divide the room into four quadrants and use one sheet of graph paper for each quadrant.

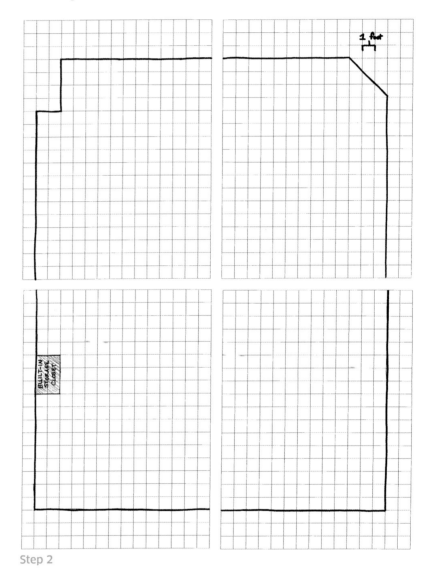

Step 2

Step 3: Define Immovable Elements

Measure and draw to size on your graph paper where the following elements are located in the room:

- Storage closets, cabinets, sink, built-in bookshelves, desks, tables
- Doors: note if these swing into or out of the room.

- Windows: note the height from the floor if there will be a piece of furniture in front of the window.
- Electricity: write an *E* where each outlet is located and an *S* for each light switch.
- Heating or air-conditioning vents: note with a *V*. In cafeterias, libraries, and gyms, the heating and cooling vents are often located in the ceiling; this will be important when you look at air flow.
- Ceiling/fire sprinklers: note with an *F*.

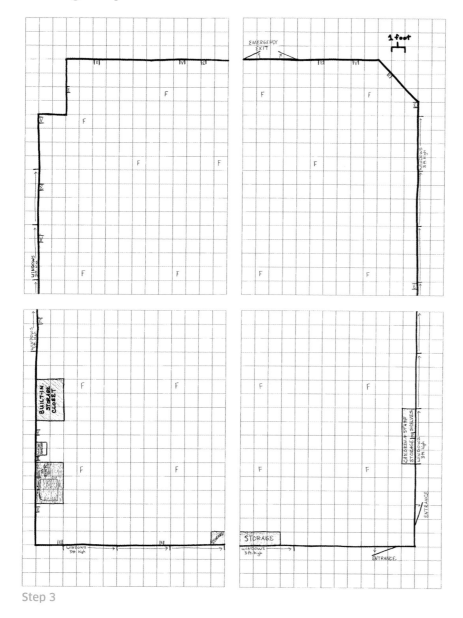

Step 3

Step 4: Determine Where to Place Each Area

For this step, you first need to decide what areas will be included in the space and then define how children and staff will get to and from each area. The third part of this step is to measure each area's furniture and account for the space used.

To start Step 4, create a list of the areas you want to include in your program space. Write the names of these areas on paper squares or rectangles of different colors and sizes, depending on the configuration of your program space and children's needs; larger shapes indicate a bigger play area, while smaller ones indicate littler areas. For example, you may have observed that many children visit the dramatic play area, but only a few visit the library area at a time. The dramatic play area will then have a larger shape than the library area. Next, arrange these cutouts on your graph paper according to where you feel they are best located in your space. It is okay to have the shapes overlap if co-locating the areas will not lessen their effectiveness.

Moving these paper cutouts around is much easier and quicker than erasing or creating multiple sheets for the space (or moving actual carpets and pieces of furniture in the room itself). There is no right or wrong way to arrange space, but keep in mind the function and approximate size of each space. Use the following suggestions as a guide:

- Keep homework and quiet relaxation areas away from loud and active areas.
- Locate science, art, snack, and sensory areas near a cleanup sink; they also are best located by windows.
- Merge separate learning areas together or locate them next to each other when they support integrated learning experiences, such as music and dramatic play, homework and computers, indoor active play and music and movement.
- Consider lighting needs in your arrangement. Areas where close work is done need natural or high-intensity light; quiet relaxation areas are best located away from windows and bright lights. (See chapter 9 for more information on lighting.)
- Try to locate the learning areas as close as possible to their stored items.
- Incorporate open space throughout the environment to allow children to move easily and encourage their creativity.
- Leave some of the open space undefined for children to spread out and play. This no name area invites creativity and gives children control over the environment.
- Open spaces that are too big are often as inappropriate as those that are too small. Oversized open areas cause some children to feel smaller and less confident, while others tend to run and chase.

When you have established all the areas and placed them on the grid, it is time to make sure they work where you want them to be. Much like a city planner who designs roads depending on the number of cars using them and shops and buildings based on the needs of the community, think of the overall physical arrangement of your space as a collection of places and pathways. Be intentional about planning pathways to avoid collisions and confusion. Lay long pieces of string or yarn over the paper circles to help you visualize how children and staff will move from one area to another. Having too many pathways takes up space that could be used for activities; having too few discourages the children from exploring various areas because there is no way to get from one place to another. Avoid creating paths that enable children to run in areas or from space to space, which can lead to injury and disruption of play. If necessary, rework the placement of the shapes and check the pathways again.

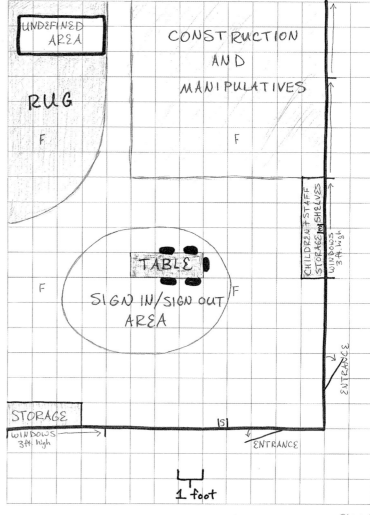

Step 4

Once you are happy with the placement of areas and pathways between them, measure the furniture for each area and make paper templates. Draw these to the same scale as the graph paper (one square for twelve inches), and cut these out. Remember, these paper furniture templates will need to be placed in each square or rectangle you draw for each play area. You can tape or glue these within the shape to give you an idea of how much furniture you will have in each area. (All shapes and yarn pathways need to be fastened to the graph paper.)

If possible, take your completed paper arrangement into the applicable room or area before you start the actual move in process. Some programs have displayed their paper arrangement templates and lived with them for a while before going on to the next step. Take your time and do not rush through this step. It may be difficult to visualize the paper layout, so do not hesitate to move the furniture within each shape or move pieces around on the paper template until you find what you think will work in your program space.

Arranging Furniture

As you consider the arrangement of furniture pieces in the program space, consider the following suggestions:

- Use furniture to help define areas, creating boundaries between them.
- Ensure that tall furniture and room dividers do not block staff's line-of-sight supervision.
- Avoid creating large open spaces by not placing all furniture against outer perimeters.
- Eliminate some furniture if it creates small alcoves where children will be overcrowded or not easily supervised.
- Keep program space flowing freely with the fifty-fifty rule: half the floor space has furniture; half remains open.

Photo 8.14

Photo 8.15

Left: The square pattern on this floor defines and gives interest to a large open space. It helps staff arrange and maintain a consistent environment by guiding placement of activity areas.

Right: Active play games and equipment have been grouped together to encourage children to use and move between them. Since everything is portable, they can be rotated and stored easily.

Step 5: Evaluate Each Area and the Space Arrangement as a Whole

Once you have completed a rough design, take time to review it carefully. Ask yourself the following questions:

1. Are learning areas included that reflect the children's ages, abilities, and interests?

   - Are there places for children to play as a group? By themselves?
   - Are there places older children can be by themselves?

- Does the space arrangement merge overlapping learning areas to support the children's integrated learning experiences?
- Is there accessible storage to support materials needed for planned activities?

2. Is the floor plan functional, organized, and safe?

- Are you arranging materials in play areas in other ways than just on shelves?
- Do you have grab-and-go (movable or portable) learning caddies in the environment?
- Are there clear pathways to encourage children to move without running from place to place and to go safely to the exit doors?
- Are there open spaces to keep from overcrowding the children?
- Does the arrangement give children easy access to all areas to invite their independent exploration and learning?
- Can staff maintain line-of-sight supervision in all areas to ensure safety?
- Can the room environment be changed easily as the enrollment changes?

Look at your answers to the questions posed. "Yes" answers indicate your proposed plan will enable the children to be happily busy with materials and with each other. "No" answers mean you have some kinks to work out in your design. Ask other stakeholders, such as the children, family or community members, and the program host, for their suggestions. More heads are better than one to help you see these challenges from a different perspective.

This shared space program has given careful thought to how children move and use the room. The large area rug adds color and identifies where the grab-and-go (containered) materials are to be used. The pop-up tent is semi-enclosed to let children be alone while still allowing staff to maintain supervision at all times.

Photo 8.16

Photo 8.17

Photo 8.18

Rearranging Spaces and Testing the Changes

Once you have finalized your plan on paper, it is time to physically arrange the space using your completed grid sheets as a guide. If possible, ask the children to assist with this activity. As you move furniture, double-check that you are not blocking access to light switches, ventilation, electric outlets, an egress, or storage.

When you (and the children) have finished rearranging, test out the changes. Observe whether the children can move smoothly from one area to another. Watch as they interact with the environment and each other. Ask for their feedback and suggestions.

Now you are ready to play in each space. This step in redesigning the environment is best accomplished by adults. School-age children are opinionated and even critical. Sometimes you need to make decisions you know are right without their input. To get a good idea of what children see and feel as they move from place to place, get down on their level. Stop for a while to play in each area just as children do. Looking at the environment through children's eyes will give you a better idea if this space invites and welcomes them to explore and learn. If the physical environment does not seem inviting as you are moving in it, take a few photographs from the children's eye level. Look at these critically as a school-ager would. Remember, children need to feel connected to the environment and have a sense of belonging for it to be effective. Make adjustments by thinking like a child.

If the arrangement is clearly not working, try the following:

- Begin small: choose the area least visited by children.
- Find something functional in that area and keep it as a starting point.
- Put everything else in the center of the area or remove it completely.
- Think like a child and ask yourself (or the children): *What happens in this area? Is the scale of the furniture appropriate for the children?*
- Either with or without children's assistance, reshape the area by gradually bringing back only the materials that you know children will use, that are purposeful, and that are age appropriate.
- Ensure furniture is not all against walls, leaving an overly large open area in the middle of the room.
- Ensure the furniture is not contributing to overcrowding by creating alcoves that are too small.
- Ensure that tall furniture and dividers do not prevent staff from having line-of-sight supervision.

Remember that the physical environment needs to be fluid. Change, combine, expand, or reduce play areas according to the size of your program and the needs and interests of the children. The most important part of the process is setting up an environment where children want to be and stay to learn. There are no set guidelines or regulations to follow—it is not a one-size-fits-all concept. Rather, you must decide what you want your environment to include based on the goals for the children and the space in your program.

Arrangement of the Physical Environment in Shared Space Programs

If you are in shared space in which you cannot move furniture, creating a fifty-fifty balance can be challenging. Likewise, creating paths for the children to move independently while minimizing running can take some creativity. In a typical cafeteria setup, the tables are arranged in parallel lines with four to five tables in a line. If you locate the art table at the end of one row, you can place an art easel or chalkboard across the walkway between the rows to indicate a clear boundary for the art area. This also prevents children from running down the walkway. Similarly, placing a cart with books at the end of another row and placing mats on the floor to create your reading space also eliminates a running path. In addition, use colorful tablecloths and signs to define specific areas. Put all quiet activities at one end of the room and noisier activities at the other end.

Photo 8.19

If you are in shared space in which you can move furniture, arrange tables or desks to divide the space. In this way you can separate quiet activities, such as homework and reading, from noisier ones, such as building and dramatic play. See chapter 9 for tips on reducing noise.

If you have open space with no furniture, place pillows or a beanbag in the reading area to create a comfortable place to read or do homework. These are easy to store on top of a storage cabinet or in a rolling garbage can. Make sure pillows and beanbags are covered with removable or easily cleaned materials. If you can add a soft chair, the

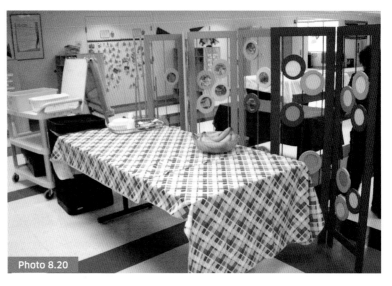

Photo 8.20

Using colored tablecloths within an area creates an inviting, homelike space for children.

The placement of this area rug adds color and definition to this shared space environment and promotes a variety of learning activities. The small lamp adds softness and a homelike appearance.

Photo 8.21

reading or homework area is a great place to do that. (See the Shared Space section in chapter 1 for more suggestions on defining areas when you have no furniture.) Additionally, small rugs create boundaries, add definition to play areas, and give a homey appearance to large or institutional spaces.

To create a place for the children's belongings in shared space, use the tables and chairs that you do not need for program activities. Let the children each use one chair to hang their coat on the back and place their book bag on the seat. Other items can go in front of the chair. If you do not have empty chairs, you can line a wall with laundry baskets labeled with the children's names, and they can place their belongings in their baskets. The baskets are easy to stack for storage.

Arranging and Displaying Materials

Once you have completed the general arrangement in your program, think about how materials are included in each area to answer the question *What happens here?* (At this time, we are not considering the selection of materials for each area; that will be discussed in chapter 10.)

One goal of a well-arranged physical environment is to promote children's independent interactions with materials and learning. To support this goal, materials need to be accessible to all children so there is less confusion and possibly less aggression, greater interaction of the children with materials and each other, and greater freedom for children to be independent. Include enough resources to support children's play and learning but not so many

These puppet show materials are stored together and brought to any location when they are needed.

Photo 8.22

Photo 8.23

balls

Photo 8.24

Label locations where materials are to be stored so staff and children can find them and put them away easily after they are used.

that they are overwhelmed or the area is too crowded or cluttered (see chapter 11 for more about de-cluttering the environment).

Not all materials need or should be arranged on shelves. Children love whimsy and variety. In addition to shelves, use containers such as a small plastic sandbox, a wading pool, a toy cart (with wheels removed to keep it in one place), open-top plastic pumpkins, and small baskets or sand buckets with handles to arrange materials in an area. These containers are both exciting and functional.

Grab-and-go caddies are ideal for shared space programs or programs with limited play areas but equally effective in all programs. These portable containers store materials when floor space is limited or when program space changes regularly. Arranging materials on a rolling cart, see-through storage bin, box, bag, or basket allows staff to grab the materials and go wherever the children are, inside or outdoors. A grab-and-go caddy can support an existing play area that has a defined function or designated activity by bringing in additional materials to extend the children's interest and involvement. Materials can be switched out within minutes, depending on the children's interest or even the weather.

Evaluating Furniture

Furniture is one of the most important and visible aspects of your school-age environment. Once you have identified what furniture pieces you have on hand to use in your physical environment, you can think about what you can add to improve the functioning of your program space and indicate this is a fun place for children to be and learn. A functional arrangement of furniture can go a long way toward improving your physical environment, but the usefulness of the furniture itself also affects the success of your physical environment. In one school-age program, the staff purchased study carrels for the new computer lab. After months of fundraising and anticipation, these arrived, were assembled, and fit perfectly in the room. As the children eagerly bounded in to use these long-awaited additions to the environment, it became apparent quickly that no one had considered the size of the children in relationship to the height of the chairs and desks. The youngest children could barely see the screen, and their legs dangled midway down the chair legs. This example points out the importance of knowing both the needs and the ages of the children as you select any type of furniture.

The following suggestions can guide your evaluation and selection of furniture:

- **Size:** Choose furniture scaled appropriately for the ages, heights, and weights of the children. A fifth grader would be uncomfortable in a preschool chair. Conversely, a kindergartner would have a hard time in an adult-sized folding chair. Ensure cabinets and shelving are easily

The furniture and materials in this art area provide storage and display areas for children's artwork.

Photo 8.25

reached by all children and cannot be tipped over. When purchasing a large storage item, look at it from a child's perspective. Kneel in front of the unit to see how easy it is to reach the shelves. If you can reach the highest shelf when kneeling, so can the average five-year-old or a person using a wheelchair.

- **Adjustability:** Purchase tables that can be raised or lowered. Some manufacturers make tables adjustable to different heights for use by toddlers through preteens. This flexibility allows your environment to change easily when the ages and sizes of children change. An eight-inch height difference between the seat of a chair and a table is most comfortable.

- **Movability:** Selecting chairs not attached to the table allows you to remove a chair so that children with a walker or a wheelchair can be included in activities. In addition, you will have more flexibility for moving furniture and redesigning space as needed.

- **Storage ease:** Folding or stacking chairs and collapsible futon sofas cut the amount of storage space you need.

- **Climbable equipment:** When purchasing lofts or other furniture for climbing activities, consider the scale of the piece in relationship to the sizes of children, the ceiling height, and the placement of light fixtures, sprinklers, and ceiling vents and ductwork. Do not forget to plan adequate fall zones; protection under and around climbers or lofts is needed to prevent injuries from falls.

Photo 8.26

A variety of arts and crafts materials are stored on the shelves and walls to be accessible to all ages of children.

- **Modular furniture:** These pieces can be purchased in a variety of sizes and configurations and used in various locations. They offer great flexibility for arranging and rearranging. They can be used alone, stacked, or attached to other furniture to create boundaries or play barriers.
- **Wheeled pieces:** If your program is in a shared space facility, wheeled furniture enables staff to move and arrange the environment easily. Note that wheels must be in the locked position when located in children's play areas.
- **Safety:** Make sure any wheels can either be locked or folded up. Choose furniture that is sturdy and durable and can be cleaned easily.
- **Comfort:** When possible, avoid furnishings that give an institutional impression. In quiet areas, include some furnishings or accessories that are soft and comfortable. Choose upholstered furniture with textured fabrics in calm, soothing colors that coordinate easily with other colors in your program. Unless you are tying furniture directly to a theme or learning activity area, avoid thematic furniture, such as upholstered chairs or sofas with footballs or unicorns, lofts that look like spaceships, and ceiling drops that look like mini-castles. (See chapter 9 for more information on selecting fabric.)

Staff have shown their creativity by decorating this art material storage cabinet with their handprints. This touch adds a bit of whimsy and personalizes the environment too.

Photo 8.27

Activities and Questions

If you have already worked through the five steps and have your program space arranged, think about the look of the physical environment in your program. Use the questions below to think critically about how it supports children's learning. If you are still in the planning stages of arranging a physical environment, use the concepts presented in the questions to guide your thinking.

1. What can you do to improve your overall program space?

2. What can you do to improve your floor plan or arrangement of areas in the space?

3. Which area in your program is the most popular? Is it large enough to accommodate all children who want to play there? If not, how can you expand or relocate this area to give opportunities to more children to play there?

4. Which area is the least popular? Should you eliminate this area or redesign it?

5. Walk around on your knees throughout your program space and see the environment from the viewpoint of a child. What do you see that looks inviting? What would you change and why?

6. Using graph paper, follow the five-step design process outlined in this chapter to draw your program space and arrange areas in your program. Once this is complete, choose a problem area or a new area you would like to add, and make the change.

CHAPTER 9

The Physical Environment: Creating Sensory-Rich Spaces

THIS CHAPTER EXAMINES the sensory details of lighting, color, pattern, texture, sound, and smell. Often we are not even consciously aware of these details, but they appeal to our senses of sight, touch, hearing, and smell. Whether our senses are aroused positively or negatively affects how we feel in the environment.

The feelings the physical environment evoke affect people's behavior. If children are overstimulated, they may want to crawl into a corner and shut down, or they may bounce in an overexcited and frenzied fashion between people and places in the environment. If your physical environment has a negative effect on the children's behavior, then your temporal and interpersonal environments will not function as smoothly as you would like. Sensory design details affect how comfortable and welcome people feel in your program environment. Good sensory design helps facilitate smooth transitions from one activity to another and supports individual needs. It helps calm children and supports their social competence skills. You know your sensory design needs attention if children are frazzled, frenzied, quick-tempered, or argumentative. Through carefully reflecting and making decisions about lighting, color, pattern, texture, acoustics, and clean air, you are paying attention to more than aesthetic elements. These design details are sensory stimulants that can invite children's engagement, wonder, and imagination.

Photo 9.1

This small boat and upholstered furniture encourage children's quiet play and reading activities. The neutral wall color almost disappears next to the bright accent colors of blue and red.

Lighting

Some places we go make us feel uneasy, unwelcome, scared, or depressed. Think about it for a minute—was it a dark or foreboding place? Typically, the presence or lack of light affects the feeling of the place. Light can affect children's sense of security and comfort when they are away from their homes (Schreiber 1996). Light also influences the level of activity, health, emotions, and personal safety. Anita Olds, an expert on children's environments, believes that light has more to do with the spirit, or feeling, of a place than perhaps any other factor (2001). Learning environments for children should be energized with light. This section discusses the two sources of light to consider in school-age programs: natural and artificial.

Photo 9.2

Right: The choice of color and lighting supports learning activities by helping children focus on their homework or project work.

NATURAL LIGHT

Natural light comes from the sun and the moon. Sunlight has a warming and positive effect on our lives. We just feel better when we are in sunlight. By incorporating daylight into your school-age program environment, you encourage active play, which is one of the most effective ways to stimulate learning. (See chapter 6 for more on the benefits of play.)

Having an outdoor play area is an ideal way to expose children to sunlight, physical movement, and the natural world all at once. Exposure to natural light is so important that some children who do not get enough exposure to sunlight develop the fatigue and irritability associated with seasonal affective disorder (SAD). The main treatment for SAD is bright light therapy from full-spectrum artificial lighting, which emits wavelengths that are similar to sunshine.

The uncovered windows combined with textural materials help connect children with the great outdoors.

Photo 9.3

In an ideal environment, children can still get exposure to natural light even when inside. If at all possible, give children the opportunity to look out windows and enjoy the sunshine and the outside world from inside. While you may not be able to add windows or skylights, you can maximize the natural light by opening blinds, curtains, and window shades. Be aware, however, that direct sunlight pouring through a window or door can cause glare and reflections at certain times of the day or year.

ARTIFICIAL LIGHT

Artificial light comes from lightbulbs. It supplements or replaces natural light to support indoor activities and outdoor safety. The type and intensity of artificial lighting you use depends on the intended activity. There is a general tendency to overlight institutional settings. Many facilities where school-age programs operate have a uniform grid of lighting,

Photo 9.4

Children need encouragement from staff and a challenging outdoor environment to promote vigorous play. Fresh air and sunshine help keep children healthy and fit.

usually strings of fluorescent lights that cover ceilings. Often these give an institutional or sterile feeling to the environment. While you may not have choices about or control over the lighting, understanding its possible effects will help you to determine whether it is negatively affecting any of the children. If possible, include a wide range of lighting options to both define different areas and meet the needs of the activities in various areas.

Criteria for selecting artificial or electric light depend greatly on the purpose of the space. In general, it is best to use full-spectrum or fluorescent bulbs that create a warmer or more natural look in indoor spaces. Using the proper wattage lightbulbs for specific tasks or activities in each location protects the children's eyes. To avoid eyestrain, high-wattage light is needed in areas with limited natural light and in areas where children read, use manipulatives, and work on projects or homework. Filtered or less intense light is appropriate in areas where children are less active; softer light encourages relaxation, quiet play, and quiet conversations. If you change the color and type of lighting, you will find the color of walls, toys, and furniture change too. The whiter the light, the purer other colors will appear.

Research has shown that intense or high-wattage lights used throughout an indoor setting have a negative effect on children's behavior (Grangaard 1993). Fluorescent lighting, for example, produces a glare when reflected light bounces off shiny objects, such as brightly colored plastic toys and furniture, which can make it difficult for children to concentrate. Reflected light can contribute to a more active, even frenzied mood in school-age programs.

Light reflections can also lead to eyestrain, nervousness (especially in children with special needs), and stress in children and adults alike. Additionally, fluorescent lighting reduces shadows and shading, which limit children's depth perception.

The quality and intensity of the light depend on the type and wattage of the bulb or tube you use. There are many indoor lighting options from which to choose. You will want to consider the following types, depending on what activities will take place in an area and how much natural light is available in these locations.

Photo 9.5

Track and spotlights are easily positioned according to where light is needed or to define a space.

Fluorescent lighting: Some research suggests that flashes from fluorescent lights can cause hyperactivity in children and trigger seizures in individuals who are seizure-prone. If you have fluorescent lights and cannot remove these, choose bulbs or tubes that provide the color mix that is most similar to daylight (available at lighting and hardware stores). In addition, you can install covers over fluorescent light fixtures to lessen the harsh glare. Add ceiling swags or other sources of lighting to add a warmer tone to fluorescent light.

Compact fluorescent lights (CFLs): Designed to replace incandescent bulbs, CFLs are more energy efficient, last longer, and do not get as hot. Unlike older forms of fluorescent lighting, CFLs produce a soft white light similar to incandescent light. They also come in a variety of color temperatures and levels of brightness. CFLs can be used in nearly all light fixtures designed for incandescent lightbulbs. A drawback, however, is that they contain trace amounts of mercury, so they need to be properly disposed of as hazardous waste.

Light-emitting diodes (LEDs): This type of lighting gives off more light per watt than either the traditional incandescent lightbulb or fluorescent lighting, making LEDs the most energy-efficient option available. Recent improvements in LED technology have produced a warmer color of light. LED bulbs come in shapes and sizes that are interchangeable with incandescent bulbs and fluorescent tubes for replacement in existing lighting fixtures. To light a large space with LEDs, multiple lamp fixtures are needed. While the cost for LEDs has dropped considerably since they were first introduced, currently the overall cost is still higher than other lighting options.

Halogen lighting: These lightbulbs last longer and are more energy efficient than incandescent lights. Because of safety issues, however, halogen bulbs should not be used in any place where children can get to them. Halogen bulbs get extremely hot, and if touched, the bulb can explode from the oil on fingers. Keep in mind that safety is the number one factor to consider when choosing lighting for your program.

Photo 9.6

Track lighting: If your budget allows you to add or change lighting, install track lighting to direct light to the specific places where it is most needed and to aid in defining the purpose of an activity area. Track lighting also allows you to create soft, indirect light in areas where children are involved in quiet activities. Additionally, track lighting is easy to adjust either individually or as a cluster of lighting.

Recessed lighting: Capable of producing a soft, indirect light, recessed lights are tucked into the ceiling rather than hanging from it. These lights work especially well in areas with low ceiling height or in active play areas where there are flying balls, beanbags, or other airborne play items.

Photo 9.7

Table lamps and floor lamps: Whether you use incandescent or CFL bulbs, table and floor lamps give the warmest feeling of all types of lighting and can be used in your program space as long as all parts of the lamp (excluding the lightbulb) are of a nonbreakable material. Plastic lamps are the best and most widely used for children's environments. The bottom of the lamp should be weighted so it does not tip over easily. If possible, screw a table lamp base to the furniture to reduce the danger of it falling on a child. If this is not an option, use industrial-strength Velcro to fasten the lamp base to the furniture top.

Electrical Safety Precautions

Reduce potential electrical safety hazards for the children in your program:

- Secure all electrical cords completely out of reach of children.
- Position table lamps so that the cords remain safely tucked out of sight from inquisitive hands.
- Select freestanding lamps that are bottom heavy, not top heavy, and that are made from nonbreakable materials.
- Keep table lamps from toppling over. Either screw the lamp base to the furniture or install industrial-strength Velcro on the lamp base and the furniture top.
- Purchase tubes called *conduit raceways* to hide electrical cords. Mount the raceways on walls and along baseboards to encase cords.
- Do not use halogen bulbs in places where children can reach them. These bulbs get extremely hot and can explode when touched.
- Handle fluorescent bulbs with extreme caution. If one breaks, follow the Environmental Protection Agency (EPA) guidelines for clean up and disposal at www2.epa.gov/cfl/cleaning-broken-cfl.

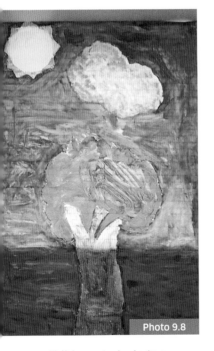

Photo 9.8

Child-created window shades reduce sun and glare while letting light into the program space and allow the children to make the space their own.

EVALUATING AND IMPROVING LIGHTING

Take a few minutes to assess the lighting in your program space:

- Does a majority of light come from ceiling light fixtures?
- Are windows covered with blinds, curtains, window shades, or anything else that prevents sunlight from streaming into the room?
- Look at various areas of your program space during different times of the day to evaluate glare and reflections from natural light. Get down on your knees to see areas from the same angles as the children. Do you see any glare or reflection bouncing off furniture or floors that might distract or irritate children?
- Are children typically wound up all day? Do they have difficulty separating from their families or complain of headaches? Any of these problems may indicate problems from high-intensity lighting.

If you answered yes to any of these questions, it is time to consider changing light sources. Here are some inexpensive ways to adjust lighting to promote children's learning and overall well-being:

- If you have fluorescent tubes in your ceiling lights, replace white tubes with warm tone tubes to create a softer, more welcoming feeling in the environment. Consider LED replacements for fluorescent tubes to create a more natural light.
- Change clear lightbulbs with lower wattage to frosted ones to reduce intense light in areas where children gather for informal group or social activities. (Remember: halogen lightbulbs are not recommended for school-age programs due to safety hazards.)
- Replace ceiling fixtures with track lighting so that you can direct light where it is needed. Use different wattage bulbs for each track fixture to add definition and change the intensity of the light in different areas.
- When you need to repaint the ceiling, use a warm, neutral color rather than a stark white. This helps to soften the light and makes the ceiling height appear lower; these in turn make the room feel warmer and cozier.
- To reduce or filter direct sunlight that creates glare, install light-filtering shades over windows. These shades block reflections while allowing filtered natural light into your space. Window films also reduce intense sunlight while blocking ultraviolet rays and passive solar heat.

Color

Like light, colors have a big impact on the look and feel of your school-age program. Changing the color scheme is one of the easiest and least expensive ways to transform your program environment. But before you make any changes, you should understand the effect that colors have on the mood and behavior of children. Colors can support children's ability to think, create, and learn. Selecting appropriate colors is a critical component as you redesign your program environment. Even if you are in a facility in which others make decisions on color choices, you can still find ways to introduce color as a positive element in your program.

The colors of walls, furniture, floor coverings, and equipment either stimulate or mellow everyone in your program environment. Colors of all hues and intensity are key elements to how stimulated or tranquil we feel in a location. Cool colors, such as pale green or blue, have a very calming effect. Warm colors, such as red and yellow, stimulate activity. Considered colorless and neutral, gray has very limited color-mood associations. It is a restful color that fades into the background of the environment and is the perfect color for walls. Bubblegum pink is another calming color. It was found to subdue violent

Bright colors add interest and excitement to the environment but should be used as accent colors in small amounts. Dark or pure tones used as background colors on bulletin boards highlight signage.

prisoners in seconds by reducing their muscle strength and calming their behavior (Olds 2001).

Most children love bright colors—especially red and yellow. But while children need visual stimuli, vibrant colors can make children hyperactive and exhausted or even cause them to shut down their senses against the intensity of the color. Vivid colors make it difficult for children to focus or concentrate on one thing for long. When the intensity or sheer amount of color overloads the environment, the activity level of school-age children can spiral out of control.

COLOR SPECTRUM

The bright colors that children love include the three primary colors: red, yellow, and blue. Primary colors are pure colors: each is composed completely of one color. All other colors are derived from these three primary colors. Bright colors also include the three secondary colors, orange, green, and purple, which are made by mixing two primary colors together in equal amounts. The vibrancy of primary and secondary colors has a place in your school-age environment, but these colors should be limited to 20 to 25 percent of the colors used.

Colors are like children—each one has its own personality. Most colors create a feeling, either positive or negative. Colors can create moods and define activity levels. The following table shows the effects and appropriate uses of various colors in school-age environments.

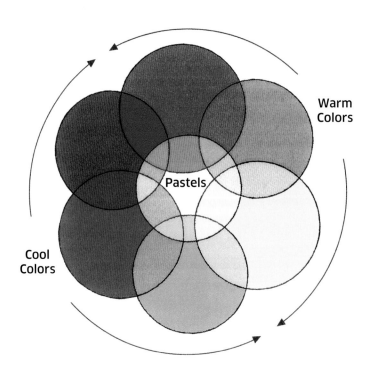

Using Color to Achieve Various Effects

	COLOR	EFFECTS	RECOMMENDED USES
Warm Tones	**Reds**	catch attention energize create warmth stimulate appetite, encourage activity	active play areas eating areas
	Oranges	stimulate appetite create warmth encourage activity	eating areas large-group or active play areas
	Yellows	promote well-being and happiness stimulate the brain and conversation	collaborative learning spaces group or gathering areas visually expand small areas
	Browns	aid concentration and reflection warmth and comfort	flooring homework areas accent color or to define space

	Violet (purple)	evoke varying feelings depending on shade/tone
		
		   pastel violet: peaceful
		
		   blue violet: frustration
			accent color or to define space
			
			use very sparingly

Cool Tones	**Blues**	soothing calming suppress appetite	accent color (pure or high-tone blues) quiet or rest areas
	Greens	calming reinforce self-esteem	quiet or rest areas brighten dim areas
Neutrals	**Creamy whites** **Beige** **Light gray** **Black**	reflect light fade into background restful on the eye some tones may cause sadness	ceilings walls visually expand small areas

NOTE: Accent colors are used in small amounts on walls (20 to 25 percent of the total wall space), on furniture, and on wall displays and display boards. They can create a dramatic and exciting look to the environment when used together with more neutral or low-tone colors in a space.

Earth tones and small checked fabric are used in this quiet spot to give it a warm feeling. Photos of the children and their families add a personal touch to the area.

Photo 9.10

EVALUATING AND APPLYING COLOR IN YOUR PROGRAM ENVIRONMENT

Knowing that children react to color in ways that affect their behavior and learning, you can carefully evaluate the colors that you currently have in your program. Are they bright and bold? Subtle and subdued? Visually chaotic? What overall feeling do you get when you walk into each program area? What is the typical behavior of the children in each place?

Color defines spaces. It can be used to tie places together, to create boundaries, or to define territory. Use colored tape on flooring to define a play area.

This large program uses different accent colors on activity room doors, hallway walls, and floors to identify the location in the building. Each room in a hallway has a different tone of the same color.

Categorize and store different materials in various colors of storage bins. Designate activity rooms or older children's areas with brightly colored stripes, shapes, or silhouettes in hallways. This color coding can help children find activity areas and return toys, games, and books to the appropriate places. For example, yellow might define the active play area, while orange defines the area for meals and snacks. Keep in mind, however, that using too many colors to define activity spaces can create an overwhelming kaleidoscope of colors that actually does more harm than good. Color should be kept in balance and used purposefully to support children's learning and well-being.

Children often remember bold colors better than warm, mtuted tones. But their preference for bright colors like red and yellow should not be a guiding factor when choosing a color scheme. Start with soft, neutral colors as a foundation on walls, furniture, and flooring. Creamy whites, light grays, and light pastels are best for the broad expanses of walls and ceilings. Then introduce more color

Photo 9.11

through accents on furniture, pillows, and storage units and through background colors for bulletin boards and wall displays.

In school-age programs, accents are usually bright and pure colors, but accents such as red need to be used in small amounts. Just a little bit goes a long way. These splashes of color help give definition to your color plan without overly stimulating the children. Avoid using warm, bright colors in areas where children rest or focus their attention. Cool colors like muted greens and soft blues are good for rest and quiet areas.

Choosing a color scheme does not need to be difficult. Many colors are appropriate for your program space. Balance is the key. For inspiration, look to nature's peaceful and harmonious color palette and choose colors that blend well together, with no one color dominating another. The following steps will help you plan your color scheme:

Step 1: For each program area, write down words that describe the mood you want it to have. For instance, you may write *nurturing* or *quiet* for homework or reading places, and *energetic* or *fun* for active play areas.

Step 2: Refer to the color table earlier in this section. For each program area, choose two accent colors that support the mood you want in that space.

Step 3: Visit a paint store or paint department in a hardware store that has a variety of wall color cards. Select color cards you feel may work. Start with soft, quiet colors as a foundation on walls and furniture. Then look for the accent colors you identified in step 2. Some stores sell small containers of paint that allow you to paint a small test section. Whether you use color cards or sample paint, make sure to test colors in the light in your program space.

Step 4: When you test colors, involve children, staff, and parents in the color choices and in painting the walls. Their input and feedback are important in determining what effects the colors will have.

Step 5: Decide on a paint finish. This determines how dull or shiny the paint will be. Note that matte finishes absorb light and make the area more saturated with color; glossy finishes reflect light and are more durable and washable. Between these extremes are finishes that can offer the best of both: washable without adding glare that is hard on the eyes.

Step 6: Once you have reached a consensus about your color plan, buy the paint and transform your space.

The accent colors you choose for each program area can be introduced in a variety of ways. In addition to paint, you have many other options:

- quilts hung on the wall
- murals created by the children in active play areas or hallways
- displays of children's artwork matted on brightly colored paper
- bulletin board backing
- pillows
- area rugs
- nonpoisonous plants, cut and silk flowers
- painting small walls, alcoves, and room dividers in a bright color

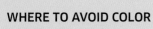

WHERE TO AVOID COLOR
Do not paint window frames or door frames in bright colors. You want to avoid drawing children's attention to these openings and changing their focus.

Pattern

Sometimes people spend time in a place, and they suddenly get light-headed or feel they need sunglasses. They may be reacting to an environment painted in a frenzy of bold stripes in bright colors on walls and floors, or containing furniture and curtains with large polka dots and checks. The eye cannot help the brain process and make sense of all the stimuli, so it simply shuts down. The end result is visual chaos and often nausea or headache. This is exactly what happens to children when they are in an environment where too many elements compete for their attention. The environment creates sensory overload and ultimately undermines their ability to concentrate and to learn.

A pattern is a single motif or unit of design that is repeated for visual interest. Patterns are seen rather than felt (as is texture). Stripes, plaids, and polka dots are all examples of patterns used on fabrics, rugs, wallpaper, and painted areas. Patterns can be used to add interest in your program; however, keep in mind that smaller patterns, usually one inch in diameter or less, are best because they are easy on the eye and more calming visually. Patterns should be used to balance a space, not distract from it. Too many patterns, like bright colors, can be far too stimulating and even distracting for school-age children. Introduce pattern through a variety of furnishings and accessories:

- pillows
- area rugs
- storage bins
- curtains that can be pulled back or valances to let in natural light
- furniture
- flooring (tiles, painted design on concrete)

Choose items with patterns carefully. Children's toys and play mats often sport a variety of patterns. Many so called "learning rugs" have too many stimuli in their design and can cause visual overload in children. A better choice is an area rug that has a variation of the same color—a pattern with tone on tone, for example, beige with tan or gray with black. Then use these in places needing definition or boundaries, such as a floor activity space, library, or quiet area.

Photo 9.12

Photo 9.13

CARPETING MISHAP

In one program, the staff eagerly anticipated the arrival of new carpeting that was left over from a recent installation. On the day the carpeting was installed, the staff discovered to their dismay that it was the remnants from the new movie theater. The visual chaos of the bold design and patterns made the children dizzy, since so many activities took place on the floor.

The staff quickly learned firsthand the role that flooring can play in helping children maintain focus and concentrate for long periods. Plain area rugs and blankets were spread over the boldly patterned carpet to enhance children's concentration and reduce visual stimuli. After these minor changes, the staff observed children staying with activities longer and needing less assistance.

Patterns or geometric designs on flooring can add interest when used in small areas; however, they can be distracting to children when used as floor covering as shown in photo 9.12. Cover high-contrast flooring with a solid-color area rug to aid children's concentration as shown in photo 9.13.

Even posters and other wall displays with patterns should be limited. You may be surprised to find that many wall displays are not important to the children, and when you take them down, the space appears much larger and more organized. Try to limit displays to those that have interest and meaning to children, such as their own artwork and photos taken of them. A general rule of thumb is to leave 60 to 80 percent of each wall empty. Let the neutral wall tones dominate to open up the environment.

Children need to be able to concentrate in their environments. Often patterns and vivid contrasts of colors make it difficult for both staff and children to concentrate for any length of time. Evaluate the patterns in your school-age environment by answering these questions:

1. How many objects in each area or room have patterns? Look at curtains, rugs, pillows, furniture, wall displays, flooring, and carpet.
2. How many different colors are in each of the patterns?
3. How many patterns have bright and bold colors?
4. How many patterns have soft and subtle colors?
5. How many large patterns (over one inch in diameter) do you find?

An area rug is a visual reminder of the purpose of this science center about sea life. It adds a bit of whimsy and color to this learning area.

If you answered more than two to any of these questions, your program environment is too visually stimulating for children. Avoid a kaleidoscope of patterns that is visually chaotic and competes for the children's attention. In so doing, you enable both staff and children to concentrate in your program environment. Here are some suggestions to create a calmer, less stimulating atmosphere:

- Use patterns in limited amounts and with a purpose.
- Introduce no more than two different patterns in each area or room.
- Select patterns that are less than one inch in diameter.
- Ensure that patterns balance the space, not distract from it.
- Leave windows bare or use neutral-colored curtains.
- Use patterned rugs only in places where they are needed.
- Choose area or individual rugs that have variations of the same color (that is, tone on tone) or that are harmonious with other colors in your environment.
- Cover all pillows in a pastel or neutral-colored pattern to create a soft, calm feeling.
- Keep only those wall displays that have meaning to the children and families or that are needed to comply with licensure standards.
- Leave 60 to 80 percent of the wall space blank.

Texture

Did you know that our skin is the largest organ in the body and a vital source of stimulation? It is commonly thought that of all the senses, touch is the one first experienced by a baby at birth and the last one experienced prior to death. Textures offer children important learning experiences, especially since they spend so much time exploring through touch. School-age children love the feel of fuzzy pillows, stuffed toys, and live animals. Nutritional experts agree that children benefit from being able to touch and explore food textures (Hendrix 2008). From cool tiled floors to cushy area rugs, textures in your school-age program add yet another dimension to the physical environment.

Sensory Defensive and Hypersensitive Awareness

Some children are sensory defensive to materials or foods with distinctive odors, textures, or tastes or are hypersensitive to other types of sensory input, such as sound and movement. These children may have difficulty using some materials, entering into certain activities, and interacting in certain areas of your program space. Be respectful of these children's sensitivities and do not force them to use any materials or to be in any location they find disagreeable. Provide alternative places and materials that are more comfortable (or appropriate) for these children to keep them involved and successful.

School-age children need to be exposed to a variety of textural materials in the environment. Look around your program and consider the following:

- What covering is on your floors: wood, tile, carpet, or a combination of these?
- What types of ground cover are in the outdoor play space: grass, wood chips, asphalt, sand, concrete, or a combination of these?
- How many different textures, such as ribbed, nubby, furry, or soft, can children touch during the course of a day?
- Are most items that children use or feel made from plastic? How many textural materials are represented?

If you notice a lack of a variety of textures, add some touches of texture in places where children can feel them. If the majority of items in the environment are made of plastic or a material without texture, consider adding wood, metal, cloth, shell, stone, wicker, fabric, or any other textural material. Once

Photo 9.15

Found objects and pieces that are textural connect children with nature and enhance their appreciation of natural materials.

you have added materials with various textures, watch how the children interact with them. Record notes that address the following questions:

1. Were the additions of textural materials noticed by children?

2. What textures seem to be most appealing to children? How were these items used?

3. Do the children gravitate to or use textural items more often than those without texture?

4. Do children tend to feel or hold on to textured materials more than ones without texture?

5. How can you use textures to help children's learning?

6. How does the texture or finishes of playthings, furniture, or carpeting affect the appearance of your program space?

7. If you added textured floor covering in some areas, do children appear more comfortable or spend more time there?

Photo 9.16

Plastics, metal, and vinyl are often
the choice for finishes in school-age
environments because they are
easy to clean and durable. Too often
items made of fabric are excluded
due to the misconception that they
harbor unhealthy contaminants.
Washing and disinfecting textural
materials and fabric accents regularly will reduce unease about their
cleanliness. The greater the variety
of textural materials you offer the
children, the better. Provide various
soft textures, which are both soothing and interesting to school-age
children, within reach as much as possible, especially in quiet areas where
they relax or work on homework. Hard textures are more suitable for play
areas where lively activities occur.

Photo 9.17

Open wicker baskets help
children find and return
items easily and keep the
environment looking neat
and orderly. Wicker bas-
kets used for serving food
create a homelike feeling
but must be sanitized after
each use.

Add texture to your program environment with materials like these:

- a variety of flooring, such as wood, tile, and carpeting of varying styles
  (looped, clipped, high-low pile)

- wicker baskets for children to carry or store various small items in
- pillows and furniture covered with natural fabric such as burlap, nubby cotton, and flannel
- area rugs made of clipped, looped, Berber, or braided material
- furniture and play items in a variety of tactile surfaces, such as plastic, wood, leather, rubber, and cloth
- natural items that offer a rich source of textures, such as pebbles, plants, cork, seeds, moss, driftwood, seashells, and pinecones
- two or more different types of ground cover in the outdoor play area (grass, mulch, and shredded tire chips are great for softening falls and feel good on children's knees and hands)

Sound and Acoustics

Sounds help us understand where we are even without our vision. Some sounds are pleasant and even happy; others alert us to danger. Sounds evoke strong physiological and psychological reactions. When we hear a siren, we may become more alert. When we hear children's laughter, we may smile. When we hear a signal to evacuate a building, we may become anxious about a possible danger. Sounds that are too loud are harmful to our ears and, according to some experts, even elevate blood pressure and bring on headaches.

At some schools in New Zealand, signs hang in prominent places, stating, "It is not noise that we must justify in this place; it is silence." Anyone who works with school-age children knows learning is anything but quiet and calm. Learning is active, exciting, thrilling, and usually downright noisy. Children's laughter and voices are most definitely sounds we want to hear in a school-age environment—not noises coming from sources such as airplanes, highway traffic, and construction machinery. Nevertheless, for a child to successfully hear, understand, and participate in a school-age program, their voices must be kept at normal conversational levels. These are in a range of sound measured at thirty-five to sixty decibels. Various areas of a school-age program have different levels of noise. When rearranging your program environment, locate noisy and active areas away from quiet areas. Some program sites pose greater challenges for controlling noise than others. Rooms with high ceilings, plaster ceilings and walls, and floors covered with a hard surface (especially concrete or tile) cause sound to reverberate and voices to echo. Especially in programs where care is provided in a gymnasium or cafeteria, noise can be a major environmental issue.

Photo 9.18

Large open rooms such as gymnasiums and cafeterias can be echo chambers where sounds become distorted or amplified. This program has added sound-absorbing material on walls and the ceiling to keep noise down and communication up.

Photo 9.19

Area rugs provide a visual boundary to define play space and contribute to a softer and quieter physical environment.

According to the U.S. General Services Administration's (GSA) *Child Care Center Design Guide* (2003), there are three categories of acoustical concerns in settings where children are in group care:

- controlling exterior noise entering the space
- modulating and controlling interior noise generated in the space
- controlling interior noise as it moves between locations in the facility

While some of these concerns are not within your control, look for ways to lower the overall sound load, protect children's hearing, and ensure they can hear conversations and announcements. Children's ability to hear and understand what is being said is vital to their concentration, focus, and learning.

Fabric and other soft materials absorb sound and can be economical ways to reduce noise. Following are some tips to help keep sound in your program environment at a moderate level (adapted from www.asha.org):

- Hang fabric swags or banners from the ceiling.
- Tack felt or corkboard to the walls.
- If your budget allows, install acoustical wall or ceiling panels.
- Use portable partitions.
- Add area rugs or small rugs, carpet squares, or gym mats.
- Select furniture covered in heavy fabric.
- Mask unwanted noise with wind chimes, sound machines that create pleasant sounds, or small water features.
- Dampen exterior noise by adding plants and bushes next to the building.
- If your budget allows, install acoustically laminated glass in window or door panes.
- Avoid toys, musical instruments, playing devises, and games that generate sounds higher than eighty-five decibels.
- Place latex-free soft tips on the bottoms of chairs and tables. (Do not use tennis balls to soften the sound, because these are made from latex, which can cause allergic reactions in some individuals.)

Smell

Do you remember the smell of your grandmother's house? How about your house after you have cooked broccoli or baked cookies? What about the smell of the beach, the forest, or fruit trees in full blossom? Our sense of smell is a recognition function or, in simpler terms, a memory maker. According to psychologists, the olfactory sense affects our emotions more than sight, hearing, or touch (Vincent 2010). Smells signal the part of the brain that controls our emotional reasoning. We are constantly testing the environment through the air we breathe for potential danger (smoke), food (broccoli or cookies), and another person close by. A smell that is pleasant is called an *aroma*, while *odor* is often unpleasant; naturally, the reaction to smells is unique to each of us. We want to stay in places that smell fresh and clean and cannot get out of places fast enough when the smell is not pleasant.

Researchers tell us that children respond to smell much as they respond to color. It affects their mood, memory, and even physiological body functions, such as heart rate, blood pressure, stress levels, and breathing. Unpleasant smells can affect children's concentration, health, and comfort and generally increase their dislike for a particular environment, while pleasant smells of flowers, popcorn, or just baked cookies create wonderful memories. The following elements and practices in your program affect the scent of the environment:

- **Ventilation:** Open windows to allow fresh air to circulate; keep heating, ventilation, and air-conditioning (HVAC) filters clean and the system operating according to the manufacturer's guidelines to ensure recirculated air flows freely throughout the program space (especially in bathrooms and food preparation areas).
- **Food preparation:** Keep air circulating at all times; clean exhaust fans, filters, and screens.
- **Cleaning process and products:** Ensure all floors are cleaned daily or as needed; empty trash cans and remove trash from program space at least daily; use hypoallergenic cleaning solvents that do not have a heavy residual odor; follow manufacturer's or licensure guidelines when mixing cleaning solutions.
- **Air fresheners:** Resist the temptation to have solid or liquid air fresheners in program space, because they mask odors and are an irritant to individuals with allergies.

Activities and Questions

Creating a visually appealing physical environment that supports children's learning involves attention to lighting, color, pattern, texture, and smell. Use the following questions to help you use all of these effectively in your school-age program.

1. When you are in your program space, how does it make you feel? Is this a feeling you want to keep or change?

2. What is the primary light source in your program? Does this lighting give the program a cozy feel or a more institutional look? Is there a way to capitalize on natural light or add area lighting?

3. When looking at your wall space, how much is covered with displays, posters, and artwork? Are the children interested in the displays? Do the displays connect to a learning outcome or support a current activity area?

4. What colors are used in your program space? Looking at the description of colors in this chapter, what three colors would you choose to incorporate into or to repaint your space? How will those colors support the intended activity in each area or help define the area?

5. How can you use the information from this chapter to create an environment that supports children's learning through all five senses?

CHAPTER 10

The Physical Environment: Toys, Materials, and Equipment That Promote Learning

THE PHYSICAL ENVIRONMENT includes the materials and the equipment you place in your program's learning areas. Some materials you choose for a given area teach children a skill; some help children practice a skill; others encourage creativity and a love of learning. Your intentionality as you choose and place materials and equipment in each area creates an environment in which children can be children while exploring, learning, and creating.

This chapter explores the role of a variety of areas that can be incorporated into a school-age program. Each section of the chapter discusses ways to facilitate play in that area and then outlines potential learning opportunities and suggested equipment and materials. By *materials* we mean those things that are consumable, such as art supplies, and those items that will rotate in and out of the area. *Equipment* refers to those items that are always in the area, such as shelving. Bring your own creativity to each area by adding any additional items you feel will enhance the learning opportunities in your program. You may find it difficult or even impossible to include all the areas and items listed in this chapter. What is important is to choose items based on what you know about the children in your program. As children's interests change or a new skill needs to be taught, change the materials in the environment to facilitate the learning or interest.

As you evaluate and redesign your environment for learning, be sure you are establishing a balance between active and quiet areas, between small- and large-group areas, and between child-directed and adult-led activities. By *adult-led activities* we mean those where an adult is teaching a skill (such as dribbling a basketball), brainstorming ideas, role-playing, or introducing a new game or activity. Both your physical space and your planned activities should enable children to experiment, to explore, and to master concepts taught in the school day.

The environmental design and activity choices listed in this chapter are only suggestions. Using creativity, community resources, and resource materials, you can set up your learning areas to meet the individual needs of the children. When choosing materials for your program, ensure they are respectful of the diversity of families in your program and the greater community. Program designs are as unique as the children, program staff, and space.

Creating Learning-Rich Spaces for Children

A goal of any afterschool program should be to support academic performance at school. In no way, however, should your program replace school or become another school after the time spent at school. Building relationships with the school to understand the academic expectations for the children in your program is a great beginning. Talking to teachers and understanding what is being taught in a given week help you provide activities to enhance what is discussed during the day. Children often need time to practice, test, and retest theories taught during the school day.

While adults often have a say in what they will do next, children are often shuffled from one activity, subject, or program to another. Within each portion of the day, children are required to conform to preset norms and behavior expectations. While afterschool programs have behavior expectations too, children should not be forced but should rather be encouraged to participate in activities and to use the resources and materials the program offers. Just as adults who work all day need time to refocus, relax, and de-stress, so do children. Afterschool programs can be a wonderful place for children to do just that.

When designing space, remember school-age children's interests are ever changing. Re-creating spaces and rotating materials will increase the engagement of children and keep them coming back to see what is new. In chapter 4 you learned about the developmental characteristics of school-age children. Couple this knowledge with an understanding of the needs and interests of the children in your program to create a program space that is inviting and stimulating and that meets the needs of all children.

Knowing children's needs and getting their thoughts help you decide what learning areas to include and how to frame the look and feel of each area. One afterschool program, for example, let the children help design an area where they could relax and be alone. The children named the area "Cozy Corner" and made a sign that stated, "When we are in this place, we choose to be by ourselves." Another program asked children to come up with their own ideas and names for areas based on what they wanted to do while at the program. Their responses included "Come and Play with Me" for the active play space, "A+ Grades" for the homework area, and "Imagination Station" for the science and discovery area. The ideal environment reflects the mood or spirit of the children.

Organizing and Storing Materials

Keeping materials neat and organized facilitates children's learning opportunities. This can be a challenge in any school-age program. Developing a system to maintain order is essential, regardless of whether your program is in shared or dedicated space. Label shelves with both pictures and words so that nonreaders and those for whom English is not their first language can be successfully independent when choosing and returning materials to the shelf.

Photo 10.1

Tape a list of materials inside the box for games that have multiple parts so children know what items go in what game. Create an inventory of available materials and their location to help staff know where they can be found. Refer to this list when reordering and purchasing new items. Place a container labeled "Lost and Found" in the center of the program space to provide children and staff with a place to put found pieces and to look for missing pieces.

For smaller materials and consumable supplies, such as those used in arts and crafts projects, use sectioned plastic dishes. These make preparing activities easy, and they allow children easy access to materials. The sections allow you to group like materials, such as cotton balls and pom-poms, side by side while keeping them separated. Use clear plastic shower caps to cover these dishes so that materials do not fall out if tipped in storage or while setting up the environment.

Photo 10.2

This is a visual reminder for the children to place found pieces in this container and to look in the container when missing a piece to a game.

Creative Art

Art offers children the opportunity to translate their feelings into a tangible product, such as a painting, sculpture, or drawing. For this reason, children both need and deserve opportunities to learn and master skills in the arts. When planning an art project, make sure children choose to participate and are not forced to engage in that area. While some children enjoy making art projects, you do not have to plan one for every day. You may want to alternate art projects with other activities, such as cooking. Let the activity interests of the children be your guide.

As you plan your art activities, consider the ages of the children in your program and what types of resources are needed to support their learning. Regardless of how often you conduct a planned art project, creative art materials should be available to the children every day. To facilitate the creative process, you should provide a plentiful variety of materials, though not all materials may be available every day. This gives children the freedom to explore self-expression through process-based art, rather than expecting them to replicate a modeled artwork. Avoid projects where the children's end products could be judged as either right or wrong. In addition to the typical mediums of paint, clay, pencils, crayons, and markers, add materials such as fabric, sand, magazines, glue, and wood to extend the learning and offer open-ended possibilities. This allows the children to change the dimension and explore their own creativity within the art process. Providing materials such as yarn, lace, and buttons lets children embellish a painting or collage in their own unique way. If children ask for materials that are not currently out, provide these materials and you will see their creativity blossom. Supplying the requested materials enables you to connect with children and to support their creativity.

Allow children to explore various artists' techniques. Children can learn about a variety of ways to use art mediums from looking at the works of famous artists of the present and past. For example, Michelangelo laid on his back to paint the Sistine Chapel, so tape paper under a table and allow the children to create a picture while lying on their backs. Amy Shackleton uses the process of dripping and gravity to create her art pieces. Alexander Calder used the science principles of balance, symmetry, and motion as he created his world-famous mobiles. Replicating the art techniques of these and other artists combines art processes with science to create unique works of art.

You should give directions to a small group of children (no more than six). To avoid stifling creativity, limit your directions to basic expectations and guidelines they need to be successful. These might include where the project can be done, what the end goal of the project is (for example, a chalk drawing),

EXPLORING THE ART PROCESS

Plan long-term, multiday art projects for children. Giving them the opportunity to produce more complex art challenges them to delve deeper into the art process.

what materials you have provided, and the cleanup procedure. The facilitator's role is not to guide them step-by-step but to provide materials and allow them to freely create.

Always consider safety when planning an art activity. If a project requires an iron, glue gun, or other heat source, plan for extra staff supervision and reduce the size of the group doing the activity. Make sure all art products are nontoxic, and provide the proper ventilation with materials that have strong odors.

Locate the art area near a water source for easy cleanup. Ideally, the floor in the art area should be tile or another easily cleaned surface. If the floor is carpeted, cover it with a plastic covering such as a drop cloth or clear shower curtain before starting messy art projects such as painting, papier-mâché, or glitter art. Placing a rubber bath mat on the floor will help prevent children from slipping and falling if water gets on the floor. Provide paper towels so children can dry hands before going to the next activity. Placing a small amount of dishwashing liquid in tempera paint makes for easy cleanup and helps paint come out of clothes more easily.

An area for displaying children's artwork allows them to decorate their space and feel appreciated for their work. Some programs use wooden frames to display children's artwork so children understand their work is valued. One program has each family bring an eleven-by-fourteen-inch frame, and the child's name is written on the frame. Children can place their artwork in their frame and change it as often as they like. Since not all creative art projects fit in these frames, some projects are displayed in hallways or other locations in the program.

Photo 10.3

Framing children's artwork sends the message that you value it.

When your budget limits the materials you can purchase, compile a wish list and give it to parents. Ask them to purchase art supplies for the program instead of a gift for staff or to bring in their throwaways and recycled materials, such as coffee cans, egg cartons, paper towel rolls, fabric remnants, buttons, lace, and yarn. Often families have these items and are more than willing to donate them to the program rather than throwing them away. The key is telling families what you can use.

This art area in a shared space is defined with a tablecloth, and materials are organized and easily accessible to the children.

Photo 10.4

Providing smocks in the art area that can be easily reached by children allows them to be independent.

Photo 10.5

POTENTIAL LEARNING OPPORTUNITIES

Art helps children develop the following knowledge and skills:

- **Social-emotional:** self-expression through open-ended, process-based art; collaborating and cooperating on group projects; working in a variety of art mediums; self-control to finish a project
- **Physical-motor:** hand-eye coordination; small muscle development
- **Cognitive:** understanding patterns and sequences; understanding the properties of various mediums and how to use them; understanding color families, proportions, perspective, shading, and principles of composition
- **Language or communication:** self-expression through various art mediums; learning to appreciate the work of other artists; learning art vocabulary
- **Creativity:** gaining an appreciation of the arts and various art forms; using a variety of mediums in creative expression

SUGGESTED EQUIPMENT

- brushes
- child-sized table and chairs
- corkboards, three-sided boards, or display cases for children's artwork
- displays of great works of art
- drying rack
- easel (for chalk, dry-erase marker, or paint)
- hole punch
- paint jars with lids
- painting shirts, smocks, or aprons
- pottery wheel
- shelf or cart for supplies
- sponges
- trash can

SUGGESTED MATERIALS

- chalk
- clay
- construction paper (including flesh tones)
- craft sticks
- crayons, fat and thin markers, pencils, pens
- erasers and pencil sharpeners
- drawing paper, writing paper, notebooks, cardboard
- egg cartons
- fabric, felt
- feathers
- glitter
- glue, paste
- lace, pom-poms, ribbon, yarn, string
- magazines, newsprint
- margarine tub lids
- modeling materials such as clay or playdough
- modeling tools such as rolling pins, cookie cutters, and plastic knives
- newspaper
- multicultural markers, pencils, and crayons
- paint (watercolor, tempera, fingerpaint)
- paintbrushes, thick and thin
- paper: construction, tissue, newsprint, magazines, stationery, gift wrapping
- pipe cleaners
- plastic needles and blunt-end needles
- poster board
- recycled objects such as corks, buttons, twist ties, egg cartons, and milk cartons
- rubber stamps and ink stamp pads
- sand
- scissors, staplers, and staple removers
- sponges
- stencils and tracing items
- stickers
- string
- tape (various types and colors)
- wood

CREATIVE WRITING SURFACES
You can easily create your own washable, erasable surfaces on which children can draw and write. Purchase chalkboard paint and apply in many layers to walls, a tabletop, the back of a bookcase, or a wooden board. Some chalkboard paints are even magnetic if metal dust is mixed into the paint.

Blocks and Building Area

Building areas allow children to learn the math, science, and engineering concepts of spatial relationships, creativity, structure, balance, and symmetry. Design the environment of a building area with plenty of open space for unstructured building and creative expression. Ensure that the open space is large enough for more than one child to play in the area to facilitate friend-

Photo 10.6

ship building and social skill development. An area designed for building or block play can be located on the floor or on a table. Some programs use carpet or rubber mats to minimize noise, while others choose a hard surface to facilitate block play.

Provide blocks and other building materials in a variety of sizes and shapes to facilitate science and math learning opportunities. Rotate materials regularly to keep interest and learning high. Minimize arguments among children by making sure you have enough materials for the number of children who can play in the space. A good variety and quantity of materials will meet the skill levels of all the ages and abilities of the children you serve. Providing a combination of wooden blocks, Lego and Duplo sets, and K'NEX will span the small-motor development of a multiage group. The addition of accessories such as toy animals, people, cars, trucks, and traffic signs allows children to extend their construction play and fosters their creativity. Link materials in this area with the current lesson plan themes to provide children with another way to process content and extend learning. Allow children

Photo 10.7

to take pictures of their creations or allow the construction to stay up for the remainder of the day, the next day, or even the week if possible. This will foster children's pride in their creations, encourage their creativity, and provide an opportunity for them to share their creations with family and friends.

Photo 10.8

Providing a variety of construction materials allows something of interest for all children.

POTENTIAL LEARNING OPPORTUNITIES

Construction play helps children develop the following knowledge and skills:

- **Social-emotional:** collaborating, compromising, negotiating, communicating, and problem solving with peers to build and rebuild roads, buildings, and neighborhoods
- **Physical-motor:** fine-motor development, hand-eye coordination
- **Cognitive:** understanding cause and effect; understanding math principles such as proportions, equivalence, volume, geometry, and balance; understanding science and engineering principles such as gravity, mechanics, and structural integrity; incorporating math principles into three-dimensional construction projects
- **Language or communication:** communicating, cooperating, and collaborating with peers
- **Creativity:** designing and building structures, roadways, and neighborhoods

SUGGESTED EQUIPMENT

- small play mat or rug depicting a neighborhood or a raceway
- small storage containers
- storage shelf

SUGGESTED MATERIALS

- animals: bugs, dinosaurs, farm animals, zoo animals
- blocks of all kinds, including cardboard, hardwood, foam, plastic, and hollow
- boxes of all sizes
- cardboard rolls from paper towels and gift wrap
- dolls and people figures
- Erector sets
- flat wooden boards
- K'NEX
- Lego and Duplo sets
- Lincoln Logs
- model cars or boats
- plastic plumbing pipes in various sizes
- playing cards
- stacking bears
- Tinkertoys
- traffic signs
- unit blocks
- vehicles: boats, cars, planes, trucks, trains

Dramatic Play

Dramatic play gives children the opportunity to act out daily life and try out new situations in a nonjudgmental, supportive space, which helps them make sense of the world around them while building their socialization, communication, and problem-solving skills. Intentionally plan time for children to play without interruption. Provide materials that are both familiar and unfamiliar to expose children to experiences they have not had before and to help them master new skills. For instance, if you have a music store in the dramatic play area that includes instruments from around the world, children can play those they are familiar with and experiment with those they are not.

Photo 10.9

Housekeeping in dramatic play provides a familiar homelike setting where children can act out the events of the day.

Your primary role as a dramatic play facilitator is to guide and encourage children's creativity by providing a rich assortment of materials. Equip this environment with realistic materials from daily life to set the stage for learning and engagement. Be open to children's ideas, encourage them to redefine the area, and include them when adding new materials. This gives them ownership and enables you to include materials that reflect the children's specific interests. Provide materials that support small-muscle development, such as clothes, kitchen utensils, phones, writing materials, and shoes with shoestrings or fasteners. Offer opportunities for school-age children to engage in the full process of producing a play: creating sets, making costumes and props, and acting. This process teaches children that things take time. Help the children feel competent by being available as an adviser, by procuring materials, and by championing their successes.

When outfitting a dramatic play area, plan a variety of themes and then collect materials that are appropriate and related to each theme. Children are a great resource for theme ideas. The most recognized dramatic play theme is housekeeping, but other possibilities are virtually endless, limited only by your imagination. Use the following list as a starting point, and go from there when thinking of ideas for dramatic play themes:

- airport
- camping
- castle
- doctor's office
- flower shop
- grocery store
- housekeeping
- music store
- newspaper

- ocean/beach
- office
- pet shop
- pizza restaurant
- post office
- shoe store
- theater
- veterinarian's office

Once you have created a list of themes, go through them one by one and list the materials you need to gather for each theme box, or prop box, as it is sometimes called. As you develop the contents for each theme, ask the children what they think should be in the box. This gives them a leadership role in creating and exploring the topic and ensures their interest in the contents. Place an inventory list on the outside and inside of each box to indicate the contents and alert you to items missing or needing to be replenished. A sample prop box inventory list follows.

PIZZA RESTAURANT PROP BOX INVENTORY

___ three cardboard rounds
___ four small plastic plates
___ one Big Deal Pizza Shop sign
___ one container of cheese (white yarn cut into two-inch pieces)
___ one container of green pepper (green felt *C's*)
___ one container of small pepperoni (1½ inch diameter circles of red felt)
___ three pads of paper
___ three pencils
___ one "Pizza Sold Here" sign
___ red-and-white checkered tablecloth
___ three crusts (white flexible canvas)
___ three red felt rounds (tomato sauce) as large as the canvas crusts
___ two aprons
___ two menus
___ two phones
___ two pictures of pizza
___ various denominations of play money

NOTE: A liquid laundry soap box (four bottles per box size) makes a great pizza oven if you are unable to use a housekeeping oven.

If you are using a housekeeping oven, make sure the cardboard pizza rounds fit inside it.

Last date used in the program: _____

Replenished on _____ by _____

Theme boxes help keep dramatic play materials organized, but they have other benefits as well. Sometimes children need an idea to get them started in a learning area they have not explored before. Theme boxes give children clear ideas about what they will find in the dramatic play area. Theme boxes can be one way to support a child's interest, such as wanting to take pictures. Furthermore, because theme boxes for dramatic play store all materials needed for a specific theme in one place, they allow for a quick changeover of an area in a limited time.

Photo 10.10

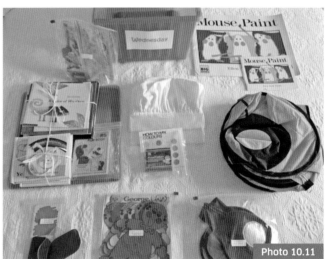

Photo 10.11

Using a variety of containers to make theme boxes allows you to choose a container that can store many or few items in each theme area.

POTENTIAL LEARNING OPPORTUNITIES

Dramatic play helps children develop the following knowledge and skills:

- **Social-emotional:** problem-solving skills; ability to feel empathy and understand others; self-esteem and self-confidence developed through role play; self-regulation developed by staying within a role
- **Physical-motor:** hand-eye coordination; fine- and large-muscle development when making and using puppets and learning to button, tie, and use zippers
- **Cognitive:** comparing and contrasting different items located in dramatic play; problem solving with peers; identifying roles; experimenting with props
- **Language or communication:** collaborating and negotiating skills with peers; determining behavior expectations through trial and error
- **Creativity:** making props; writing scripts; building sets; exploring new roles

SUGGESTED EQUIPMENT

- chest of drawers or shelving unit with containers for holding dramatic play accessories
- child-sized table and chairs
- coat tree or furniture piece for hanging dramatic play clothes
- cooking utensils
- dishes, cups, and glasses (unbreakable)
- dolls (multicultural and ones with disabilities)
- housecleaning items (brooms, feather dusters, scrub brushes)
- housekeeping items (sink, refrigerator, stove)
- living room items (child-sized sofa, end tables, upholstered chair, coffee table, table or floor lamp, decorative or floor pillows, CD player for listening to music)
- mirror, full-length (unbreakable)
- puppet theater
- other equipment needed to support theme ideas

SUGGESTED MATERIALS

- aprons
- computer keyboards
- costumes for play performances
- dress-up clothes (male and female) that represent multiple cultures, family types, and careers
- empty food cartons and tin cans
- hats (male and female)
- items related to various careers or the greater community
- magazines and books
- masks
- multicultural items such as clothing and cooking items
- paper and pencils
- phones, real and play or old (nonworking) cell phones (have more than one)
- place mats
- play food (make sure to include ethnic food as well)
- puppets (hand, finger, sock, marionette)
- purses
- scarves
- shoes (male and female)
- suitcases, briefcases, and cloth shopping bags
- sunglasses
- toolbox
- writing paper and pencil

Cooking Activities

Cooking is a fun way to model good nutrition habits and help children learn life skills such as preparing food, reading a recipe, and learning the difference between a teaspoon and a tablespoon. Cooking activities also allow children to experience new foods and discuss food origins. Inviting families to share their favorite food is a great way to get them involved in the program and provides opportunities for children to learn about each other.

Locate cooking activities close to a water source for hand washing, food preparation, and cleanup. If your program is licensed by a state or local agency, check to see what, if any, requirements exist for preparing food with the children in your program. If a commercial kitchen is available in your space, make sure you have permission to use it and know the cleanup procedures. Above all else, safety should be considered first when planning cooking activities. To maintain safety, work with small groups of no more than six children and at least one adult. This ensures the children's use of equipment is monitored carefully and the adult can provide more individual attention. Ensure sanitary conditions for preparing and serving food by providing a clean work space and establishing hand-washing rules. Selecting recipes that produce a single-serving snack can also help maintain sanitary conditions since each child makes and eats his own.

Facilitate cooking activities by providing a recipe and the necessary ingredients and equipment. You can provide cooking experiences that range from simple trail mix, which requires no heating element, to a full meal. Select the recipes based on the physical and cognitive abilities of the children. For example, you may want to have recipes that includes pictures for children with limited reading skills, recipes that do not require cutting or the use of an oven for younger children, and recipes that do not require mixing or small measurements for children with limited small-motor skills. Allow children to read the recipe, measure ingredients, mix, and cook according to directions. For children who are learning to read, provide verbal instruction or use a large-print storyboard with pictures and words to enable independent cooking activities.

Help ensure that cooking is a positive experience for everyone by establishing clear behavior expectations. In addition to hand washing, children should clean up after themselves, washing the utensils and dishes they use. This is not the responsibility of staff. Give children a clear message that when you dirty dishes, you clean them. This expectation also gives children a sense of responsibility and ownership in the program. Likewise, allowing children to make their own snack gives them ownership of their food choices and portion sizes. Decorating cookies and cupcakes and displaying vegetables and fruit are opportunities for children to be creative and express themselves.

A RECIPE FOR SUCCESS
Help ensure successful cooking experiences for both staff and children by working in small groups of no more than six children and at least one adult per group.

POTENTIAL LEARNING OPPORTUNITIES

Cooking helps children develop the following knowledge and skills:

- **Social-emotional:** working cooperatively; taking turns; experiencing self-esteem from a project well done and self-control by following cooking area rules and finishing a project
- **Physical-motor:** small- and large-muscle development as children measure, stir, mix, sift, pour, squeeze, mold, and crack eggs
- **Cognitive:** understanding the properties of different cooking materials; predicting what will happen next; problem solving; observing changes in physical shape, volume, and texture; understanding cause and effect; understanding differences in the measurement of dry and liquid materials; understanding and following a sequence
- **Language or communication:** reading and interpreting step-by-step directions; learning cooking vocabulary; experiencing a new type of written communication
- **Creativity:** experimenting with foods and food preparation; decorating and arranging foods for display

SUGGESTED EQUIPMENT

- cookie cutters
- cookie sheets
- cutting boards
- electric mixer, blender, or food processor
- electric slow cooker
- hairnets or disposable hats
- heat source (hot plate, electric skillet, griddle, microwave, stove, toaster oven, or oven)
- measuring spoons and cups
- mixing spoons and bowls
- pans and skillet
- plastic knives (pumpkin carving knives work well)
- rolling pin
- table and chairs
- vegetable peelers

SUGGESTED MATERIALS

- child-sized aprons
- cookbooks, recipe boards
- food needed for cooking projects

Indoor Play

Indoor games bring children enjoyment, offer opportunities to build both large and small muscles, and develop higher-level thinking skills. This area includes both large-motor activities and tabletop games. Ensure that children can participate in large-motor activities each day—even when the weather is too inclement for outdoor play. Indoor activities can be adult directed or child initiated. The ideal space for large-motor activities is a large open area with seamless flooring and bright ambient lighting. It should be large enough to support active games for all of the children in your program. This space can be located in your primary program space or in another room in your building. When an alternate space is not available, some programs use the hallway to play eraser shuffleboard, trash can basketball, and balloon volleyball. In such a case, you may have to rotate children into and out of the hallway so it does not become overcrowded and unsafe. Think creatively about the space you have to determine different ways to use it for active game play. Make modifications to tried-and-true games and to children's favorites to adapt them for play in the space you have.

Choose games that both challenge them and develop specific skills, such as communicating and problem solving. Rotate games to keep children engaged, and include cultural games such as Mancala, Nine Men's Morris, pick-up sticks, Chinese jump rope, and hopscotch. This allows the children to experience a variety of games and to learn that some of their favorite games have origins in other countries. Balance competitive with noncompetitive games, such as charades, and with group activities, like a scavenger hunt that requires the children to work as a team. Providing a variety of choices helps children become independent. Help children find and return materials and supplies to the correct place by labeling where various items go, and then instill the expectation in them to be responsible for the materials.

Tabletop games can include purchased boxed games and those made by the staff or children. Children can create new games, adapt old ones, or decide how the game will end. Using a simple deck of cards and their imagination, children can create a new card game or make changes to a favorite game. Staff and children can make board games using discarded game pieces and lightweight poster board (sometimes referred to as *oak tag*) or a file folder. Write down the new game rules and share them with others. This tells the children you value their ideas.

Adults playing games with children provides time for conversation, turn taking, and teaching game rules.

Photo 10.12

Photo 10.13

Children playing together learn communication skills, friendship making, strategy, and negotiation.

Board games can be a simple fifteen-minute activity or can be played for weeks in a championship or an Olympics fashion. To keep all items together for a game, make sure to repair ripped boxes or place all pieces together in a resealable plastic bag. Labeling the bags with the name of the game and the number of pieces helps children to know what pieces go with each game and makes cleanup easier.

When introducing any new game, make an announcement that you have placed a new game in that area and explain the rules of the game. Explain the game often or post the game rules during the first few days. Be available to answer questions about the game. Remember that not everyone plays a game your way. Find out if any of the children have played the game before, and get an understanding of how they played it. Let the children decide what version they want to play. Save other versions for another day or another group of children.

POTENTIAL LEARNING OPPORTUNITIES

Indoor play helps children develop the following knowledge and skills:

- **Social-emotional:** taking turns, encouraging peers, following rules, gracefully accepting winning and losing, taking risks, pursuing opportunities to socialize with others, developing responsibility to find and put away games and to take care them

- **Physical-motor:** developing small muscles by picking up pieces, moving pieces on the board, placing puzzle pieces, rolling dice, spinning a spinner, holding multiple cards at one time, shuffling, dealing cards; developing large muscles by throwing, catching, and running
- **Cognitive:** Setting rules and understanding rules, problem solving, recognizing spatial relationships, anticipating consequences, using strategy
- **Language or communication:** engaging in conversation, reading rules, listening to others
- **Creativity:** creating new games, developing new rules, adapting games for different settings and situations

SUGGESTED EQUIPMENT

- air hockey table
- balance beam
- basketball hoop (for indoors and adjustable)
- beanbags
- cones
- exercise mat
- foosball table
- hopscotch mat
- hula hoops
- parachute
- pool table (can be tabletop)
- ring toss
- sensory table
- table tennis table (can be tabletop)

SUGGESTED MATERIALS

- board games
  - checkers
  - chess
  - Clue
  - Connect Four
  - dominoes

- Life
- mah-jongg
- Mastermind
- Scrabble (junior and regular)
- Stratego
- TriBond
- Trouble
- card games
  - regular decks of cards to use for the games above and for games such as rummy, golf, and Kings in the Corner
  - specialized decks of cards for Crazy Eights, Go Fish, Old Maid, and Uno

Music and Movement

Exposing children to a broad variety of music and dance helps them to appreciate different styles of music and music that originates in various cultures. Introduce the children to instruments from around the world. Hearing new sounds and experiencing the beat expands children's knowledge of the many ways to make music and can spark their imagination to create their own musical instrument. Invite parents and community members to the program to share their musical or dance talents. Ask a dancer from the local ballet company or a parent who teaches dance to help children experience dance and promote lifelong interest in music and dance. Make sure your music and movement area has an open space that is large enough to accommodate dancing. Locate the area away from quiet activities and homework.

Equip the music area with a variety of prescreened recorded music and playback equipment. Include cultural, classical, and folk music as well as current music favored by the children. Encourage children to bring in music to share with the group. Always prescreen all audio media to ensure you are eliminating any undesired words, offensive lyrics, or descriptions of behaviors that are unacceptable or too mature for the children in your care. Secure playback equipment such as MP3 players, CD players, and multi-touch players to large pieces of wood or plastic so children do not walk away with equipment when they leave the program space. These types of digital players should have earphones that are easy to disinfect. Children should keep their own players at home to minimize the chance of loss and breakage. Some children enjoy listening to music while doing homework or just relaxing. If you provide this option, make sure children have earphones so as not to disturb others. Karaoke machines are very popular with children in school-age programs. They allow children to sing along with the music as words are displayed for them to follow along. Having a karaoke party is fun and allows children (and staff) to test and display their musical talents.

In addition to equipment for music listening, provide children with instruments to make their own music. Include a variety of instruments, and allow the children to experiment with creating different sounds, beats, rhythms, and tempos. Store the instruments on low shelves to help prevent falls and include multiples whenever possible so that more than one child can play at a time. Teach the children how to operate and care for the instruments.

Encourage creativity in both music and dance. Often children will create wonderful music and lyrics when given the opportunity. Provide blank music staff paper for the children to compose their own music. Encourage children to make their own instrument using gourds, buckets, boxes, sticks, sandpaper, and rubber bands. The variation of sounds that can be created is inspiring. Be open to other items the children would like to use to make instruments. Store these materials in a container in the music area so that children are free to create and modify creations. Experimentation with a variety of materials helps children understand the creation and manipulation of sound. For dancers, include a variety of costumes and props, such as streamers, scarves, and ribbons. Encourage children to choreograph dance moves to different types of music. Dance is also a great way to encourage large-muscle development and physical activity.

These three girls are collaborating to make music that includes beat, rhythm, tempo, and timbre.

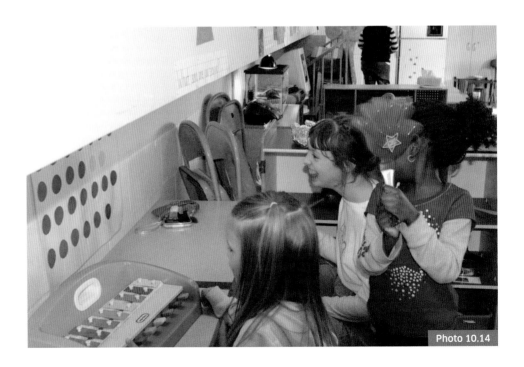

Photo 10.14

Music and movement helps children develop the following knowledge and skills:

- **Social-emotional:** building community by dancing, singing, and enjoying music together; appreciating music and dance as a means to soothe, relax, and relieve stress; expressing emotions through music and dance
- **Physical-motor:** developing large muscles when dancing, developing fine motor skills when playing instruments
- **Cognitive:** gaining an appreciation for a variety of music and dance styles; recognizing differences in pitch, rhythm, timbre, and mood; understanding the role of cause and effect in creating various sounds; understanding spatial awareness
- **Language or communication:** creating lyrics, setting words to music, relaying meaning and feelings through dance
- **Creativity:** telling stories through music and dance, expressing emotions through music and dance, writing lyrics, composing music, choreographing dance moves, making musical instruments

SUGGESTED EQUIPMENT

- bells and rhythm sticks
- CD players
- CD storage rack
- headphones
- instruments from around the world or made by children
- karaoke machine
- keyboard or piano
- microphones
- storage cabinet or low shelves
- tambourines
- triangles and cymbals
- xylophone

- dance outfits
- dance props, such as streamers, ribbons, fans, and scarves
- dance shoes (tap, jazz, and ballet)
- music staff paper (blank)
- paper, pencils, and pens
- prerecorded music (jazz, classical, opera, big band, ethnic, popular, children's songs)
- recordable blank CDs
- sheet music
- songbooks with notes and words to encourage singing along and playing an instrument

Small-Muscle Manipulatives and Sensory Play

Sensory and manipulative activities are especially beneficial to children—both younger and older—who have not had sufficient opportunities to develop their small muscles. Not everyone who comes to your program will have had experiences digging in dirt or sand or playing at a water table, nor will everyone be able to hold a pencil correctly or lace beads. Manipulative and sensory play allows children to understand the attributes of everyday materials while developing small-muscle control and hand-eye coordination. Through sensory exploration, children experiment, test, and develop theories about the various materials offered. Manipulatives encourage the development of hand-eye coordination and of small muscles used in writing, cutting, and pincer movements as children stack blocks, put together puzzles, and move their markers around a game board.

Items that require use of small muscles and hand-eye coordination are typically found throughout afterschool programs. Math counters can be placed in the homework area, and puzzles, lacing cards, and playing cards can be placed in the game (or indoor play) area. Dominoes, Legos, and foam and hardwood blocks can be placed in the construction area; and musical instruments, in the music area. Activities such as craft and cooking projects also develop small-muscle movement.

Keep all manipulative materials in small, sturdy, see-through containers located on easily accessible shelves to encourage children to use them independently. The containers should be small enough for children to be able to move them easily to a table or floor space and return them to the shelf when they are finished. Manipulatives can be used by one child or in small groups, so provide enough materials to facilitate uninterrupted play and reduce arguments among children. Label all activity containers with the name and a picture of the contents along with a simple written description of the activity. This type of labeling allows children to independently find what they would like to play with. Rotate these materials often to maintain interest. Using small containers will make rotating the materials easy and also allow you to quickly see if additional materials need to be added.

A sensory play area provides additional small-muscle opportunities while also allowing children to engage in experimenting, testing, and developing theories about the variety of sensory materials offered. You can stage these experiences in a variety of ways, depending on your space and your resources. Options include a manufactured sensory table, individual plastic containers, a small plastic swimming pool, and a sandbox. Sand, bubbles, snow, pea gravel, plastic grass, water, dirt, shells, pinecones, and leaves are examples of great sensory materials. If you fill a sensory table with sand, a child will learn its properties, such as volume, weight, and texture, and how fast it moves through a funnel or sieve. In water play, children learn that certain things float while others sink. These explorations can be the beginning of an interest in science later in life.

Photo 10.15

Facilitate children's sensory exploration by asking open-ended questions and providing extended time for children to learn by trial and error. Observe children's progress, and be prepared to enrich a sensory activity by adding additional objects or changing the medium to expand the children's knowledge. For instance, if you start out with dry sand and a variety of tools such as funnels, sieves, cups, and spoons in the sensory table, the children learn that sand flows through these implements with ease. When you add water to the sand, you create another aspect to the sand play that will challenge the child's thinking about how sand flows

Photo 10.16

Sensory materials can provide children with opportunities for exploration and an introduction to scientific concepts.

through the funnel. They soon will understand that wet sand does not flow as easily as dry sand. Rotating sensory materials and adding other dimensions to them builds interest and provides additional learning opportunities.

POTENTIAL LEARNING OPPORTUNITIES

Small manipulative and sensory play helps children develop the following knowledge and skills:

- **Social-emotional:** making friends and socializing while working side by side, sharing, community building while working together
- **Physical-motor:** developing small motor muscles by sifting, measuring, pouring, squeezing, and molding
- **Cognitive:** understanding the properties of different sensory materials; developing and testing theories; experimenting; predicting what will happen; problem solving; observing changes in physical shape, volume, and texture
- **Language or communication:** explaining processes, discussing and comparing results with peers and staff
- **Creativity:** experimenting with sensory materials; using support materials, such as funnels and sieves, in innovative ways

SUGGESTED EQUIPMENT

- easy-to-clean floor covering (vinyl drop cloth)
- plastic tubs or sensory table
- shelves
- storage containers
- tables and chairs

- artificial plastic and silk flowers, petals, and leaves
- balls in various sizes
- beads (various sizes)
- boats that float
- bubble liquid and various sizes of bubble wands
- buckets, scoops, shovels, spoons
- cups
- Easter grass
- funnels (various sizes)
- items that sink and float
- jewelry-making materials: string and items that can be strung together, such as metal nuts, buttons, or plastic straws cut into one-inch pieces
- lacing cards
- leaves
- nuts and bolts (various sizes)

- pea gravel
- Peg-Boards
- pinecones
- plastic cups
- plastic interworking gears
- playdough
- potholder-making materials
- potting soil/dirt
- puzzles (of various difficulty)
- sand
- shells
- sieves, strainers
- snow (artificial or real)
- things to sort and count such as counting bears, plastic bugs, buttons, shells, and different colored milk jug lids
- watering cans
- waterwheels
- weaving loom

KEYS TO WOOD-WORKING SAFETY
- Review safety rules before every activity.
- Demonstrate proper use of tools before every activity.
- Use safety equipment, including goggles and nail aprons.
- Place a rubber bath mat or carpet square on the work surface.
- Always have an adult in the area during activities.

Woodworking

Woodworking provides an outlet for creativity as children take an idea and use wood to make a three-dimensional representation. In addition, woodworking develops hand-eye coordination and large- and small-muscle movements. Safety is paramount in woodworking endeavors. Set the tone of "safety first" from the very beginning. If you feel uncomfortable in this role, bring in a person knowledgeable in woodworking—a parent or a local cabinetmaker—to explain safety rules and demonstrate the proper use of tools. Safety goggles and tools sized for children enable them to be creative in a safe environment. Ensure successful experiences by modeling, actively teaching, and posting safety rules and proper use of tools at all times.

Stock your woodworking area with a variety of sizes, types, thicknesses, and shapes of wood. Often you can obtain wood for free or a reduced price by asking parents, builders, carpenters, the local hardware store, or lumberyards. Be sure that the wood you acquire is not coated with toxic chemicals such as creosote, lead-based paint, or other potentially harmful substances. Provide plenty of nails, sandpaper, screws, glue, wood, and tools so children are not limited by the amount or variety of materials. Equip the area with real tools in children's sizes to help ensure success.

For children who have not done woodworking before, start small by letting them begin with a sheet of Styrofoam, a hammer, and golf tees. This activity helps children become familiar with a hammer and what it can do. Hammering roofing nails into a large tree stump is another beginner project. Have children place a rubber mat or carpet square under the object they are working on to cut down on noise, preserve tabletops, and keep items from slipping when they are pounding or sawing.

Once children have mastered the fundamentals of woodworking, you can set up more advanced projects, such as birdhouses, treasure boxes, table trivets, and jewelry boxes. An adult must be in the area at all times to assist the children and ensure safety. If you or another staff member cannot do this, ask family members interested in woodworking or employees at your local lumber company if they can help.

Learning and practicing skills help children develop a love of woodworking. Using real tools and making usable items give children a sense of purpose and productivity. Extend their learning by encouraging them to use art supplies such as paint, glitter, and string to personalize their wooden creations. These additional materials help make the project more open-ended, giving children the freedom to create, take their projects apart, re-create, and make a wooden sculpture that is uniquely theirs, limited only by the supplies provided and their imaginations.

Providing woodworking activities inside and out with appropriate tools and materials enhances the experience for children.

Photo 10.17

Photo 10.18

POTENTIAL LEARNING OPPORTUNITIES

Woodworking helps children develop the following knowledge and skills:

- **Social-emotional:** developing self-esteem and a sense of pride from successful use of tools and from displays of completed projects, working collaboratively, sharing tools, developing a hobby that can provide relaxation and an outlet for coping
- **Physical-motor:** developing large- and small-muscle skills, developing hand-eye coordination
- **Cognitive:** problem solving; understanding balance, cause and effect, and the properties and limits of materials; understanding the need for safety and the use of safety materials such as goggles and nail aprons
- **Language or communication:** increasing vocabulary by learning new words related to woodworking, using new vocabulary to describe their work and the names of tools and supplies that are needed for their next project, compiling written lists of materials needed, completing drawings of projects with labeled parts
- **Creativity:** thinking creatively, expressing self and problem solving to produce embellished wooden objects

SUGGESTED EQUIPMENT

- chisels
- clamps
- coping saw
- golf tees (two inches long)
- hammers (thirteen to sixteen ounces)
- miter box
- nail aprons
- pliers
- rack for hanging tools or a toolbox
- rubber mats or carpet squares to place on tables underneath wood projects (bathtub mats work great)
- safety goggles, both child- and adult-sized
- screwdrivers (Phillips and straight-head)
- Styrofoam sheets, three to four inches thick
- T square
- tape measures (twenty feet)
- vise or vise grips
- woodworking space, table, or bench

- nails and screws (variety of sizes)
- paintbrushes in assorted sizes
- sandpaper of various grades
- scraps of wood (two to ten inches)
- self-adhesive letters
- short pieces of lumber (twelve to eighteen inches)
- tree stump
- various art supplies, such as string, feathers, glitter, yarn, fabric scraps, and beads
- water-based paints in a variety of colors
- wood glue

Quiet Social Area

School-agers are social creatures. They love to hang out with friends, gossip, and giggle; sometimes they like to just *be*. Children need a quiet place to be alone, unwind, and socialize. Friends become an important factor in school-age children's lives. They need to be liked and part of a group. A priority in your environment must be to create places that support this aspect of their growth. A quiet social area requires materials and furnishings that create a cozy, homelike environment. A comfortable temperature, warm lighting, and soft furnishings help children feel safe and relaxed. Having a sense of safety and privacy helps children learn to trust others and increases their ability to socialize with friends. In this quiet space, children can be social without the expectation of being involved in an activity. School-agers want the space to be about them and what they like.

Locate this space apart from the active areas and closer to quieter activities. Places somewhat private or off the beaten track meet children's need to take a break from large groups for a while and can even be used to get back their self-control. These spaces should always be within the staff's line of sight and easily supervised.

Have children help design the space so they feel a sense of belonging and want to go to there and chill. Use comfortable furniture, beanbag chairs, floor pillows, and gym mats to provide a relaxed feel. Some programs use crib mattresses—either singly or clustered together—for quiet (and movable) spaces. Covering the mattresses with crib sheets makes them colorful and easy to keep clean. Hang posters that the children connect with; this goes a long way in promoting their sense of feeling valued and accepted. Provide

Quiet spaces provide places for the children to relax and socialize.

journals and diaries to encourage children's creative writing and reflection. Journals also provide an opportunity for children to de-stress and regain control. Put out reading materials of interest to children but different from the typical library books, such as age-appropriate newspapers and magazines; these materials create a different feel to your quiet social space and expand children's knowledge of the world around them. Older children like games that provide challenge, so supply higher-level thinking games, such as checkers, Stratego, Blokus, Brain Quest, and chess. Posting a riddle or logic problem for them to solve will engage them while challenging their thinking. Be sure to announce the names of those who participated in the activity (and the correct answer) in the parent newsletter or post the list in the parent center. You can store these games on a shelf within your program space, but children should be able to take them to different areas of the room. These games should be rotated in and out of the program to maintain interest.

If your program includes older children, usually ages nine to eighteen, you may choose to create an additional quiet space for them located in a more private, yet easily supervised, area. By providing a more private area for older children, you establish trust and send the message that you know they can conduct themselves appropriately. Furnishings and resources for this area need to reflect the ages, the interests, and even the personalities of the older children. Make the area feel older and different from the rest of the program. Include games that require a higher level of knowledge to indicate you know they are no longer in primary grades, while challenging their thinking and increasing their problem-solving skills. Place age-appropriate, prescreened music as well as acceptable posters in this space to encourage older children

PERSONALIZING WALLS IN SHARED SPACE
If you are unable to attach posters to the walls in your program space, glue them to foam core boards and place them in the quiet social area when setting up the space. The boards can easily be stored on top of a storage unit.

to come to your program. Include the local newspaper and magazines to help connect the children with the events in their community.

Remember that older children want to feel valued and like to do activities with a purpose. Provide them with opportunities for peer mentoring, tutoring, and community service to make your program a place where they feel valued and important. Older children often love to be with a large group of peers. The physical environment can support these children by providing a variety of spaces that allow for many activities that might be of interest to them, such as drama, dance, media design, and service projects for the greater community. Use community service projects to increase their understanding of others and their ability to make a difference in the world around them. In addition, community service projects provide opportunities to take on leadership roles and a sense of being valued in the local community.

POTENTIAL LEARNING OPPORTUNITIES

The quiet/social area helps children develop the following knowledge and skills:

- **Social-emotional:** friend-making skills; listening; establishing trust with peers; sharing information; feeling secure; building community; feeling empathy and compassion for each other and for community service recipients; gaining a sense of connectedness to the local, national, and international communities through print
- **Physical-motor:** developing small muscles
- **Cognitive:** understanding of game strategy, rules, and cause and effect; gaining an awareness of local and world events through newspapers and magazines
- **Language or communication:** broadening literacy skills through non-traditional reading materials
- **Creativity:** journaling, writing stories and plays, composing poems

SUGGESTED EQUIPMENT

- area rugs
- beanbag chairs
- carpeted area
- ceiling drop or canopy, such as see-through netting, fabric swag, kite
- child-chosen acceptable posters
- computer

- floor mats
- floor pillows
- semi-enclosed structure with clear line of sight to the inside (such as a small tent or a cutaway cardboard appliance box)
- soft furniture (couch, overstuffed chair, crib mattress)
- tables and chairs

SUGGESTED MATERIALS

- games for older children: chess, Blokus, Brain Quest, Stratego, Monopoly
- games for younger children: Clue, checkers, charades, Candyland, Chutes and Ladders, Scatergories, Boggle
- headphones and equipment to play recorded music
- journals and writing tools
- logic problems
- magazines (teen, auto, model, computer, comic)
- newspaper (local)
- prescreened music
- variety of games, including higher-level thinking games

Media and Technology Area

Media and technology are a part of children's everyday lives, and media literacy has become an essential skill set. Access to media devices can support a child's learning, but it can also provide inappropriate images and knowledge. Taking this into consideration will guide you as you include media opportunities as part of the activities you provide. That being said, it is important children have access to computers and other technology in your program. School-age staff need to be receptive to the use of computers in the program. Often children are more educated about the use of the computers than adults; let them teach you. Invite a parent proficient in computer software and keyboarding or someone from a local newspaper to talk to the children about how to use the computer to write an article or to research information. Computers are great tools to maximize learning and provide many up-to-date learning resources.

Children can use computers to play games or to write school papers, poems, stories, and newsletters. If children can access the Internet on your program computers, be sure to install a firewall or cyber nanny to limit their access to inappropriate websites. Some afterschool programs have educational software already installed on computers; some have word-processing programs and editing software; still others allow the children to choose a learning game to upload from a prescreened collection of CD-ROMs or some other external storage device.

If you do not have funds to purchase a computer, try contacting families and local businesses to ask for a donation when they upgrade their computers. If you receive any donated computers, check that the hard drives have been completely wiped of all previous files and operating systems to ensure that children do not discover inappropriate information. You (or a computer technician) will then need to install operating systems and software programs, including antivirus software.

Some school-age programs use multi-touch mobile devices because they are portable, allowing the children to move units from space to space. The use of a pictured menu allows nonreaders to navigate this system. If you choose multi-touch devices, purchase a childproof storage unit to protect your investment. Other programs prefer desktop computers because they are larger, stationary, and tend to last longer.

Facilitate the children's use of technology by training them how to use the computer and explaining what can and cannot be done. Post simple instructions in words and pictures near the computer to help the children when they get stuck or forget how to operate it. For some children, the use of a computer for communication is an everyday occurrence; however, for children who have physical or cognitive challenges, staff may need to provide additional instructions on the appropriate use of the computer. Children may increase their written communication when they use the computer to create stories and poetry, complete a school report, or put together a program newsletter. Older children have great fun when they can use their creativity to design computer games.

Video recorders and digital cameras are popular ways to document activities and events in the program, and letting children use this equipment empowers them and builds ownership in the program. Taking pictures and videos is a great way to engage older children. Children and staff can snap a photo or record a performance, a game, or children at play to share with families. Teach the children the proper use of digital equipment. Using a tripod minimizes fuzzy pictures and videos that move too quickly from one spot to another. Provide editing software to enable children to be creative as they illustrate stories and poems, add pictures to the program website or newsletter, or make creative changes to the final product. You should have a photo release before posting or sharing children's images in your written or digital information.

The idea of using television in an afterschool program is controversial. Parents and staff have different ideas of what is appropriate television or movie watching. So much of what children watch depends on their age as well as their temperament and interests. We do not advocate putting children in front of a television unless it is tied to a learning objective. Using small clips that help teach a skill or reinforce a lesson theme is a great way to enhance learning. Some organizations have policies about the use of television during the program time. If your program is affiliated with an organization, check to see what the policies are before using television or movies in your program. When selecting television programs or movies to enhance learning, view the entire program before the children do to ensure it meets the desired learning outcome.

Research published by the American Academy of Pediatricians (AAP) indicates the amount of time children spend in front of equipment with screens has an effect on their development, attention span, behavior, and rates of obesity (AAP 2013). School-age children can become more attached to screens and other battery-driven devices than to peers or adults. For some children, what they see on the screen is more exciting than any other activity, often leading them to spend more and more time fixated on these digital devices. Although some screen time is educational, much of what children view is not. The AAP recommends children's total media time for games and entertainment should be limited to fewer than two hours a day (2013). The amount of time a child in a school-age program spends in front of a screen may be difficult to monitor. To curb screen time, create and display policies and procedures. Following are some suggestions:

- Display your commitment to following the AAP's daily recommendation of fewer than two hours a day of screen time. For example, a posted sign might read, "We care about the health and well-being of children and subscribe to the recommendation from the American Academy of Pediatrics that children spend fewer than two hours a day in front of any device with a screen."
- Provide exciting and challenging activities that are screen-free.
- Plug in or bring out devices with screens for a limited period of time each day.
- Limit both the number and locations of devices with screens.
- Set filters on computers or install only software programs with an educational focus.
- Require children to log in and out after using plugged-in devices to monitor their screen time.
- Set a good example and establish the expectation that all children and adults (including visitors and parents) will turn off cell phones and other portable screen devices while in your program space.

Photo 10.22

Computer areas can provide a space where children can create plays and poems and tap into a variety of learning games to support their academic success.

Photo 10.23

POTENTIAL LEARNING OPPORTUNITIES

Media and technology help children develop the following knowledge and skills:

- **Social-emotional:** collaborating and negotiating with peers while playing games, building community by sharing photos and videos of the program, gaining self-esteem from the value others express for digital documentation of the program
- **Physical-motor:** developing small-motor skills by using electronic devices, typing on a computer keyboard, and operating a mouse
- **Cognitive:** developing strategy and understanding cause and effect while playing computer games; sorting, comparing, classifying, problem solving, and using higher-level thinking skills when using educational software; gaining spatial awareness and understanding lighting, composition, and symmetry when taking pictures or filming events
- **Language or communication:** communicating while working together to write stories, poems, plays, newsletters, and articles and while filming presentations or editing video
- **Creativity:** creating stories, plays, poems; editing photos and videos; laying out newsletters; illustrating stories; creating computer games

- cameras, disposable or digital
- CD/DVD burner
- chairs and tables
- computers
- headphones
- multi-touch mobile devices
- printer
- scanner
- storage cabinet or shelves
- television
- tripod (height adjustable)
- video camera

SUGGESTED MATERIALS

- copy paper
- external computer storage device, such as a flash drive, portable hard drive, compact flash or SD (secure digital) card
- paper, pencils, and pens
- photo albums
- photo paper
- recordable DVDs and CDs

Math, Literacy, and Science

Many children are curious about the how and why of their environment. School-age programs provide an opportunity to experiment in a fun and non-judgmental way with ideas and concepts taught during the school day. This interweaving of math, literacy, and science into your program helps instill in children a lifelong love of learning and establishes a foundation for the higher-level thinking required as they continue on in school and in life. You do not need to be an expert in science, math, or literacy. Bring in experts from local schools, park districts, businesses, and libraries to help maximize children's understanding and learning. Tapping into these community resources will help you expand your activities and connect the community to your program. Develop a partnership with schools to share information and support the learning of the children enrolled in your program.

Plan some projects that combine math, literacy, and science. For example, have children take apart old radios, computers, and electrical appliances with the cords removed. This allows them to see inside and look at parts that make the appliance work. Have children use reference books to guide them as they take apart machines, radios, and other small appliances. Incorporate math by having children sort and count the various parts. Once several items have been taken apart, have children create a new appliance using the parts they have sorted. Incorporate literacy by having children write an advertisement describing their new product. Extend this activity further by having them create a short commercial.

MATH

Math is everywhere, which makes it easy to include real-life math situations in your program. Have children determine how many plates and napkins are needed for snack or how much money is needed for a field trip. Have children conduct a bake sale, and let them help decide how to use the profits. From this they learn how to budget money, how to research the cost of items, and how to get the most out of their dollars. Preparing items for the bake sale gives them practice using fractions. Baking is also a good way to help children understand the scientific changes in materials as they mix different ingredients together. Transition times offer another great opportunity to include math activities. While the children line up to transition to another area or activity, use math facts to keep them engaged while waiting; they are learning without knowing it. Equip the math area with manipulatives such as counters and handheld calculators to help children become independent and successful when doing math problems.

LITERACY

To support literacy development, design a print-rich program environment. Label shelves with pictures and words to help children associate the written word with the picture. Provide reading materials for a variety of ages, interests, and proficiency levels. Display books in bilingual formats, especially if you have any children whose first language is not English. Place printed materials throughout your program; for example, place books about building in the construction area and books about various creative processes in the art area. Change reading materials frequently to expose children to various formats, authors, and interest areas. All types of written materials, from the local newspaper to picture books, encourage the exploration of words and can

Photo 10.24

kindle a love of reading. The public library is a great resource. A librarian can put together a collection that meets the children's needs.

Facilitate writing by providing creative opportunities in a nonjudgmental environment. Encourage the children to write poems, plays, and stories. Suggest that they write their own stories based on what they see in a picture book, or plan specific story starters to inspire creative writing. These can be as simple as a picture that the children use as a starting point to write a story. A more complex story starter might address a bullying situation; ask the children to write how they would handle it.

Some programs use journaling for children to write about their feelings or to give input about the program. If you would like to use journal writing but cannot persuade the children to visit your literacy area, have them make their own journals. They can bring in their favorite cereal box to make a cover. Cut the box into two pieces and trim each slightly larger than paper size. Then take blank paper or filler paper (depending on the age of the children), punch holes through the cereal box covers and the paper, and tie the journal together with string. Covers can also be made from cardboard. This method allows children to decorate their own covers, making them uniquely theirs. Encourage children to journal for pleasure and relaxation. They can draw, write stories, or describe their day or how they feel about a certain situation. Ask them

Books displayed for easy viewing encourage children to use the reading area.

to express what changes they think are needed in your program. Set up a bin marked "Read My Journal" for children to share what they have written. If they do not want you to read a journal entry, tell them to fold the page over to signal that it is private.

SCIENCE

Some programs struggle to bring in science, yet it can be the easiest subject to include when planning activities. Watching seeds grow, studying erosion, and observing tadpoles become frogs are all science in action. Experiments such as estimating how much time it will take an ice cube to melt or guessing whether a pound of feathers or a pound of rocks will hit the ground first if dropped from the same height at the same time inspire children's enthusiasm. You can spark a lifelong interest in science when you provide these types of activities. Have children talk about or write down what they saw or what they think will happen next. Facilitate science activities by preparing easy-to-read instructions. Assign an adult to the science area if close supervision is needed when conducting an experiment. If possible, conduct science experiments near a water source to facilitate cleanup. Follow the steps in the scientific process: ask a question, research the topic, form a hypothesis, test it, analyze the data, draw a conclusion, and communicate the results. Often when an experiment flops, it can be the best opportunity to learn by trial and error. Let children repeat experiments to see if they get different results. Have them document experiments and then compare their process and results with those of their peers. (For additional science activities, see Outdoor Play later in this chapter.)

POTENTIAL LEARNING OPPORTUNITIES

Math, literacy, and science help children develop the following knowledge and skills:

- **Social-emotional:** expressing feelings, sharing and comparing information with others, communicating through appropriate verbal and written means, learning the process of trial and error, learning self-control by staying within available material resources or within the bounds of an experiment
- **Physical-motor:** developing fine-motor skills by using writing utensils and math manipulatives and materials such as a calculator, geoboard, tangrams, rulers, protractors, and compasses

Photo 10.25

Photo 10.26

Programs that offer areas that support academic subjects allow children to practice, test, and apply theories taught at school.

Create a handmade valentine for a soldier this Valentine's Day.

VALENTINES ♥FOR♥TROOPS♥

Our soldiers need to know that we love them, miss them and support them!

Photo 10.27

- **Cognitive:** computing, budgeting, estimating, measuring, theorizing, predicting, comparing, classifying, sequencing, analyzing, observing cause and effect, recognizing shapes and numbers, understanding standard and metric measurements
- **Language or communication:** reading for pleasure and information; journaling; writing creatively; writing to communicate information; documenting feelings, observations, scientific processes, and results
- **Creativity:** writing poems, stories, and plays; creating advertisements and commercials; engaging in creative thought processes such as theorizing, investigating, experimenting, testing, retesting, dismantling parts, assembling parts

SUGGESTED EQUIPMENT

- abacus
- balance or scale
- bookshelves
- calculators
- microscope
- scales and standard weights
- simple machines, such as inclined plane, lever, pulley, gears, wheels
- table and chairs
- take-apart items, such as battery-powered or electric items (old radios, toasters, clocks, blenders with cords and batteries removed)

SUGGESTED MATERIALS

- collections of natural elements, such as shells, leaves, rocks, fossils, twigs, tree bark, feathers, pinecones, seeds, nuts, and pods. When possible, choose ones that can be found in your area.
- compass
- eyedroppers
- flashlight
- geoboards and rubber bands
- graph paper
- magnets
- magnifying glasses
- observation logs (single subject notebooks work well)
- Peg-Boards
- plants and planting materials, such as seeds, bulbs, soil, pots
- play money
- prepared microscope slides with a variety of materials, such as hair, skin, blades of grass
- prisms
- protractors
- rulers and standard linear measuring tools
- spinning tops
- tangrams
- test tubes

Homework Assistance

When children arrive in your afterschool program each afternoon, they have been in school all day. School-age staff are often caught between helping children with assigned homework and ensuring they have time to de-stress and be children. They need time to rest, relax, and rejuvenate before starting homework. In today's hectic lifestyle, many parents insist that children complete their homework while in your care, because they have other activities—sports, scouts, dance, music, language classes—scheduled later. The key to making this a win-win for all involved is creating a balance by providing a well-equipped homework area and staff available to help when requested by the child and encouraging parents and students to work together to determine when and where the homework will be completed.

Most parents and educators believe completion of homework helps children succeed in school. While research has shown this to be true for children in grades seven through twelve, the verdict is less clear for younger children, according to Harris Cooper, professor of education, psychology, and neuroscience at Duke University and author of *The Battle over Homework: Common Ground for Administrators, Teachers, and Parents*. Cooper noted in an interview on March 7, 2006, in *Duke Today*, "Kids burn out. . . . All kids should be doing homework, but the amount and type should vary according to their developmental level and home circumstances" (Cooper 2006). He contends that homework for younger students should be short, lead to success without much struggle, and occasionally involve the parents. Children need to understand the benefits of completing homework as well as the consequences for not completing it, but this message should come from parents and educators. If you get caught in the middle, suggest to parents that they set up a homework contract with their child. Assure parents that you are available for children when they have questions or want someone to check their homework.

PEER TEACHING
Establishing peer teaching is one way to increase children's competence and to build community as they help each other with homework.

Encourage children's willingness to engage in homework by first allowing them time to relax, socialize with friends, and eat a healthy snack. Children often forget that the homework area is open, so remind them. Encourage—but do not force—them to do their homework. Children learn in many ways: some listen to music while doing homework; some need silence; others need to be on the floor; still others do better in small groups, using peer teaching. Offer the children flexibility, resources, and encouragement to help make homework an enjoyable and productive experience.

Design a quiet, comfortable place for homework that is separate from your quiet social area. Include acceptable posters the children like, and furnish the space with a combination of tables, chairs, and soft furniture, such as couches, beanbags, area rugs, and floor pillows, to create a homelike atmosphere where they can relax while completing homework. If you are unable to have soft furniture, be creative by using gym mats and floor pillows to create a soft space. These items are easily stored on top of or in a storage cabinet. A table and chairs defines a space for writing and drawing. Allow children to use the computers to complete homework; whenever possible, include a computer in the homework area. Provide materials children need

Photo 10.28

Providing supportive staff and materials needed to complete homework effectively helps create a program where children can be successful.

Photo 10.29

to complete homework, such as rulers, pens, pencils, markers, paper, and reference materials, such as dictionaries, atlases, and electronic encyclopedias, or Internet access.

POTENTIAL LEARNING OPPORTUNITIES

Homework assistance helps children develop the following knowledge and skills:

- **Social-emotional:** collaborating, empathizing, cooperating, and building community during peer teaching and mentoring; experiencing feelings of success, positive self-esteem, and competency when homework is completed
- **Physical-motor:** developing small-motor skills while writing, using manipulatives, and reading
- **Cognitive:** reading for pleasure, information, and comprehension; increasing reading ability; expanding concepts taught during the school day

- **Language or communication:** improving communication skills and literacy when writing, completing homework, and researching information
- **Creativity:** increasing creativity when children present materials while peer teaching

SUGGESTED EQUIPMENT

- area rugs
- beanbag chairs
- child-chosen, staff-approved posters
- floor mats
- floor pillows
- prescreened music
- soft furniture (couch or overstuffed chair)
- tables and chairs or study carrels

SUGGESTED MATERIALS

- calculators
- compass
- computer with Internet access
- erasers
- globe or world map
- hole punches
- Internet access for research, controlled with cyber nanny software
- math counters
- pens, pencils, crayons, markers, colored pencils
- protractors
- reference materials (various reading levels)
- staple puller
- stapler
- writing paper, kindergarten and composition notebook (various rule widths)

Outdoor Play

Outdoor play is as essential to quality school-age programming as indoor play. It facilitates cognitive and social-emotional development as well as physical development and encourages a healthy lifestyle. When planning outside activities, ask the children for suggestions. Allowing them to direct their own activities gives them the message that their ideas are valued and provides them with leadership opportunities. Ask for child volunteers to demonstrate

Photo 10.31

Photo 10.30

Photo 10.32

No matter the size or configuration of outdoor play spaces, they can provide large-motor play opportunities and connect children with nature.

when you explain how to play a new game and encourage questions to teach the children good listening and communication skills. If the children are not connecting with a game, ask them how to change it to make it more children friendly or more challenging. This conveys to them that you believe in their ability to find solutions. Above all, go with the flow and be flexible; the children can tell you what works and what does not.

Outdoor play spaces can be as diverse as indoor spaces. The basic requirements are a balance of shade and sun, access to drinking water, and a variety of play equipment and materials, both portable and stationary. Your equipment should facilitate large-motor play for children of all ages and abilities. Stationary equipment must be securely fastened to the ground, free of hazards, and suited to the ages of children served. To minimize injuries, large climbing equipment must have an adequate fall zone with soft ground cover such as wood chips, sand, or pea gravel. Check with your licensing agency or the Consumer Product Safety Commission for recommendations on how far to extend a fall zone. (For more information, see Outdoor Safety in chapter 3.)

If you do not have large climbing equipment available, think about how else you can encourage large-motor development. If you have a large open field, then play soccer, baseball, or tag games. Use hula hoops and a Frisbee to make a Frisbee golf course. (Using a soft Frisbee will minimize injuries from children's misthrows that hit another child.) Purchase a boccie ball, croquet, or badminton set. Multicultural games such as these also give you a chance to teach children where games originated, which helps them understand that not everything was created in their country. Staff members assigned to work outdoors often rely on competitive group games such as baseball, soccer, and basketball, but introducing noncompetitive group-dynamic games, such as the human knot or traffic jam, is equally important. These games facilitate group interaction, collaboration, and team building and minimize competition. Satisfy school-age children's craving for competition by encouraging them to compete against their own records rather than against others. Have them track and compare their own scores from day to day by charting their daily bests, such as relay race times, how many fly balls they caught, or how many times they jumped rope without stopping.

In addition to organized sports, facilitate opportunities for individual play. Provide materials for quiet activities such as reading, coloring, and board games for children who do not want to participate in large-motor activities. Spread a tablecloth or a blanket in a shady spot for those wanting to play quietly. This allows children to make their own choices and gives them other outlets for socialization.

A warm, sunny day is perfect for an impromptu beach party, as this photo shows. Staff quickly gathered materials and set them in a grassy place for children to enjoy.

Photo 10.33

Photo 10.34

When materials are placed in an easy-to-transport receptacle, staff are more likely to use them. Access to a variety of materials also encourages child-led activities.

To ease your daily setup of the outdoor environment, use a large trash can on wheels to store and transport equipment. Store items such as jump ropes, Frisbees, and quiet play materials in small canvas bags so they are easy for children to carry. Stackable plastic crates containing equipment that children can easily carry are also a solution for quickly setting up the outdoor space.

The outdoors is a great place to encourage exploration by introducing science activities and connecting children with nature. Teach science concepts in natural settings by having children plant and tend a flower or vegetable garden and by planning times for children to observe, chart, and predict the presence of wild animals, bugs, and birds in your outdoor space. Help children understand how animals live by watching how ants go to and from an ant colony. Take outside learning inside by creating an ant colony in the program space for children to observe. Cord off a section of grass for each of the children, and have them use a magnifying glass to find and document what animals they see in their section. Ask them to compare their results. These experiences provide children with many hands-on learning opportunities and cultivate an appreciation of the beauty and wonder of the outdoors.

POTENTIAL LEARNING OPPORTUNITIES

Outdoor play helps children develop the following knowledge and skills:

- **Social-emotional:** building friendships, taking turns, encouraging peers, taking chances, learning to win and lose gracefully, making choices, developing self-esteem and self-control, building teams, listening to others, following rules
- **Physical-motor:** developing small- and large-motor movements, coordinating hand-eye movements
- **Cognitive:** following rules, problem solving, recognizing spatial relationships, developing game strategies, observing life cycles, predicting what will happen in nature
- **Language or communication:** participating in conversations, listening, reading rules, explaining rules, demonstrating a game skill
- **Creativity:** adapting games, making new rules, creating games

SUGGESTED EQUIPMENT

- basketball hoop (adjustable height)
- bikes
- cart (wheeled) or plastic crates for transporting equipment
- cones
- golf clubs
- large climbing equipment
- outdoor umbrella or portable awning (to create shade)
- parachute
- sandbox
- scooters
- shuffleboard
- stilts
- tennis rackets
- volleyball net

SUGGESTED MATERIALS

- badminton set
- balls of various sizes, shapes, types, and textures
- bases
- bats
- beanbags
- bike helmets
- boccie ball set
- books (various reading levels), both reading and coloring
- box of quiet games and reading material
- chalk (outside)
- Chinese jump rope
- croquet set
- golf tees and practice balls
- hopscotch outline
- hula hoops
- jacks
- jump ropes
- large plastic tubs to use for sensory experiences
- marbles
- skates and helmets
- soft Frisbee
- tablecloth, quilt, or blanket

Activities and Questions

Use these activities and questions to assess your program space and the areas you currently offer the children in your care.

1. After reviewing the program areas discussed in this chapter, list the areas you have in your program. What areas do you offer daily, weekly, and monthly? How did you determine what areas to place in your program space? List new materials you would like to add to existing areas.

2. What areas would you like to add to your program? What materials would you like to include in these areas?

3. For the areas you would like to add, review your existing program space to decide where to place new areas.

4. Look at the list of materials and equipment in this chapter, and add things you have used in these areas that are not on the lists.

5. Do you have a space devoted to the older children in your program? How are the materials in this area different from those in the rest of your program?

6. What activities do you offer in your outdoor environment for children who do not want to participate in active games?

7. Do you use theme (or prop) boxes in your program? If so, list the name of each and where in your program you use it. If not, choose a theme, program area, or type of material or supply, and create a storage box for it. Do you have an inventory sheet for each box? If not, make one.

CHAPTER 11

Keeping the Wow!

IN GREEK MYTHOLOGY, King Sisyphus was made to roll a huge boulder up a hill, watch it roll back down, and repeat this task for the rest of his life. Like Sisyphus's task, keeping the environment exciting and wowing children is an ongoing process.

The only constant in life is change. Change can put us out of our comfort zone. You will experience both successes and challenges as your program develops and matures. Enrollment in school-age programs can change from day to day and from week to week. Some programs struggle to maintain the same staff for a program year, let alone multiple years. These changes are one reason why ongoing observations and periodic use of an assessment tool are essential. (See appendix C for assessment resources.)

Your review of the information from assessments and observations will show where your program's strengths are and what areas need improvement as well as the role and effectiveness of your work with children. Observations provide clues about what the environment needs to improve the quality of programming. They can guide the decisions of staff who plan activities, rotate materials, and determine what intentional teaching to include. The information can help identify what activities will meet the social-emotional, physical, and cognitive needs of the children and what areas need additional materials to extend learning. In addition, these notes can help determine if the schedule needs to be changed or routines need to be retaught. For example, observations may have indicated a need to train staff in making effective transitions, creating an effective daily schedule, supporting children's learning through problem-solving techniques, rotating or adding new materials or furnishings, and partnering with parents. Then you can create an action plan that lists improvement areas, possible solutions, the person responsible for making each change, a timeline for completion, and the money needed to make the change.

No set formula governs how you use your funds, so you must allocate spending according to what the children and environment need to create an exciting and welcoming program space. Be realistic about the amount of money and time needed. As with any evaluation process that reveals a need

Photo 11.1

Through carefully chosen activities, children learn social skills that help create an atmosphere where friendships can flourish.

for change, administrators have the responsibility to ensure that the budget includes funding to support environmental changes and staff training.

When changes occur in staffing, enrollment, children's health, or child engagement in program areas or activities, you need to determine what adjustments to make. Change is an inevitable part of program design, planning, and growth. If something does not work, change it! The following chart illustrates this cyclic process:

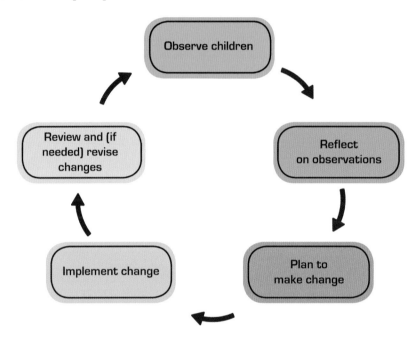

Once you engage in the process of change and purposefully schedule time to evaluate your program's temporal, interpersonal, and physical environment, you will find that continually redesigning your environment becomes easier and easier. The task becomes routine and systematic rather than something that occurs only when you have a problem. Adopting the practice of periodic evaluation enables you to nurture all the children in a safe, accepting environment with thoughtfully planned spaces, materials, and activities. The environment sends out messages in a somewhat telepathic way to everyone who enters your program. The messages from an ideal school-age environment include these top ten:

1. safe
2. homelike
3. happy—smiling faces and pleasant sounds
4. soft and comfortable
5. welcoming and inviting
6. accepting—a celebration of diversity
7. orderly and organized

8. flexible—schedules designed to meet the needs of the children
9. purposefully designed with exciting and stimulating spaces and learning activities
10. clean and fresh

Throughout this book, you have learned about how to improve the design, function, and effectiveness of your afterschool program by looking at the three dimensions of the environment: temporal, interpersonal, and physical. This final chapter discusses how to keep your environment exciting and inviting while remaining clutter-free, organized, warm, and welcoming to all.

Keeping Your Environment Exciting and Inviting

The goal of this book has been to inspire and free you to create afterschool environments that are as unique and special as the individuals who use them. Even though we all had instructions about how to write letters and words, we all write our names differently. Marketing companies even use the term *signature pieces* to refer to items that are unique or outside the standard model. There is no one way to create the wow factor in your program environment, but many components are fundamental and require ongoing attention.

Changing the environment when children have lost interest in a given area can regain their interest. If possible, make changes with children present. Do not rush the process; allow children time to adjust to new rules and consequences, new locations of materials and learning areas, and new staffing. This is particularly important for children who depend on predictable environments to maintain their sense of security and competence.

You might be asking yourself, *How will I know when to make changes to an area?* Observation is the key element in discovering the changes that will keep your environment exciting and inviting. Regularly scheduled time for observations allows you to

- pay attention to the children's lack of engagement in an activity area,
- notice when children need more educational or social support, and
- look for ways to make changes to an activity area to support the current weekly lesson.

The key to keeping any area exciting is watching the level of children's participation in that area. Use the evaluation tools in the appendixes to help guide your observations. Clues to ineffective physical environments are areas the children do not visit and materials that are collecting dust. Clues to missing links in interpersonal supports are antisocial behavior and negative behaviors. Clues that the temporal environment needs adjustment are having to move children before they have completed their activity and children wanting to continue an activity longer than scheduled. If you notice any of these signs, make some changes. Rotating materials, following fads, and talking with the children will help you keep children engaged in your program.

Rotating materials: Rotating materials regularly encourages children's participation by creating new places and activities for them to explore. Plan rotations to follow your lesson plans, always keeping the interests and needs of the children in mind. While materials are out of circulation, you can replace missing parts and make needed repairs. The regular rotation of materials is easy to do when you store them in grab-and-go bins, crates, and plastic containers. For each storage unit, compile a complete list of the contents and tape a copy of the list both on the outside of the bin and on the inside of the lid. Ensure smooth rotations by having all the contents of a bin go together—matched by theme or by learning area. You do not need to remove materials from a play area if children are continuing to use and learn through the materials. See Arranging and Displaying Materials in chapter 8 for more information on grab-and-go caddies.

When the program added materials in housekeeping that were weighted like real food products, the children once again became engaged in the area.

Photo 11.2

Following fads: Children love to follow fads. One great way to keep children engaged is to follow fads. Fads are here today and gone tomorrow, so you will need to work quickly to integrate them within the program. You will also find that not all fads will be appropriate for the children's ages or your program philosophy. The challenge will be to make sure you understand all aspects of the current fad, so investigate. For more information on fads, see Discover Children's Likes and Dislikes in chapter 7.

Staff ask for children's input about the materials in this play area and rotate materials often to encourage the children's use of them. This practice encourages children to learn through imaginative and creative project work.

Photo 11.3

Asking the children: Solicit feedback from children about various aspects of your program environment. Encourage them to give input on everything from the daily activity schedule and clubs to field trips and learning materials. Remember to periodically give children an interest survey (see appendix A). Giving them freedom within preset limits to choose field trips and materials, such as games, books, and artwork, helps to establish children's ownership in the program. For more information on getting input from children, see Discover Children's Likes and Dislikes in chapter 7.

The Clutter Bug Disease

Stop for a moment to think about the overall organization of both the indoor and outdoor environments in your program. Are the materials added to your environment to support the children's fads or current interests overtaking your program space? Are more and more materials being added but nothing taken out? Do staff and children know where most everything can be found? How long does it take to locate what you are looking for? Organization of materials should be as orderly as a deck of playing cards when they are in numerical order and sorted by suits. Afterschool programs wow children

Photo 11.4

The overall organization and clutter-free appearance of this program space encourage children to use materials and equipment respectfully.

when the environment is well organized and clean and when the materials are easily accessible.

Johnna Darragh (2008), a professor of early childhood education, advocates evaluating children's program environments from the perspective of "the view from the door." If visitors were to peek into your environment from the door, what would they see? While everyone may want a school-age program that runs smoothly and appears orderly, physical environments often become packed with stuff. They get cluttered. When clutter takes over a physical environment, it becomes a roadblock to children's learning and affects the temporal and interpersonal environments as well. A prop is added to the dramatic play area, but there is no place to store it, so it is put in a box with the costumes. Next come another building kit, new reference books, and arts and crafts supplies. Before long, you have so many materials that children need to dig deep to find something of interest, or they decide it is too much trouble, so they simply leave the area. Cleanup time becomes a battle. There is way too much stuff to put away in any kind of an organized fashion. Hallways are littered with book bags and coats. Bulletin boards have notes about football team sign-up even though that was months ago. The clutter bug has attacked. Disorder reigns in what were once functional areas.

Photo 11.5

Clutter in your program spaces sends a message to children that it is okay to leave things in a heap and not put things where they belong or take care of them.

THE PROBLEM WITH CLUTTER

Clutter is typically defined as a confusing or disorderly array of items scattered throughout an identified area. Clutter and disorganization have a negative effect on the overall effectiveness of your program environment. With so much stuff around, adults and children can become frustrated and distracted. Some clutter presents safety issues. For example, children can trip on a floor covered with toys, books, or food residue; outdoor areas littered with things that roll or that block play areas can also cause children to tumble. Other kinds of clutter pose health hazards. When fabrics are dirty or stored in confined places, dust mites breed easily. Mold and mildew spores grow rapidly from leftover and forgotten food items, and germs and bacteria live on dirty materials handled or sneezed upon by children. Often these items both look and smell bad.

Clutter is also counterproductive to the learning environment of an afterschool program. A cluttered environment distracts children. They have a hard time maintaining the focus needed to concentrate long enough to learn. When children have too many playthings to choose from, they typically choose nothing or tend to move quickly from one space to another because they are overstimulated. They may not be able to find what they are looking for, or they may say everything is boring. When you have too much furniture clogging areas, children are not involved in active play or exploration because they are overwhelmed or simply too crowded to move. Items hanging from the ceiling become flutter clutter, and too many wall displays take on the look of highly patterned wallpaper. Instead of supporting children's experiences, cluttered environments prevent learning from happening.

ERADICATING CLUTTER

By bringing order and organization to your school-age program, you free up space for new materials, and you enable children's behavior to improve and their creativity to thrive. An organized, predictable environment helps children make sense of what is around them, which gives them a sense of security and independence. Even the youngest children will become independent learners when they can find and return their playthings to the right place.

Just as clutter does not accumulate overnight, neither can you de-clutter your program space overnight. Start by removing one small bag or box of unused items from your environment. Get the children involved. They can help you decide what stays and what goes. The following checklist includes many well-proven ways to tackle clutter in your program environment (and just maybe your office, car, or home too).

SEVEN STEPS TO TACKLE CLUTTER

Step 1: Make a plan:

- Start out small—choose one section of an area to focus on.
- Set a timeline to finish this project.
- Observe and record what the children do not use.
- Gather storage containers for materials you want to keep and garbage bags for those you plan to get rid of.

Step 2: Get to work:

- Remove the items you have identified that children do not use.
- Stay on schedule—play music, dance as you work, sing along with silly songs to make it fun.
- Involve the children, or make it a staff group activity.
- Be like the Energizer bunny and keep going.

Step 3: Carry everything you have removed to a staging area and sort into three piles:

- items for charity
- items to store
- items for the trash can

Step 4: Be honest:

- Is this item worth keeping for the children?
- Will they use it in the future?
- Does it work?
- Are there other learning materials like this that the children use?

Step 5: Clean the area when you have finished removing the clutter.

Step 6: Celebrate your success! If the children have helped with this process, treat them to an extra story, longer outside time, or maybe even bring out some new materials now that you have the space.

Step 7: Repeat this process for all cluttered spaces, and keep the clutter bug out of your program for good.

STORAGE TIPS

Once you have de-cluttered, a key to keeping clutter in check is developing an effective system for storing and rotating materials. In chapter 1, we suggested some ways to tackle the lack of storage in program space, including wheeled carts that allow you to place all materials needed for each area together and to move easily and quickly to minimize setup time. In chapter 8, Arranging and Displaying Materials discusses a number of storage tricks, including grab-and-go caddies. Using stackable containers or flat under-the-bed storage units allows you to place items on top of a storage cabinet or in shelving units.

Other ideas include packing materials away in old suitcases or bags with zippers and labeling the contents; ones with wheels are especially helpful when storing materials with many pieces or heavy books. Suitcases can cut down greatly on needed storage space. For a more natural look, small wicker baskets make setup easy, and they can nest for quick storage. Using clear plastic shower caps to cover materials in wicker baskets prevents small items from spilling in storage.

Wicker baskets provide a natural element to the environment and provide containers that children can easily carry.

Photo 11.6

Photo 11.7

Photo 11.8

Photo 11.7: A rolling cart helps staff quickly set up the program environment.

Photo 11.8: Well-organized cabinets with stacking bins maximize storage space and make finding materials easy.

Keeping Your Environment Warm and Welcoming

Eradicating clutter is an important step in keeping your environment warm and welcoming. Some of the things you do to keep the environment organized add warmth. These touches include color coding or labeling shelves to help children find and return materials and using wicker baskets or fabric-covered boxes to store playthings. Other natural materials and items from nature—such as plants, shells, pets, natural-fiber rugs, and pillows—also add warmth. Refresh these items periodically by visiting garage sales and asking families to bring whatever they can to share. Before adding any used items to your environment, ensure they are sanitary and safe for children's use. From watching what children do, use, or avoid, continually make changes in your temporal, interpersonal, and physical environments that convey a sense of comfort, beauty, and calm. Remember that soft or neutral color palettes are soothing and promote tranquil activities. Create an artists' gallery to display children's artwork. Frame their paintings and drawings to hang in the gallery. Use cloth runners on display shelves or countertops for pottery, sculptures, and other art objects. Change the artwork displays regularly.

Your ongoing efforts to keep your environment warm and welcoming as well as exciting and inviting all add up to a great afterschool program in a space that wows. It is a place where staff members like to work and want to stay. It is a place where children love to be, love to learn, and never want to leave.

Activities and Questions

Keeping the environment exciting is critical to the overall functioning and success of your program. Answer the following questions to help you keep the wow factor in your program.

1. How do you determine when to rotate materials?

2. When and how do you involve the children in changing your environment? If you do not involve the children, make a plan to encourage the children's input regularly.

3. Review the last observation you made, and highlight areas that need changes. Make a list of ideas for changes and the materials needed to make the changes.

4. How will you know if the changes you made are effective?

5. Look around your program space and find an area that is cluttered. Go through the items in this area, and for each one, make a choice to keep it where it is, pitch it, or return it to its correct place.

6. Look at your storage areas. What materials are not used, not needed, or inappropriate for children's use? How can you make storage more organized and free up space?

7. Look critically at all three dimensions of your environment—temporal, interpersonal, and physical. Make a list of the positive and negative messages your environment sends out in each of the three dimensions. Refer to this list often to help assess and improve your program. Brainstorm with children, staff, and parents to make the needed changes.

Appendixes

INTEREST SURVEY 1

Name _____

Draw a circle around the things that you are interested in or what you would like to know more about. Your answers will help the staff plan activities and provide resources for areas of interest and those you would like to know more about.

acting	crocheting	movies	soccer
airplanes	dancing	music	swimming
art	dolls	painting	tennis
baseball	drawing	photography	trains
basketball	fishing	playing outside	video games
board games	gardening	reading	volleyball
cars	knitting	science	writing
chess	martial arts	sewing	
cooking	math	skating	

INTEREST SURVEY 2

Take the time to carefully complete the survey. Your feedback will help us plan activities and provide resources for areas of interest and those you would like to know more about.

MUSIC

What radio stations do you listen to? _____

Who are your favorite musicians or bands? _____

Are there any CDs you would like to have included here? _____

Do you sing or play a musical instrument? **Yes   No**
(circle one)

If yes, would you like to perform here? **Yes   No**
(circle one)

BOOKS AND PRINTED MATERIALS

What kinds of books do you like to read?

Nonfiction

books about famous people   books about animals   books about space

(circle all you like)

other _____
(add other types of nonfiction you like to read)

Fiction

adventure   comedy   science fiction   fantasy

(circle all you like)

other _____
(add other types of fiction you like to read)

CLUBS

Check any of the following clubs you would like to be a part of.

___ aerobics (floor and movement exercises, making up routines)

___ camping (learning about wilderness survival skills, learning to tie different kinds of knots, going on nature hikes)

___ drama (prop making, set designing, acting, creating costumes, producing a play)

___ macramé (learning different techniques, making a wall hanging, plant holder, or piece of jewelry)

___ nutrition (learning ways to eat and stay fit, preparing tasty and healthy foods, dental hygiene, exercises, and so on)

___ photography (experimenting with different kinds of cameras made in the club, learning techniques for better picture taking)

___ sewing (learning to embroider, cross-stitch, needlepoint; making a finished product to take home)

___ weaving (making different kinds of looms, completing small projects and large woven masterpieces)

___ other _____
(add other club ideas here)

DRAMA

Would you like to perform a play or skit for younger children? **Yes   No**
(circle one)

Would you like to perform for families? **Yes   No**
(circle one)

Are you interested in puppets? **Yes   No**
(circle one)

If you are, would you like to make different kinds of puppets? **Yes   No**
(circle one)

Would you help build a puppet stage? **Yes   No**
(circle one)

Would you like to put on a puppet show for others? **Yes   No**
(circle one)

ART

Do you want to have any of the following art activities available to do on your own?

papier-mâché   sculpture   macramé   calligraphy   weaving   wood burning

(circle all you like)

_____
(add other art ideas here)

GAMES AND PUZZLES

What is your favorite board game? _____

What board games would you like us to have that we do not have now? _____

_____

_____

Are you interested in doing a group jigsaw puzzle of 500 to 1,000 pieces?

Yes   No
(circle one)

2/3

COOKING AND FOOD

If you could make anything for snack, what would it be? _____

What do you like to cook? _____

BUILDING AND CONSTRUCTION

Do you like to work with tools to build things? Yes   No
(circle one)

Are you interested in building models or doing a woodworking project? Yes   No
(circle one)

If yes, what kinds of projects? _____

SCIENCE AND DISCOVERY

Do you like to grow plants? Yes   No
(circle one)

Do you like to use a microscope? Yes   No
(circle one)

Do you like animals? Yes   No
(circle one)

If yes, what kinds? _____

What kinds of science projects do you find interesting? _____
_____

HOMEWORK

What kinds of supplies do you need to get your homework done? _____
_____

COMPUTERS

What kinds of games do you like to use on the computer? _____
_____

What kind of computer do you like to use? _____

What do you want to spend more time doing? _____

What do you want to be able to do that you cannot do now? _____
_____
_____

3/3

This worksheet should be completed by a team of staff and parents or an advisory committee to design or redesign an environment that meets the needs of children and staff. Honest answers are needed to make this planning effective. You may find older children's input can be useful in this process too.

1. What does our program value? _____

_____

_____

_____

_____

2. What goals do we have for the children enrolled in our program? _____

_____

_____

_____

_____

3. Most of the time, our children enjoy the following activities: _____

_____

_____

_____

4. Our current environment supports children's needs in the following ways:

_____

_____

_____

_____

5. Our current environment does not support children's needs in the following ways:

_____

_____

_____

6. We see the following as roadblocks to creating or redesigning the environment:

_____

_____

_____

_____

ENVIRONMENT PLANNING WORKSHEET (CONT.)

7. The following areas are working well in our environment (circle all that apply):

indoor play area

quiet play area: manipulative, reading, small-group games, etc.

academic or homework area

creative arts area: dramatic play, music and movement, arts and crafts, etc.

toileting, personal hygiene, ill-child areas

storage

staff area

entry/administrative areas

snack/eating area

outdoor play area

other _____

8. The following areas are not working well in our environment (circle all that apply):

indoor play area

quiet play area: manipulative, reading, small-group games, etc.

academic or homework area

creative arts area: dramatic play, music and movement, arts and crafts, etc.

toileting, personal hygiene, ill-child areas

storage

staff area

entry/administrative areas

snack/eating area

outdoor play area

other _____

9. List by priority the areas in the environment that are most important to change (based on responses to #8): _____

_____

_____

_____

10. Here's our plan of action. We are willing to make the following changes: _____

_____

_____

_____

_____

2/2

APPENDIX C → **PROGRAM ASSESSMENT RESOURCES**

Program-wide Assessments

Assessing School-Age Quality

www.niost.org

This instrument was originally developed by the National Institute on Out-of-School Time (NIOST) for use with the National School-Age Association accreditation process. While accreditation is no longer a service offered by the National School-Age Association, self-study materials are still available for purchase from NIOST. This tool assesses 144 standards in six areas. Those areas include

1. human relationships
2. indoor environment
3. outdoor environments
4. health, safety, and nutrition
5. activities
6. administration

The scoring is based on a three-point scale.

Council on Accreditation (COA)

www.coaafterschool.org

The Council on Accreditation standards used the National AfterSchool Association (NAA) accreditation standards as a basis for developing its eighth edition of standards, which includes ten additional administrative standards. The standards have been wordsmithed to meet the graphic and written standards for the COA system. The system is completely online. The online system provides a variety of support documents to guide you in the accreditation process. The areas of standards are divided into three sections:

1. After School Program Administration
2. After School Human Resources
3. After School Programming and Services

High Scope Youth Program Quality Assessment (Youth PQA)

http://etools.highscope.org/assessment/PQA/index.php

The Youth PQA is a research-based instrument. It was designed to evaluate the quality of youth programs and identify staff development needs for structured programs serving grades four through twelve. It is intended to assess the quality of youth programs for the purposes of accountability, evaluation, and program improvement. The instrument has been used in a wide variety of settings, including school-age, community-based, camp, drop-in, and peer/adult mentoring programs. The Youth PQA is a dual-purpose instrument, effective for high-stakes accountability and research purposes, and user friendly enough to be used for program self-assessment. It is both an evaluation tool and a program learning tool. The tools areas are listed as follows:

1. engagement
2. interactions
3. supportive environment
4. safe environment
5. youth voice and governance
6. professional learning community

Quality Assurance System (QAS)

www.foundationsinc.org

QAS was developed by Foundations, Inc., to help school-age programs conduct quality assessment and continuous improvement planning. It is an online tool designed to be general enough for use in a range of school and community-based programs serving children grades kindergarten through twelve. It focuses on quality at the site level. Programs using the QAS start with an initial assessment from which observers identify areas of strength as well as those that need improvement. Once the assessment is finished, the tool helps develop specific improvement strategies. Foundations recommends that the QAS be conducted twice a year, at the beginning of the program year and midway through the year. The tool is based on seven building blocks:

1. program planning and improvement
2. leadership
3. facility and program space
4. health and safety
5. staffing
6. family and community connections
7. social climate

National AfterSchool Association (NAA) Standards for Quality School-Age Care

www.naaweb.org

This assessment describes the practices that lead to stimulating, safe, and supportive programs for children and youth ages five to fourteen during their out-of-school time. The *NAA Standards for Quality School-Age Care* contains concrete examples, guiding questions for staff discussion, a glossary, and an appendix. The *NAA Standards* can be used to guide a program through a quality assessment, setting goals, and determining need for staff development and provides a plan for continuous improvement. For information about the ASQ self-study process, contact the National Institute on Out-of-School Time (NIOST) at www.niost.org.

The Association for Early Learning Leaders (formerly known as the National Association of Child Care Professionals)

www.earlylearningleaders.org

The Association for Early Learning Leaders will "accredit school-age programs that are a component of a licensed program serving primarily preschool children provided that the majority of children in the school-age program are eight years old or younger." Therefore, a free-standing school-age program would not qualify for the Association for Early Learning Leaders accreditation. Only school-age groups associated with a preschool, with the same onsite director, and located at the same site with the same license can be accredited as part of the total organization by the Association for Early Learning Leaders.

AfterSchool Program Assessment System (APAS)

www.niost.org

This system was developed by the National Institute on Out-of-School Time (NIOST). This program assessment has two parts: the Survey of Afterschool Youth Outcomes (SAYO) and the Assessing Afterschool Program Practices Tool (APT). These tools can be used together or separately, depending on the specific needs of the program. This evaluation system is aimed at improving program quality and youth outcomes in school-age programs.

The School-Age Care Environment Ratings Scale (SACERS)

http://ers.fpg.unc.edu

This rating scale was developed at University of North Carolina–Chapel Hill. It is designed to assess before- and afterschool/group care programs for school-age children five to twelve years old. The total scale consists of forty-nine items, including six supplementary items for programs enrolling children with disabilities. The evaluation tool can be used to determine the program's strengths and specific areas for improvement or the total program. This tool comes complete with definition of various terms as well as directions for the scoring of the tool.

Program Parts Assessments

Early Language and Literacy Classroom Observation (ELLCO) K–3

www.brookespublishing.com

This assessment has two parts: an observation tool to gather information about five elements of the literacy environment and a staff interview that supplements the observation with staff's firsthand reflections. This tool has been designed for programs that serve children in grades kindergarten through three. The information gained allows you to determine the effectiveness of your program environment, strengthen the quality of your program and teaching practices, and improve young children's early literacy outcomes. The five key literacy elements are the following:

1. classroom structure
2. curriculum

3. language environment
4. books and book-reading opportunities
5. print and early writing supports

The National AfterSchool Association (NAA) Code of Ethics

www.naaweb.org

The Code of Ethics sets standards of conduct for the school-age staff and outlines personal and professional excellence. It encourages professional development of those working in the school-age field. The highest standards of professional competence, fairness, impartiality, efficiency, effectiveness, and fiscal responsibility are integrated within the sections. It was designed as a resource to assist the school-age professional in understanding the ethical responsibilities inherent in providing school-age programs for children ages five through eighteen. Use this document as an assessment tool to determine where your organization and staff stand on ethical issues. This document is divided into four sections that cover ethical responsibilities to children and youth, families, colleagues, and the community. In addition, this document provides a statement of ethical conduct for school-age staff that can be used with staff and shared with parents.

The National AfterSchool Association's Afterschool Core Knowledge and Competencies

www.naaweb.org

This document outlines the knowledge and skills needed by staff to provide quality afterschool care. This assessment tool allows the school-age staff to be rated at one of five levels for each of the following categories:

- child and youth growth and development
- learning environments and curriculum
- child and youth observation and assessment
- interactions with children and youth
- youth engagement
- cultural competency and responsiveness
- family, school, and community relationships
- safety and wellness
- program planning and development
- professional development and leadership

The National AfterSchool Association Standards for Healthy Eating and Physical Activity (HEPA) in Out-of-School Time Programs

www.naaweb.org

This tool was developed in collaboration with the National Institute on Out-of-School Time (NIOST) and the National AfterSchool Association (NAA). These standards are up-to-date, evidence-based, and practical, and they foster the best possible nutrition and physical activity outcomes for children in grades kindergarten through twelve attending school-age programs. According to the NAA website, there are two notable points to consider when using HEPA standards: some standards will be easy to adopt, while others will take some financial commitment and long-term planning. In some programs, these voluntary standards may be in conflict with existing regulations or licensure guidelines.

The Program Administration Scale (PAS)

http://cecl.nl.edu

This scale was developed by the McCormick Center for Early Childhood Leadership, and it assesses and improves the quality of organizational practices. The PAS provides a reliable tool for measuring the overall quality of the administrative practices of early care and education programs. The PAS assesses quality in ten areas:

1. human resources development
2. personnel cost and allocation
3. center operation
4. child assessment
5. fiscal management
6. program planning and evaluation
7. family partnership
8. marketing and public relations
9. technology

APPENDIX D → **GRAPH PAPER**

References

Afterschool Alliance. 2009. "Afterschool Essentials: Research and Polling." www.afterschoolalliance.org/documents/2012/Essentials_4_20_12_FINAL.pdf.

American Academy of Pediatrics (AAP). 2006. "Handwashing and Use of Hand Sanitizers." In *Health and Safety E-News for Caregivers and Teachers,* e-newsletter, April. http://www.healthychildcare.org/ENewsApr06.html#handwashing.

———. 2013. "Media and Children." http://www.aap.org/en-us/advocacy-and-policy/aap-health-initiatives/Pages/Media-and-Children.aspx.

Armstrong, Thomas. 2009. *Multiple Intelligences in the Classroom.* 3rd ed. Alexandria, VA: ASCD.

Boise, Phil. 2010. *Go Green Rating Scale for Early Childhood Settings Handbook: Improving Your Score.* St. Paul: Redleaf Press.

Cooper, Harris. 2006. Quoted in "Duke Study: Homework Helps Students Succeed in School, as Long as There Isn't Too Much." *Duke Today,* March 7. http://today.duke.edu/2006/03/homework.htm.

Curtis, Deb, and Margie Carter. 2003. *Design for Living and Learning: Transforming Early Childhood Environments.* St. Paul: Redleaf Press.

Darragh, Johnna. 2008. "The View from the Door." *Exchange,* Nov./Dec., 22–24.

Gordon, Ann Miles, and Kathryn Williams Browne. 2011. *Beginnings and Beyond: Foundations in Early Childhood Education.* 8th ed. Belmont, CA: Wadsworth.

Grangaard, Ellen Mannel. 1993. "Effects of Color and Light on Selected Elementary Students." Ph.D. diss., University of Nevada, Las Vegas.

Greenman, Jim. 2005. *Caring Spaces, Learning Places: Children's Environments That Work.* Redmond, WA: Exchange Press.

Harvard Health Publications. 2009. "Taking on School Bullies." *Harvard Mental Health Letter* 26 (3): 6–7. www.health.harvard.edu/newsletters/Harvard_Mental_Health_Letter/2009/September/taking-on-school-bullies.

Hendrix, Marie. 2008. "Picky Eaters." *Exchange,* Mar./Apr., 90–92.

Interior Mall. 2013. "Flame Resistant FAQ." http://interiormall.com/cat/howto/FireProof.htm.

Isbell, Rebecca, and Betty Exelby. 2001. *Early Learning Environments That Work.* Beltsville, MD: Gryphon House.

Kamrin, Michael. 2001. *The Scientific Facts about the Dry-Cleaning Chemical Perc.* Report prepared at the request of the American Council on Science and Health, July 1. New York: American Council of Science and Health. http://www.acsh.org/publications/the-scientific-facts-about-the-dry-cleaning-chemical-perc-second-edition/.

Kostelnik, Marjorie J., Kara Murphy Gregory, Anne K. Soderman, and Alice Phipps Whiren. 2011. *Guiding Children's Social Development and Learning.* 7th ed. Belmont, CA: Wadsworth Cengage Learning.

Layzer, Jean I., Barbara D. Goodson, and Melanie Brown-Lyons. 2007. *National Study of Child Care for Low-Income Families: Care in the Home: A Description of Family Child Care and the Experiences of the Families and Children*

That Use It. Report prepared at the request of the U.S. Department of Health and Human Services. Cambridge, MA: Abt Associates. http://archive.acf.hhs.gov/programs/opre/cc/nsc_low_income/reports/care_home/care_home_title.html.

National AfterSchool Association (NAA). 2009. "Code of Ethics." http://www.naaweb.org/downloads/NAACodeofEthicsJan09.newaddress.pdf.

———. 2011. *Core Knowledge and Competencies for Afterschool and Youth Development Professionals.* McLean, VA: NAA. http://www.naaweb.org/downloads/NAA%20Final%20Print%20version.pdf.

National Association of School Psychologists (NASP). 2002. "Social Skills: Promoting Positive Behavior, Academic Success, and School Safety." http://www.nasponline.org/resources/factsheets/socialskills_fs.aspx.

National Early Childhood Program Accreditation (NECPA). 2013. "School-Age Programs Policy." Accessed February 5. http://www.necpa.net/userfiles/SCHOOL-AGE%20PROGRAMS%20POLICY.pdf.

National Fire Protection Agency (NFPA). 2011. *NFPA 101: Life Safety Code.* 2012 ed. Quincy, MA: NFPA. http://www.nfpa.org/aboutthecodes/AboutTheCodes.asp?DocNum=101&cookie%5Ftest=1.

Nemours Foundation. 2013. "Playground Safety." http://kidshealth.org/parent/firstaid_safe/outdoor/playground.html#a_Unsafe_Playground_Equipment.

Office of the United Nations High Commissioner for Human Rights. Convention on the Rights of the Child. General Assembly Resolution 44/25 of November 20, 1989. Available at www.un.org/documents/ga/res/44/a44r025.htm.

Olds, Anita Rui. 2001. *Child Care Design Guide.* New York: McGraw-Hill.

Ollhoff, Jim, and Laurie Ollhoff. 2004. *Getting Along: Teaching Social Skills to Children and Youth.* Eden Prairie, MN: Sparrow Media.

Schreiber, Mary Ellis. 1996. "Lighting Alternatives: Considerations for Child Care Centers." *Young Children* 51 (4): 11–13.

Strong-Wilson, Teresa, and Julia Ellis. 2007. "Children and Place: Reggio Emilia's Environment as Third Teacher." *Theory into Practice* 46 (1): 40–47. doi:10.1080/00405840709336547.

Thomas, Alexander, Stella Chess, and Herbert G. Birch. 1968. *Temperament and Behavior Disorders in Children.* New York: New York University Press.

Thomas, Gillian, and Guy Thompson. 2004. *A Child's Place: Why Environment Matters to Children.* Report. London: Green Alliance/DEMOS. http://www.green-alliance.org.uk/uploadedFiles/Publications/A%20Childs%20Place%20Final%20Version.pdf.

United States Department of Agriculture (USDA). 2009. *Serving It Safe: A Manager's Tool Kit.* Chapter 4: A Clean and Sanitary Foodservice. Alexandria, VA: USDA.

United States Environmental Protection Agency (EPA). 2008. "Cleaning Up a Broken CFL." www2.epa.gov/cfl/cleaning-broken-cfl.

———. 2012. "An Introduction to Indoor Air Quality (IAQ)." www.epa.gov/iaq/lead.html

U.S. General Services Administration (GSA). 2003. *Child Care Center Design Guide.* New York: GSA.

Vincent, Evelyn. 2010. "Scent and the Brain: Aromatherapy and Its Effects on Emotions." http://aromatherapy4u.wordpress.com/2010/03/04.

Index

Enrollment Planning Worksheet, 268–69

environment
    creating wow factor, 253–55
    dedicated space, 6–8
    dimensions overview, 9–10
    goals for, setting, 14–17
    impact on brain development, 66, 68–69
    interpersonal dimension, 10
    learning domain supports, 71–72
    messages conveyed by, 130, 158–59, 252–53
    multiple intelligence supports, 68–69
    physical dimension, 10
    shared space, 2–6, 173–74
    temperament supports, 73–74
    temporal dimension, 10
    See also interpersonal environment; physical environment; temporal environment; welcoming environments

Environmental Protection Agency (EPA)
    drinking water safety, 53–54
    fluorescent light bulbs, 186

Environment Planning Worksheet, 268–69

equipment
    art activities, 209
    blocks and building areas, 211
    cooking activities, 216, 217
    dramatic play areas, 215
    homework assistance areas, 243, 245
    indoor play activities, 221
    manipulative activities/sensory play, 226
    math/science/literacy activities, 242
    media/technology areas, 233–34, 237
    music and movement activities, 223
    outdoor activities, 246–47, 249
    quiet social areas, 232–33
    woodworking activities, 229

F

fabrics
    acoustical properties, 200
    cleanliness of, 55, 197, 257
    fire-resistant/flame retardant, 47
    selecting, 178, 190

fads
    determining appropriateness of, 134, 255
    incorporating in lesson plans, 85, 254–55

families
    communication with, 8–9, 35, 127, 131

cultural differences and diversity, 130, 133, 145–46
    donations from, 33, 207
    gathering information about, 131, 132–33
    providing information to, 136–39, 152

family centers, providing, 138, 152

family conferences, 137

fearful children, 73, 75

feisty children, 74, 75

fifty-fifty rule for physical space, 170

fire safety, 46–47

flame-retardant fabrics, 47

flexibility
    need for, 81, 82
    in schedules, 89–90
    See also change

flexible children, 74, 75

float and sink activity, 86, 87

floor plans, developing, 166–71, 172

fluorescent lighting, 183–84, 186, 187

food preparation
    cooking activities, 216–17
    licensing and regulations, 53, 216
    smells and, 201

formal assessments, 31–32

friends, making, 109
    See also social-emotional development

funding
    state subsidies, 25
    See also budgeting and finances

furniture
    arranging, 4–6, 169, 170, 178
    evaluating and selecting, 176–77
    safety considerations, 45, 46, 47

G

games and puzzles
    challenging children with, 111
    indoor play activities, 218–21
    outdoor activities, 247
    quiet social areas, 231, 233
    skill development and, 122

goals
    of afterschool programs, 204–5
    setting for learning environments, 14–17

Gordon, Ann Miles, 10

grab-and-go caddies, 4

graphing floor plans, 166–71

Greenman, Jim, 43

group projects
    building community, 150–51
    cooking activities, 216
    maximum size considerations, 59

for older children, 144

guest speakers, 148

Guiding Children's Social Development and Learning (Kostelnik), 89

gyms
    protecting floors, 5
    shared space with, 3

H

halogen lighting, 185, 186

handbooks, 137, 138

hand washing, 52, 96–97, 216

health and hygiene
    children's health issues, 135
    cleaning and sanitizing, 46, 201, 216
    clutter and, 257
    hand washing, 52, 96–97, 216
    ill child area, 52–53
    See also safety

hearing impairments, 142
    accommodations, 28
    noise levels and, 199–200

heating ventilation and air conditioning (HVAC), 55, 201

High Scope Youth Program Quality Assessment (Youth PQA), 270–71

holidays, cultural considerations, 145–46

homework assistance, 242–45

How Welcoming Is Your Program Environment? checklist, 127–29

HVAC. *See* heating ventilation and air conditioning (HVAC)

hypersensitivity, 195

I

IEPs. *See* Individualized Education Programs/Plans (IEPs)

ill child area, 52–53

inclusive environments, 147–48

individuality, supporting, 139–41

Individualized Education Programs/Plans (IEPs), 132

indoor areas
    air quality, 54–55, 201
    assessing, 12
    lighting, 182–87
    for older children, 144
    See also physical environment

indoor play activities, 218–21

information
    about children's health issues, 135
    communicating with families, 136–39
    gathering about children and families, 132–36
    sources of, 132

National Association of Child Care Professionals, 272

National Fire Protection Association (NFPA), 46

National Program for Playground Safety, 45

Nemours Foundation, 48

newsletters and brochures, 8–9, 35, 137, 138

NFPA. *See* National Fire Protection Association (NFPA)

noise levels, 162, 198–200

note taking
    in observation process, 38–39, 77
    reflecting on lesson plans, 88–89
    by staff, 38–39

O

observations
    assessing social competence, 105
    benefits and importance of, 76, 132, 253–54
    as evaluation tool, 17, 32–33, 251
    note taking, 38–39, 77
    of physical space usage, 160–62
    steps to follow, 77–78
    See also assessments

older children
    meeting needs of, 14, 143–44
    provision of support for younger children, 151
    quiet social areas, 231–32

Olds, Anita Rui, 15, 43, 182

Ollhoff, Jim, 108

Ollhoff, Laurie, 108

openness
    in conflict management, 120
    cultivating, 129, 147–48

organization
    clutter, dealing with, 255–59
    storage, 4, 174–75, 205

organizational administrators, 19

orientation sessions, 137

outdoor activities
    assessing, 13
    designing space, 141, 246–47
    equipment and materials, 141, 246–47, 249
    knowledge and skills development, 248
    for older children, 144
    planning, 245–48
    safety, 48, 51, 246
    unsafe equipment, 48

overstimulation, 181
    See also sensory stimulation

P

parents
    informing about guest speakers, 148
    program assessment by, 32

PAS. *See* Program Administration Scale (PAS)

patterns, sensory stimulation and, 192–94

peace table/conflict resolution center, 112, 117–18

peer teaching, 243

personality, compared to temperament, 72

photographs
    as communication tool, 35
    photo releases, 35
    taken by children, 234

physical development. *See* motor skills development

physical environment
    accessibility, 140–41, 142–43
    assessing, 11–13, 170–71, 172
    clues to ineffectiveness, 161–62, 254
    dedicated space, 6–8
    described, 10
    design of
        arranging areas, 155–58, 167–71, 172
        basic requirements, 15, 161
        belongings, space for, 174
        fifty-fifty rule, 170
        lighting, 182–87
        mapping and planning, 163–71
        rugs and floor coverings, 5, 174, 193, 207
        storage, 4, 174–75
        traffic patterns/pathways, 162, 169
    effect on behavior, 158–60, 161–62
    learning domain supports, 71–72
    multiple intelligence supports, 68–69
    older children, spaces for, 143–44
    sensory stimulation
        colors, 187–92
        lighting, 182–87
        patterns, 192–94
        smells, 200–201
        sound and acoustics, 198–200
        textures, 195–98
    setting up and taking down, 3–4
    shared space, 2–6, 173–74
    temperament supports, 73–74
    water sources, 6, 207, 216
    See also environment; equipment; materials; safety; toys; welcoming environments

physical impairments
    accessibility issues, 140–41, 142–43
    accommodations, 28–29

planning
    based on observations, 77–78
    compared to doing, 78
    Environment Planning Worksheet, 268–69
    guiding questions for activities and themes, 88
    including children in, 85, 204–5
    lesson plans, 82, 83, 85–89
    physical space and program areas, 163–71

play
    outdoor activities, 48, 141, 245–49
    supporting, 122
    value of, 121–22
    See also activities; games and puzzles

playground safety, 45, 48, 141

pollutants. *See* toxins and pollutants

problem-solving
    conflict management, 117–18
    in play, 121–22

Program Administration Scale (PAS), 274

program areas
    arrangement of, 156–58, 167–71
    colors in, 187–92
    establishing balance of activities, 203
    evaluation and documentation of usage, 160–62, 172
    home base areas, 59
    lighting, 182–87
    mapping and planning, 163–71
    organizing materials, 174–75, 205
    patterns and textures in, 192–98
    smells, 200–201
    sound and acoustics, 198–200
    types of
        blocks and building areas, 210–11
        cooking, 216–17
        creative art, 206–9
        dramatic play, 212–15
        homework assistance, 242–45
        math/science/literacy, 173, 237–42
        media/technology, 233–37
        quiet social areas, 230–33

program evaluation
    formal assessments, 31–32
    observations, 31, 32–33, 251
    resources, 270–74

puppets, 117

supervision, playground, 48
supplies. *See* materials; toys
supportive environments. *See* welcoming environments

T

tax deductions, 27
technology areas, 233–37
television watching, 234–35
temperament of children, 72–76
temporal environment
    clues to ineffectiveness, 254
    A Day in the Life of Your Temporal Environment checklist, 83–84
    described, 10, 81–82
    learning domain supports, 71–72
    lesson plans, 82, 83, 85–89
    multiple intelligence supports, 68–69
    routines, 96–97
    rules and consequences, 97–101
    schedules, 89–94
    temperament supports, 73–74
    transitions, 95–96
texting, to families, 35
textures, sensory stimulation and, 195–98
thematic activities, 81, 212–14
tolerance, teaching and modeling, 119–20, 149–50
tools, woodworking, 227–30
touch, sense of, 195
toxins and pollutants
    asbestos, 54
    cleaning products, 46, 201
    drinking water, 53–54
toys
    lead exposure, 46, 53
    safety considerations, 45–46
    See also games and puzzles; materials
track lighting, 187
traffic patterns/pathways, 162, 169
transitions, 84, 95–96
translations, language, 138–39

U

United Nations High Commission for Human Rights, on value of play, 121
universal design, 143
U.S. Department of Agriculture, food preparation, 53
U.S. Department of Justice, 27
U.S. General Services Administration (GSA), acoustical concerns, 199

V

ventilation, 201
verbal interactions. *See* conversations
videos
    as communication tool, 35
    made by children, 234
visual impairments, 28, 141, 142

W

walkie-talkie systems, 59, 61
wall space, covering, 46–47, 193
water sources
    lead exposure and, 53–54
    locations of, 6, 207, 216
webbing evaluation process, 164
websites, providing information via, 35
welcoming environments
    accommodating needs in, 127–28, 139–41
    benefits of to children, 126
    characteristics of, 126, 260
    communication in, 127, 131–32, 136–39
    community building, 129, 150–52
    diversity, embracing, 128, 145–46
    How Welcoming Is Your Program Environment? checklist, 127–29
    individuality, supporting, 139–41
    for older children, 143–44
    openness, cultivating, 129, 147–48
    reducing clutter in, 255–60
    for special needs, children with, 140–41, 142–43
    tolerance and respect, 129, 149–50
wheelchair accessibility, 140, 142
windows, 182, 183, 187, 201
woodworking activities, 227–30
writing activities, 239
writing surfaces, 209